POSTCARD HISTORY SERIES

Clearfield

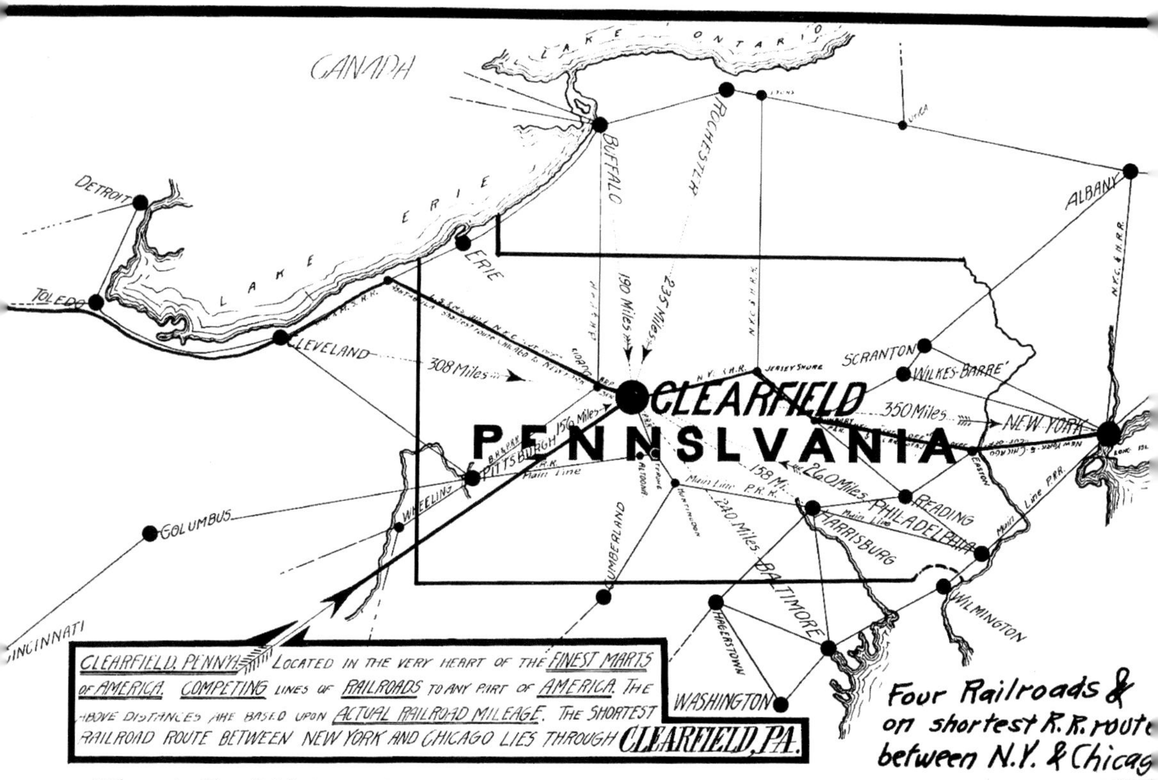

Where is Clearfield, Pennsylvania? This postcard shows Clearfield's location in relation to the railroads of the time. It boasts that the shortest route between Chicago and New York is through Clearfield. Today, the easiest way to travel by ground between those two cities is still through Clearfield but via Interstate 80.

POSTCARD HISTORY SERIES

Clearfield

Julie Rae Rickard for the Clearfield County Historical Society

ARCADIA
PUBLISHING

ISBN 978-0-7385-1113-9

Published by Arcadia Publishing
Charleston, South Carolina

Printed in the United States of America

Library of Congress Catalog Card Number: 2002109306

For all general information contact Arcadia Publishing at:
Telephone 843-853-2070
Fax 843-853-0044
E-Mail sales@arcadiapublishing.com
For customer service and orders:
Toll-Free 1-888-313-2665

Visit us on the Internet at www.arcadiapublishing.com

Contents

Acknowledgments		6
Introduction		7
1.	Street Scenes	9
2.	Landmarks	29
3.	Disasters	47
4.	Community	57
5.	Curwensville	73
6.	Industry	95
7.	The View from Above	109
8.	Neighbors	113
9.	Miscellaneous Greetings	123

ACKNOWLEDGMENTS

My sincere appreciation goes to the following, without whom this book would never have been completed.

For several years, Robert M. Kurtz Jr. has toyed with the idea of putting together a book using Clearfield postcards. He is the one who contacted Arcadia Publishing and then asked me to put the cards together and write the captions. This book is really his baby.

Whenever I had a question, Warren Fox had the answer or knew where he could find it. He spent numerous hours with me at the historical society doing research for this book and helped me to keep the facts straight.

My extreme gratitude goes to Jim Leitzinger, J. Duane Test, and the Zalno family for trusting me with their valuable collections and for their input.

Jerry Learn was an important part of this project due to his expertise in scanning the postcards.

Patricia Murphy was gracious enough to donate her time to scan additional images. Also, her enthusiasm and advice on this project were invaluable to me.

Amy Sutton and the staff at Arcadia Publishing deserve recognition for being so patient with the last-minute revisions.

The Dimeling Senior Residence was kind enough to provide photographs of the Dimeling Hotel in its heyday.

Finally, I need to acknowledge the Clearfield County Historical Society for graciously allowing me access to all of its resources.

I thank you all.

Introduction

You have just received a postcard of Clearfield from 1910, 1923, or perhaps 1940.

Located in scenic central Pennsylvania, Clearfield has a rich history that goes back to 1804. This collection of postcards documents some of that history during the early part of the 20th century.

At this time, traveling German photographers visited the area, taking many pictures that were later turned into postcards for sale in local stores. The names and trademarks on these cards vary. Some bear the "Litho-Chrome" trademark from Dresden-Leipzig-Berlin, others the "PCK Series," which lists its origin as Shave & Keller in Rye, New York, and a few others have "Rotograph Co. NY City" on them. Most were printed in Germany.

This was a simpler time when there was no e-mail and, for only a penny, one could send greetings and a photograph to a friend or relative. The first postcards of the 20th century were limited in their note writing, for the back was marked "this side for address only." It was not until after 1907 that postcards with a divided back, leaving more room for a message, were made legal.

World War I halted much of the German postcard-printing business from 1914 to 1917. Some of the companies resumed their work after the war, but by the time the United States had entered World War II, these companies were no longer producing American postcards.

The cards were sold at local five-and-dime stores, as well as at drugstores, variety stores, and newsstands. Many were stamped with the name of these local companies: Way's Stationery Store in Curwensville, Schrum's Pharmacy in DuBois, J.A. Gardner Importing Company in Tyrone, and Kurtz Stationery Store in Clearfield.

This collection includes many that were branded with the Kurtz name. They are reproduced here courtesy of Robert M. Kurtz Jr., grandson of Charles T. Kurtz, who founded the stationery store and Kurtz Bros. in 1894. This collection comes from the Clearfield County Historical Society and private collectors Robert M. Kurtz Jr., Jim Leitzinger, J. Duane Test, and the Zalno family. A few photographs have been included in order to cover important historical events.

Putting together this book has been a lesson in history for me. I hope that you too enjoy learning more about Clearfield's past through these memorable postcards.

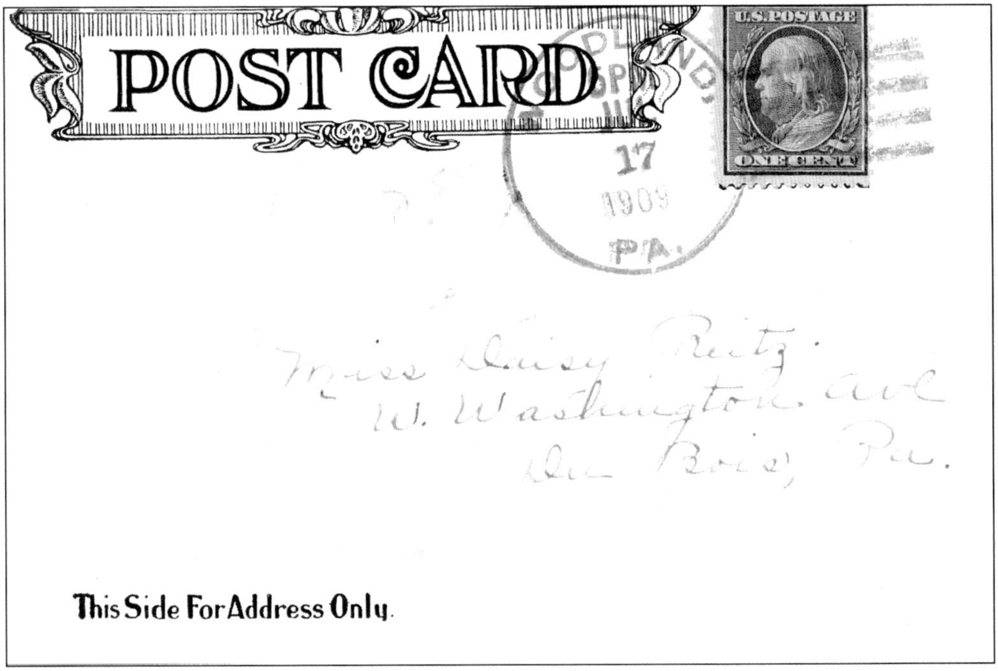

Here is an example of an early postcard before the divided card became available. Note the "this side for address only" limitation.

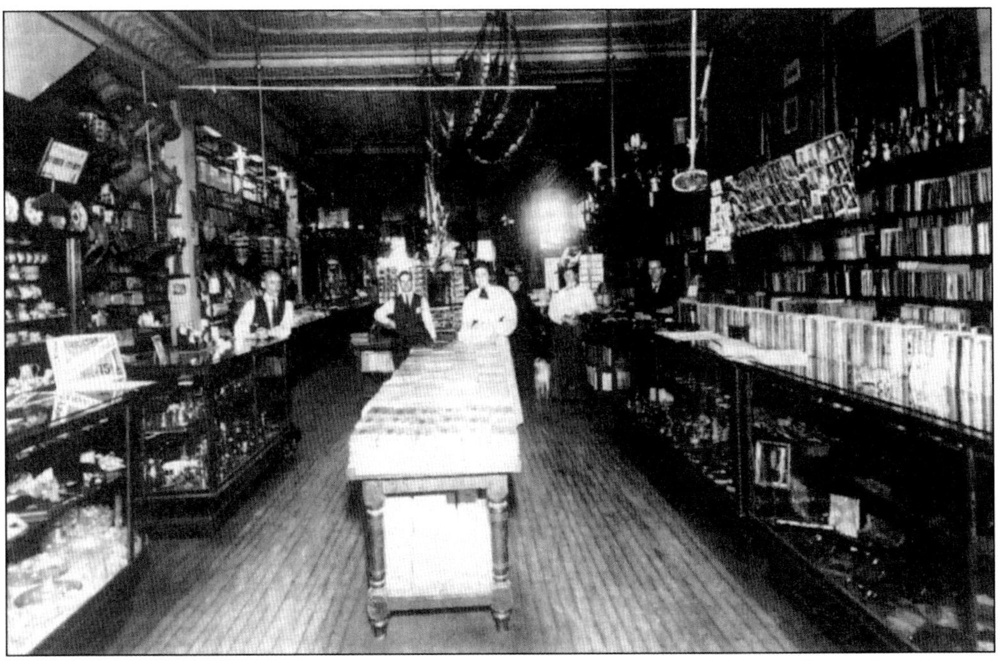

These postcards were sold at local stores like the Kurtz Bros. Store, which was located on Second Street. Kurtz Bros. founder Charles Kurtz is on the left. (Courtesy Kurtz Bros.)

One

Street Scenes

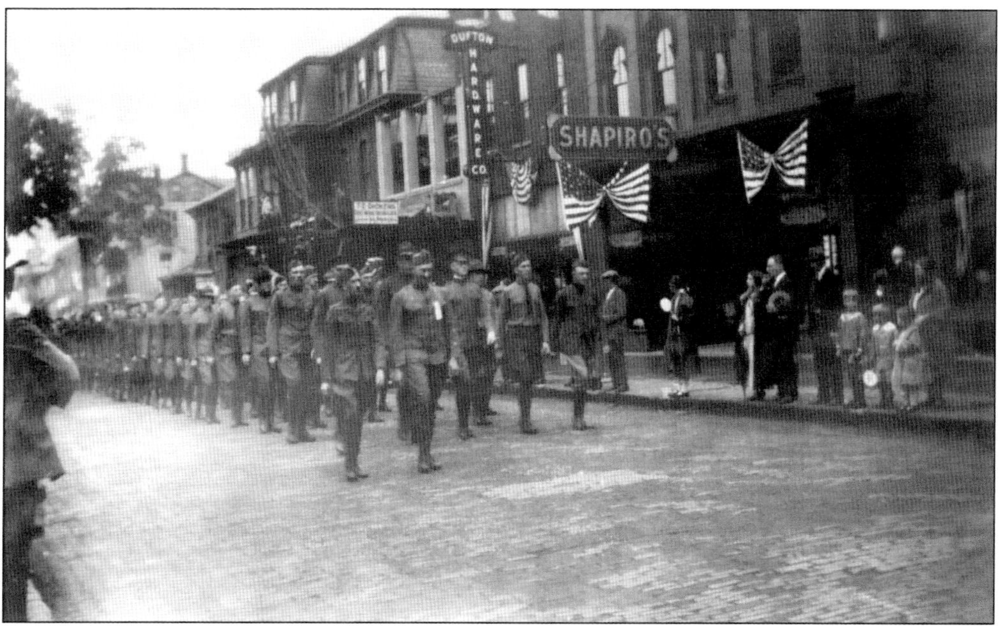

World War I veterans march down Market Street in the annual Fourth of July parade *c.* 1920. On the street at that time are, from left to right, the Hotel Windsor, Robinson's Men's Shop, Dufton's Hardware, and Shapiro's Men's Store. The streets of Clearfield were a common subject for postcards, with Market and Second being the most popular.

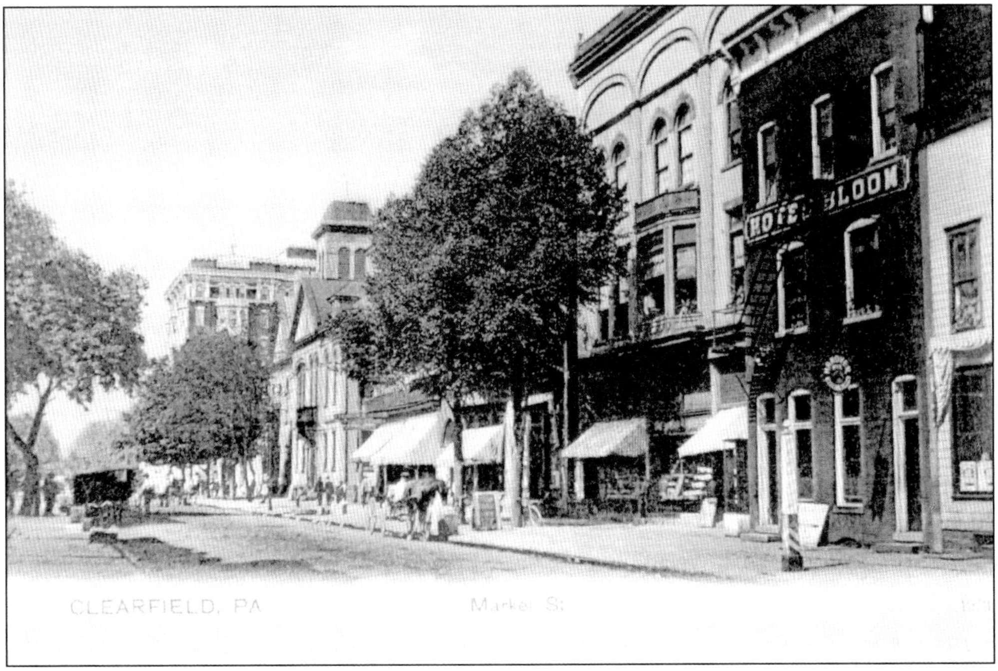

Market Street *c.* 1906 featured, from left to right, the Dimeling Hotel, the Clearfield County Courthouse, the Pie Opera House (behind the trees), Leitzinger Bros. (only three stories), and the Hotel Bloom.

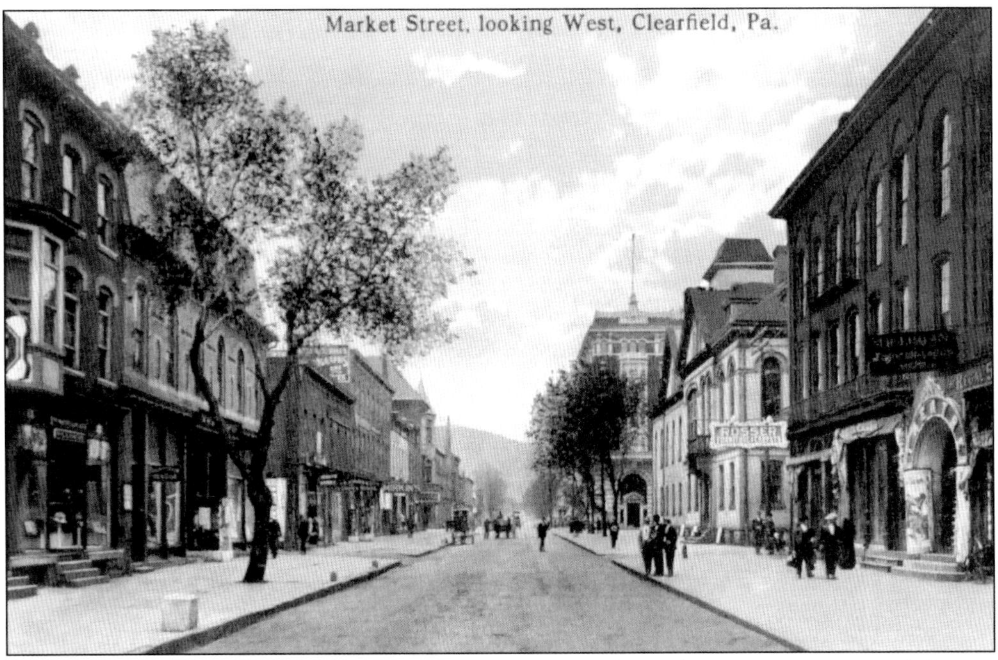

On the right is a better view of the opera house, which also housed Rosser Furniture and Carpets and the Regal five-and-dime store. Shown on the left are Shapiro's Men's Store, Daisy Johnson's Millinery Shop, and Leonardson's Department Store. This card is postmarked 1914.

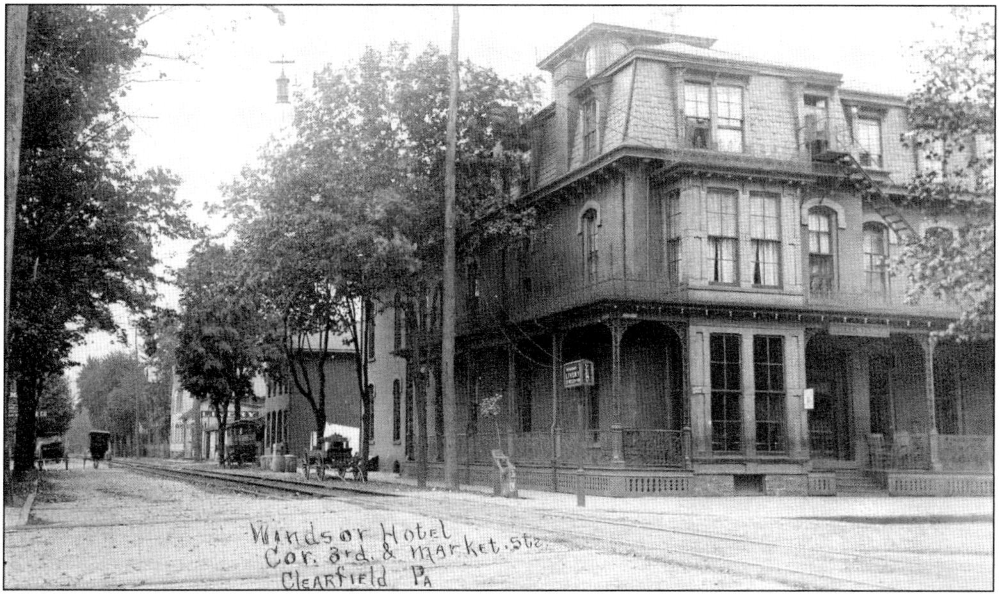

In 1911, the Windsor Hotel occupied the corner of Third and Market Streets. Today, this is the home of the Dollar General Store. (Courtesy Zalno collection.)

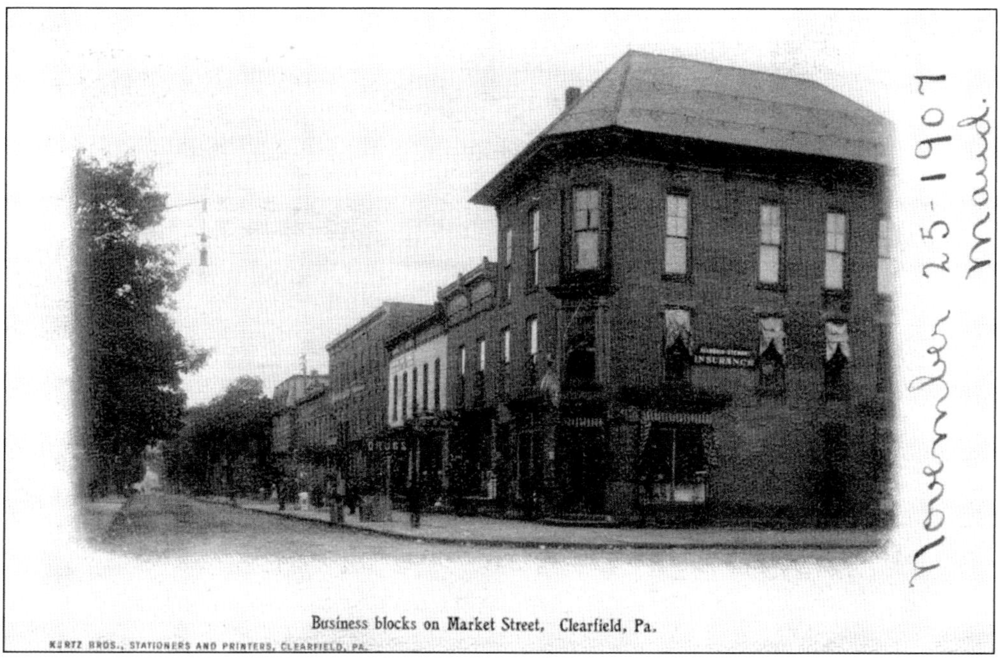

This view shows Market Street from Second Street. Hembold and Stewart Insurance is on the corner. (Courtesy Zalno collection.)

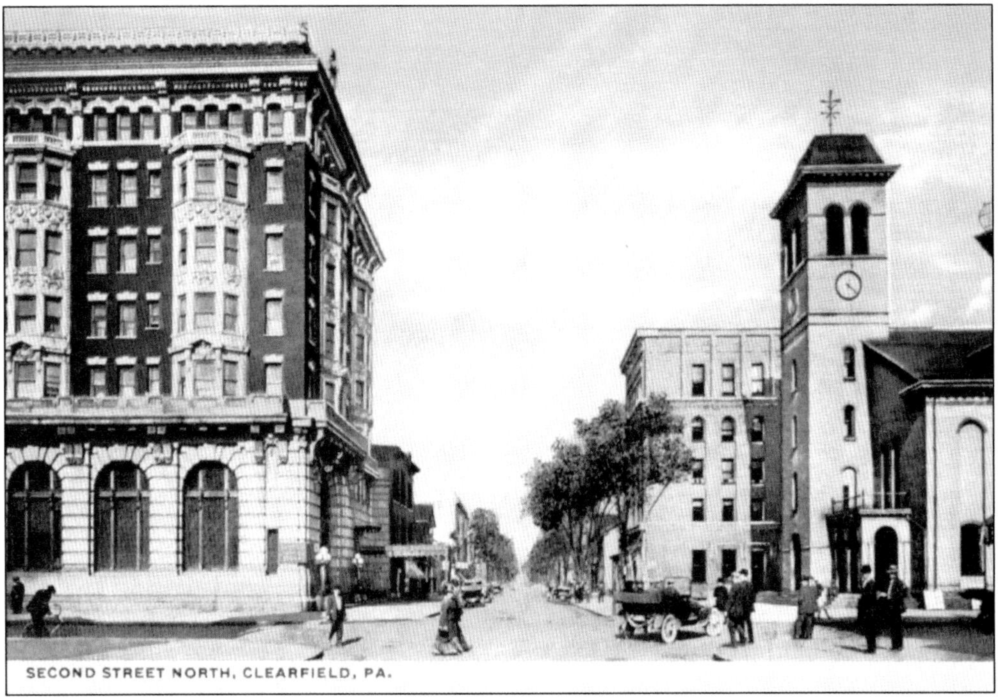

Shown here is North Second Street at Market Street *c.* 1915, looking much as it does today, with the Dimeling Hotel on the left and the Clearfield County Courthouse and Clearfield Bank & Trust building on the right. The cars and fashions have changed a bit, however.

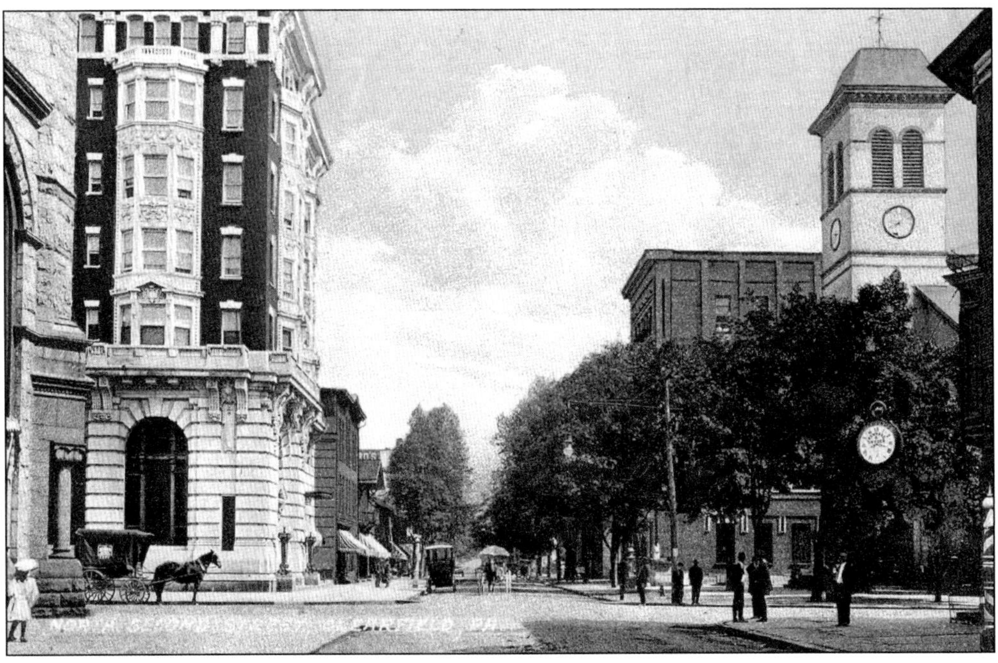

An even earlier photograph than the previous one, this view was taken when horse-drawn carriages traveled these streets. (Courtesy Zalno collection.)

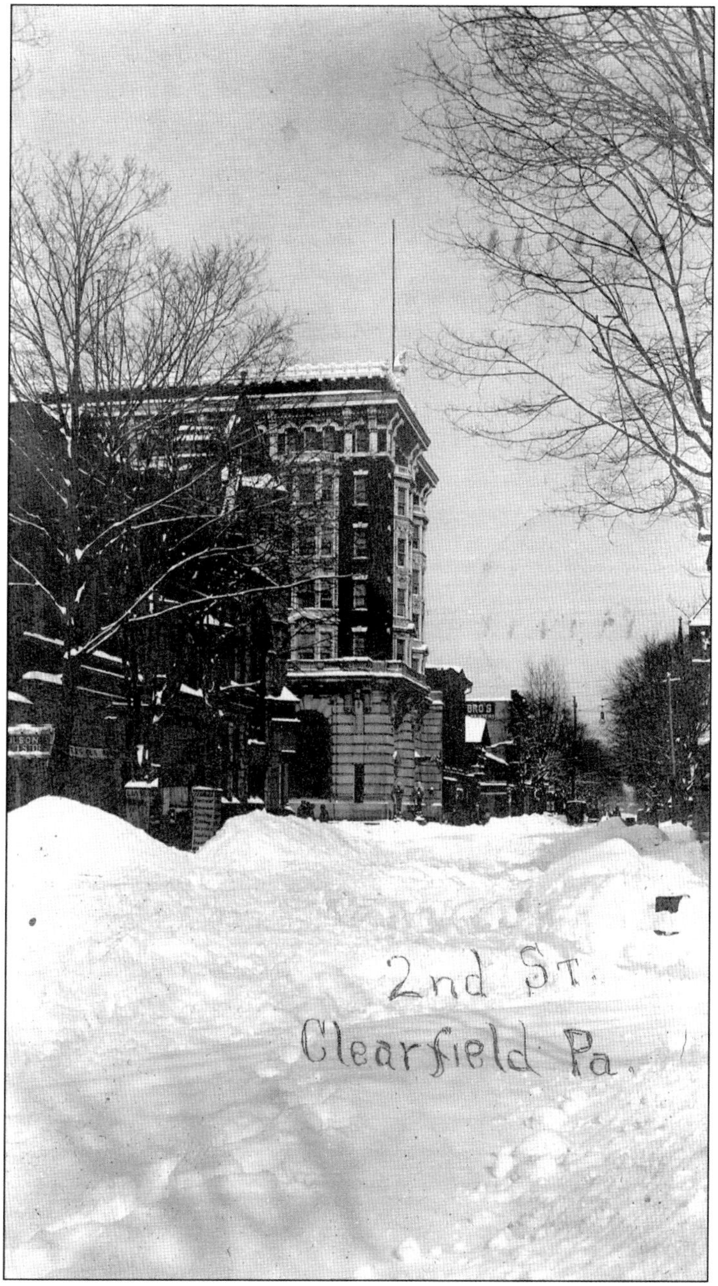

This picture shows Second Street in winter *c.* 1910. (Courtesy Zalno collection.)

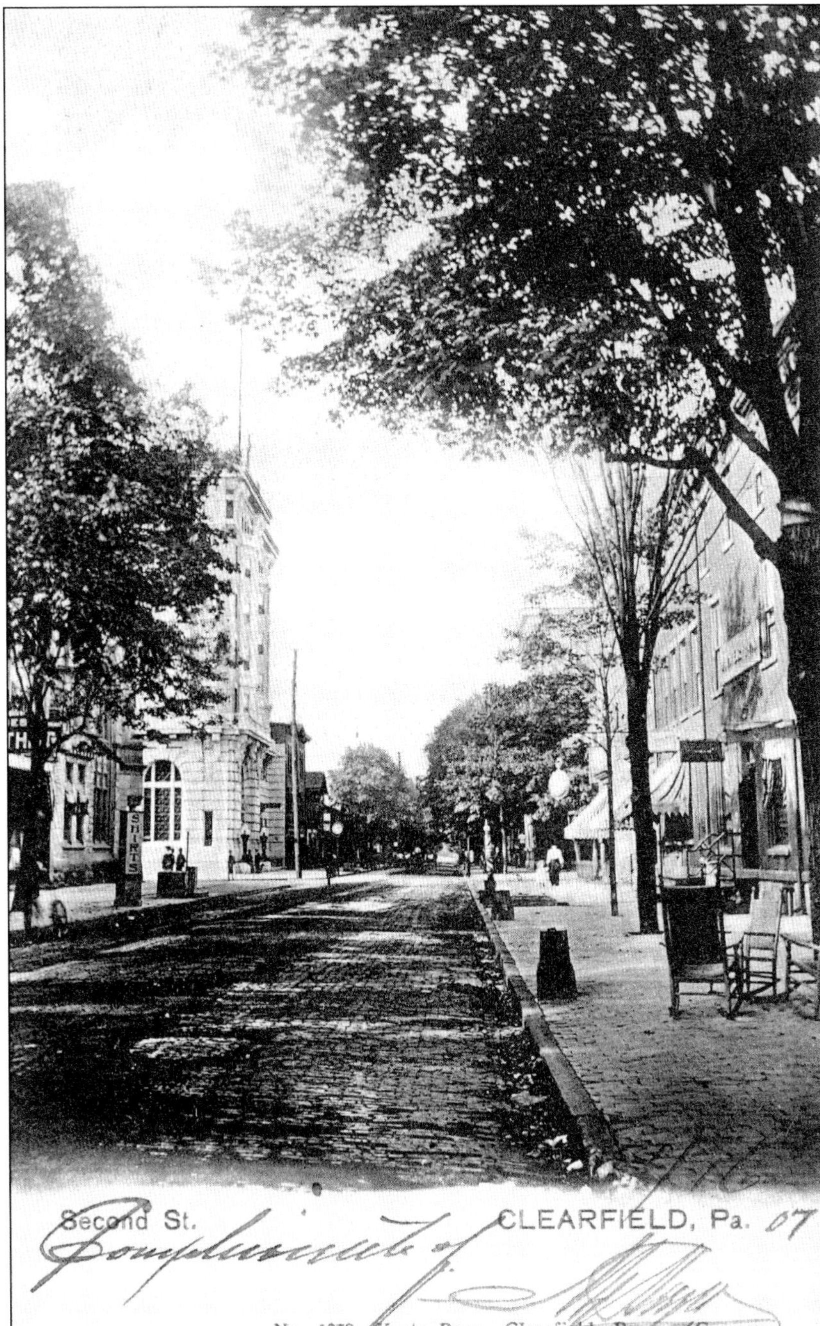

Second Street, complete with rockers on the street (right), is depicted here in a warmer season. (Courtesy Zalno collection.)

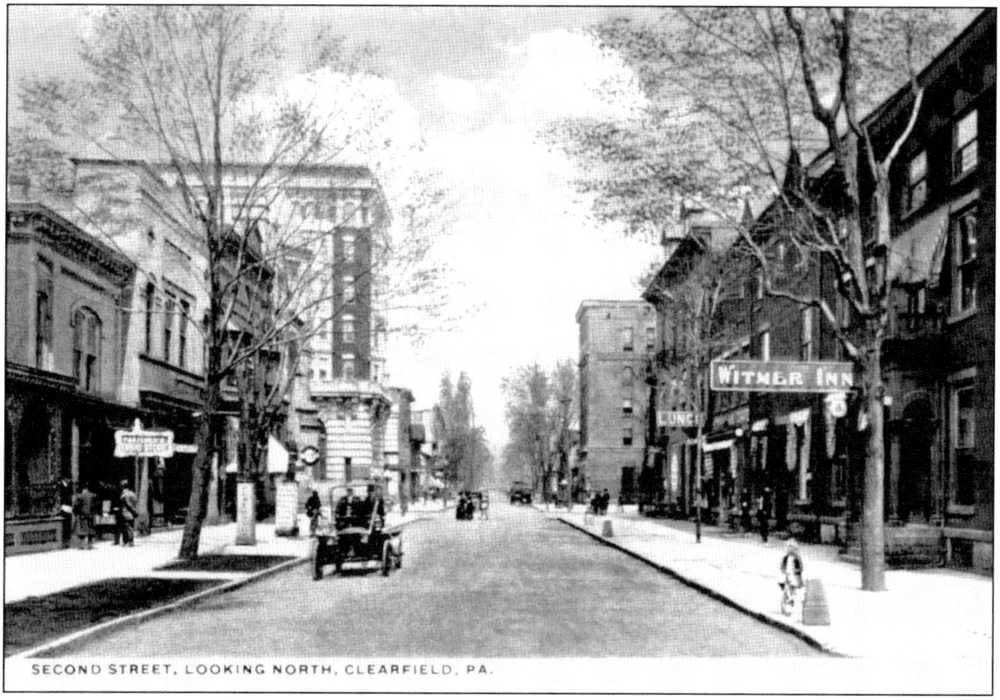

This *c.* 1920 image of Second Street shows, on the left, the County National Bank, Thatcher Drug Store, and the porch of Bertha Bigler. On the right is the Witmer Inn, which later became the Clearfielder. It was torn down in the 1970s.

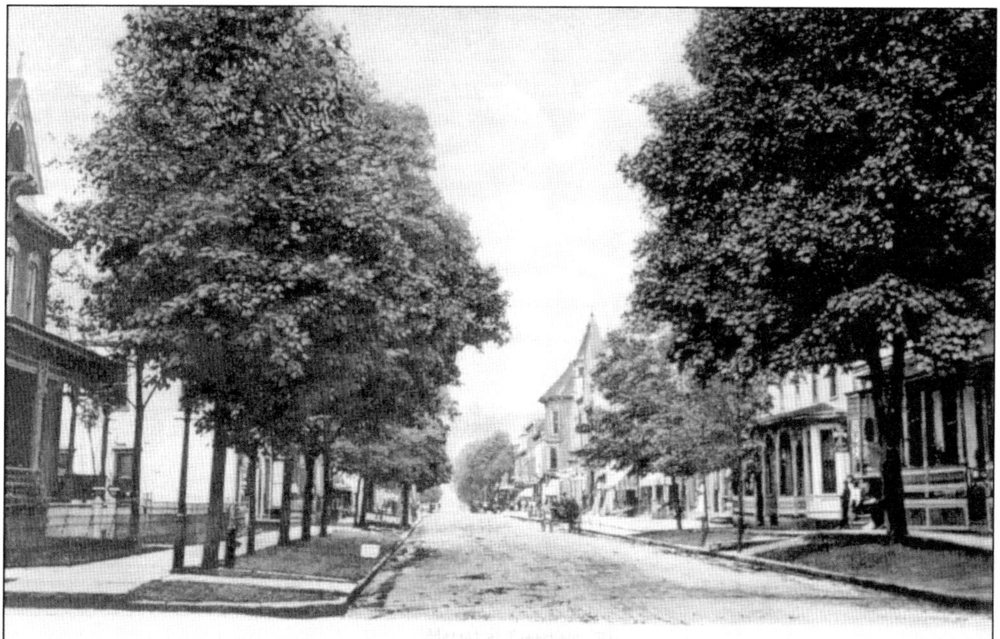

In this *c.* 1909 view of Market Street from Front Street, the top of the County National Bank building is just visible. On the right is the Shaw House, where a park and the Joseph and Elizabeth Shaw Public Library were eventually built.

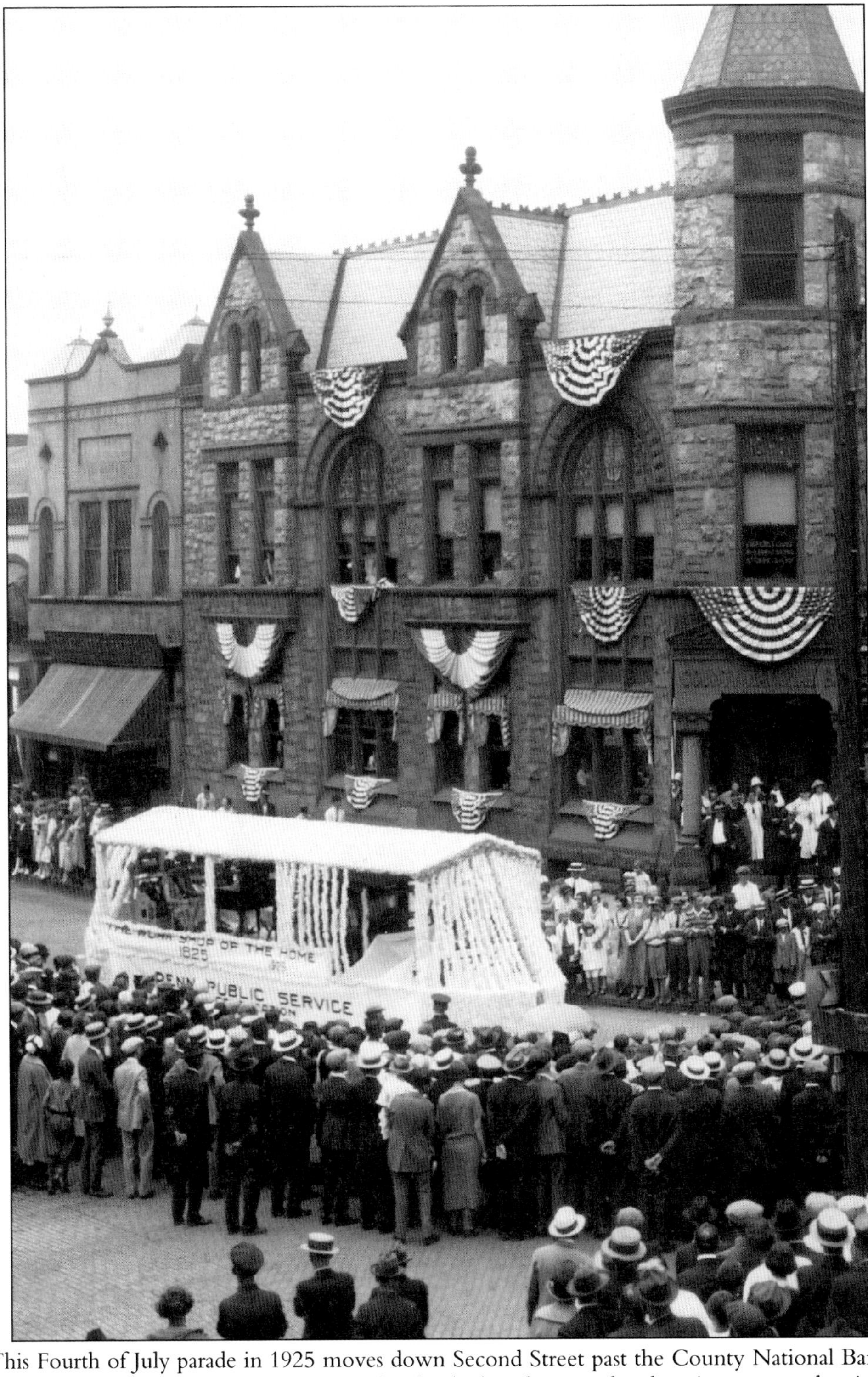

This Fourth of July parade in 1925 moves down Second Street past the County National Bank. The picture was taken by C.W. Howard, who had a photography shop in town at the time. (Courtesy Zalno collection.)

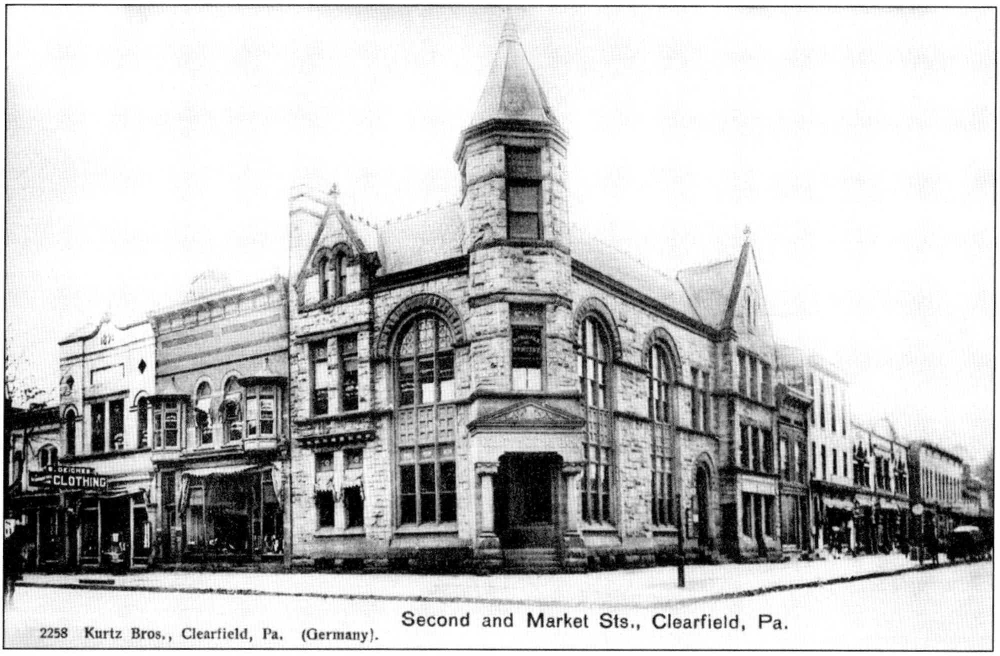

The County National Bank, built in 1890, is shown in this photograph of Second and Market Streets. To the left is A.J. Hagerty's Dry Goods and Millinery Shop.

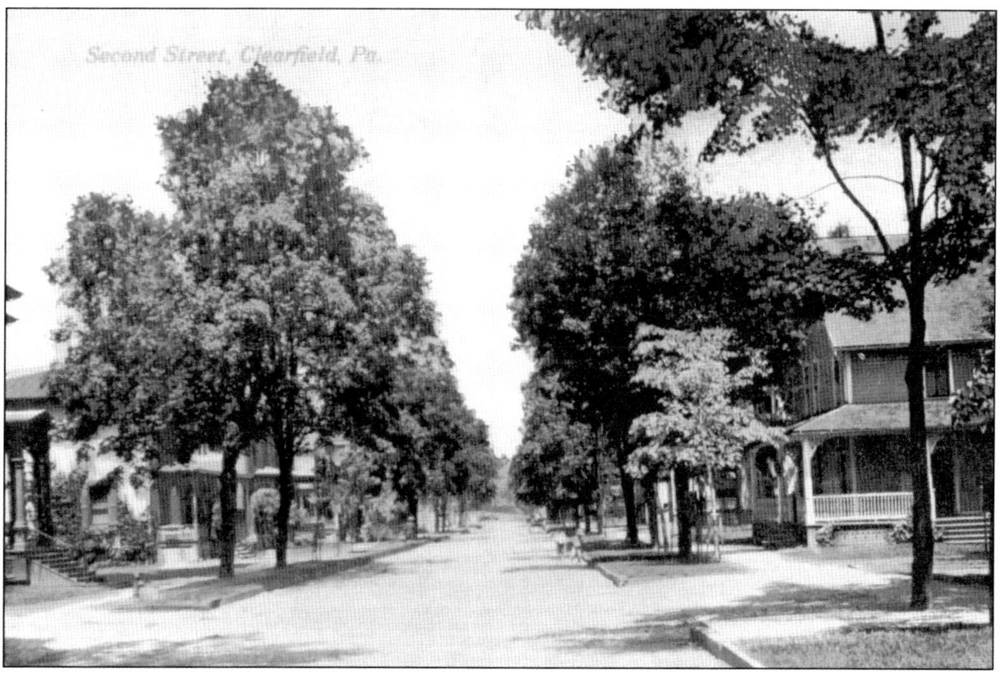

Looking north from Pine Street, this view shows Second Street.

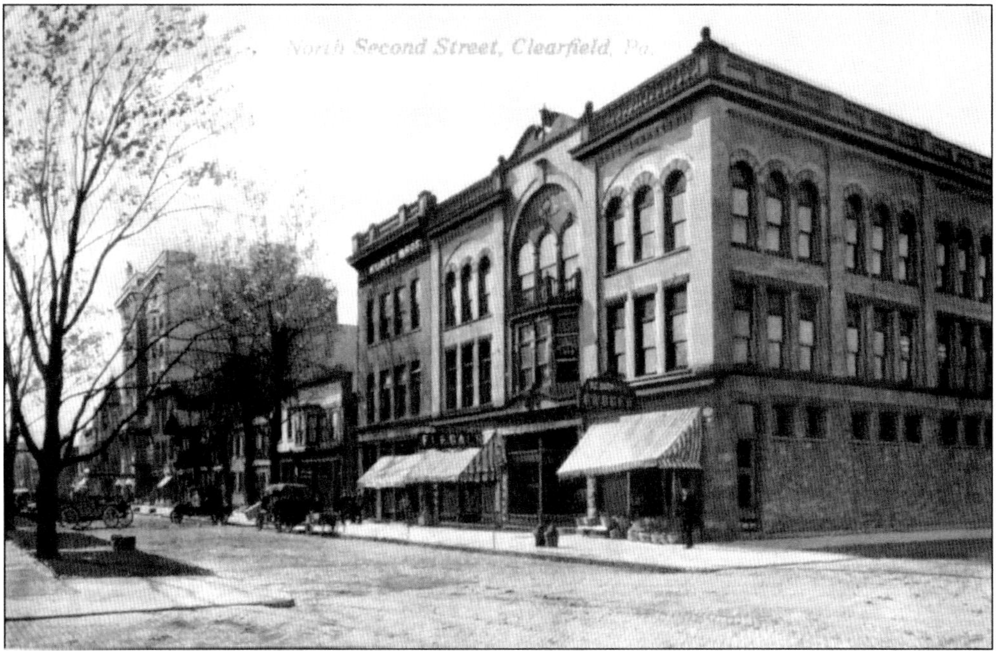

Above, North Second Street is shown from Locust Street; this view features the Keystone Building, which was built in 1900. At the time of the photograph, it housed Flegal's Grocery Store. Today, it is home to the Shoe Tree, the Republican headquarters, and Hess & Fisher Engineers. To the left of the Keystone is the Kurtz Bros. building, built in 1901. Below is another shot of the same area from a slightly different angle.

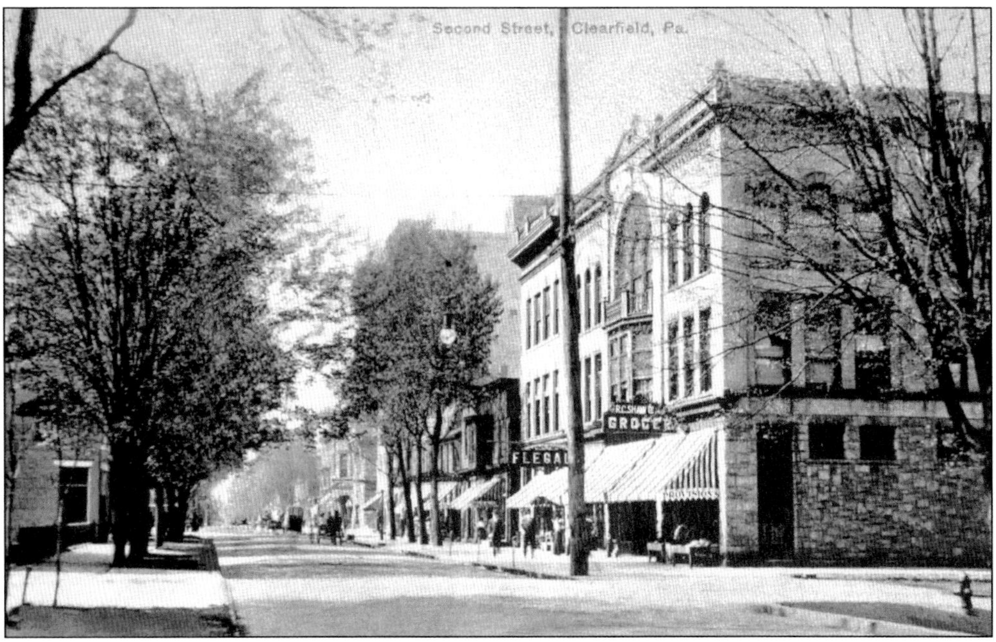

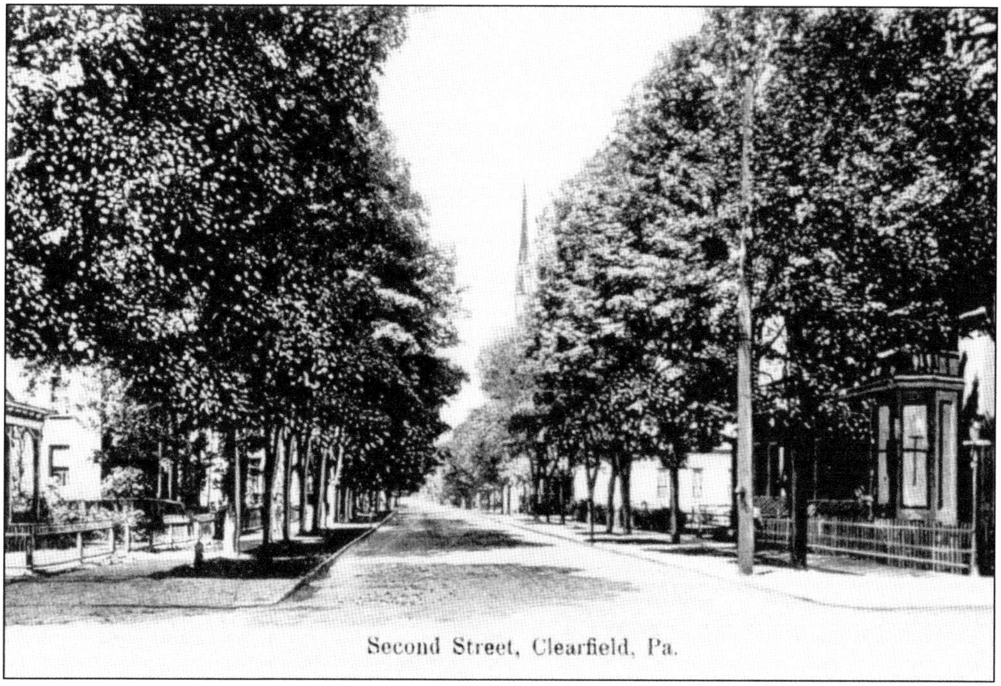

This view looks north from Locust Street toward Second Street. The steeple of the Presbyterian church appears near the center of the card.

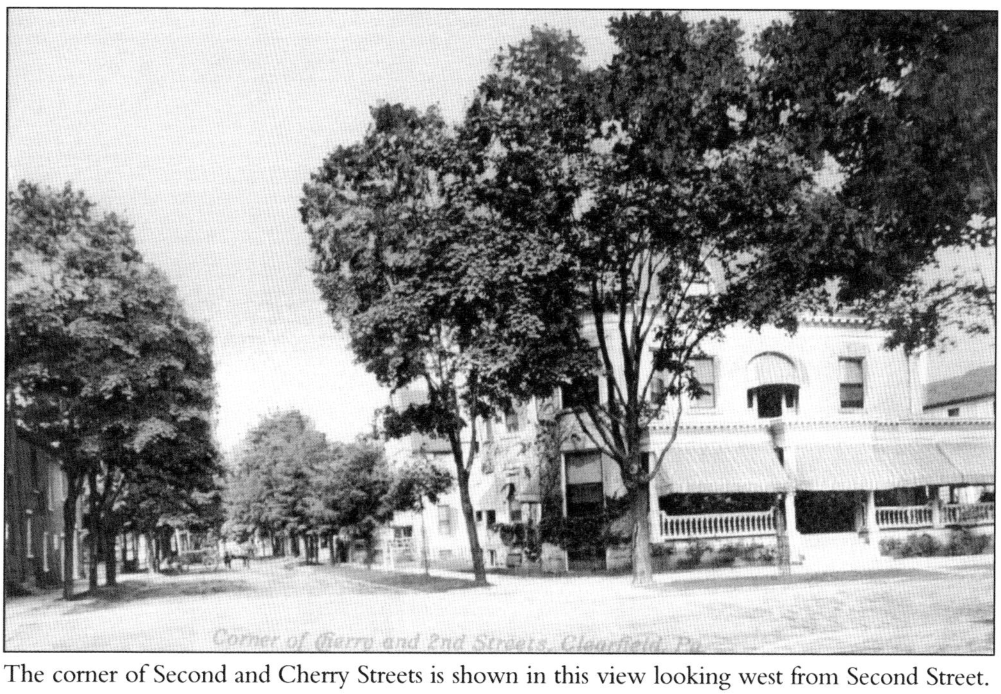

The corner of Second and Cherry Streets is shown in this view looking west from Second Street.

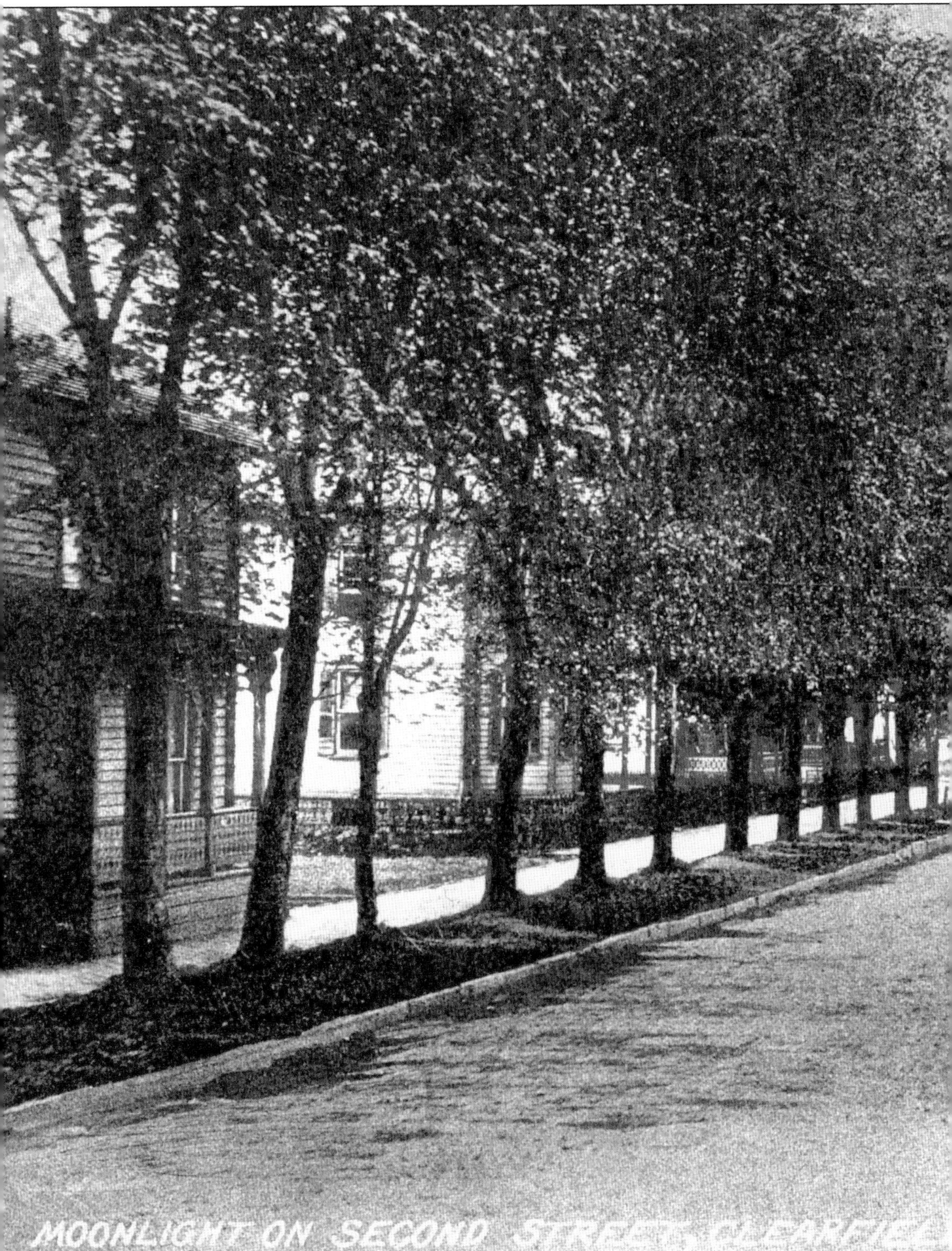

Moonlight shines on Second Street, revealing the old Clearfield County Jail on the right. Just

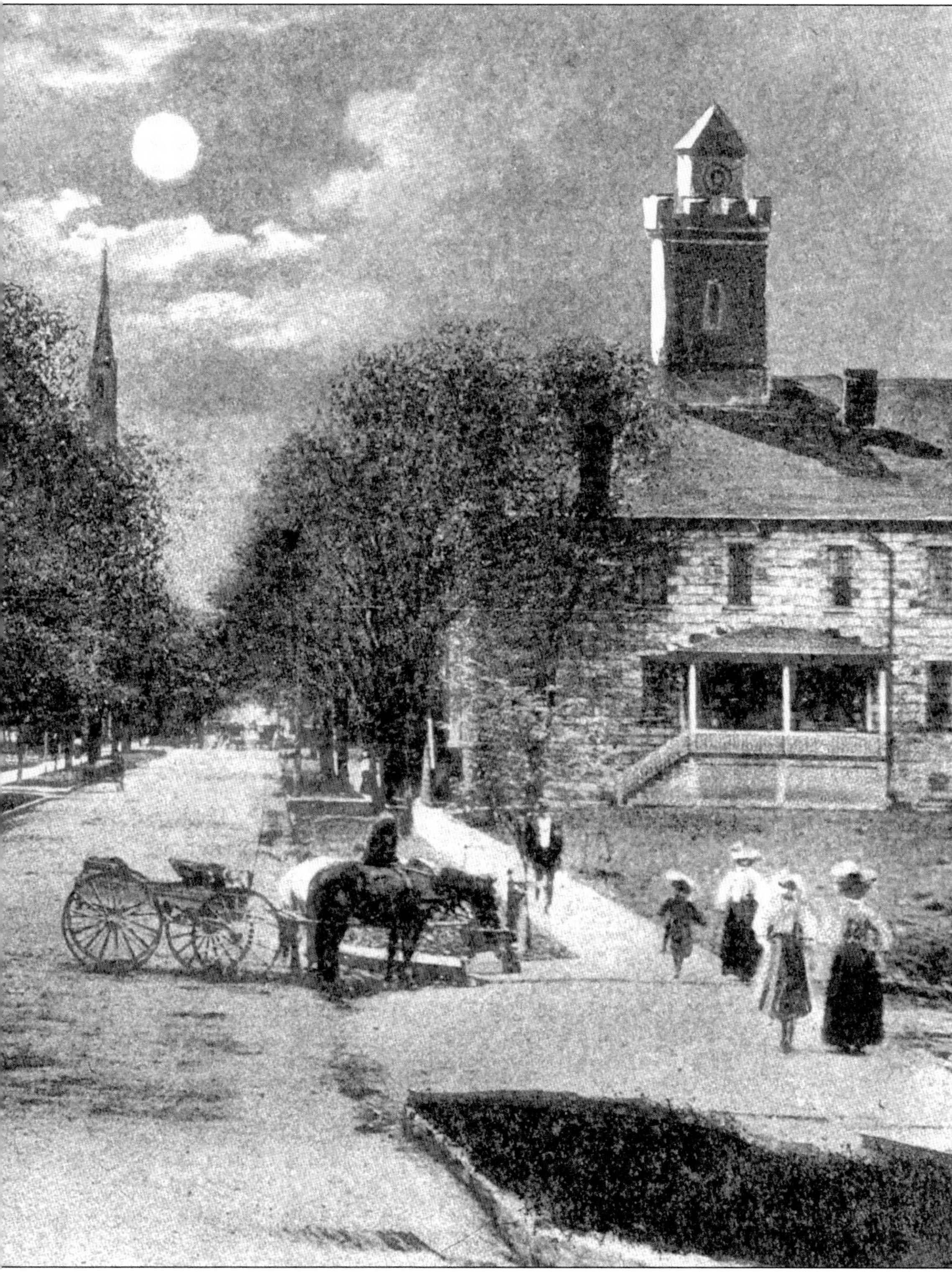

below the moon is the steeple of the Presbyterian church. (Courtesy Zalno collection.)

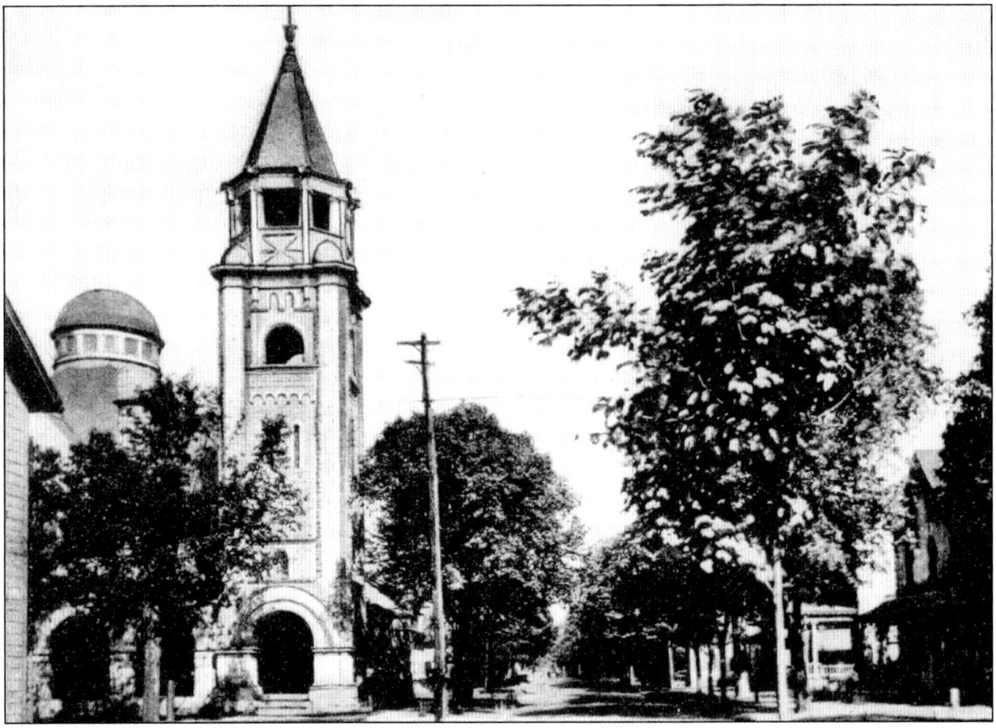

Farther down Second Street at the corner with Walnut Street stands the Methodist church, shown here in the early 1900s. The church burned in 1968 and was rebuilt in 1971.

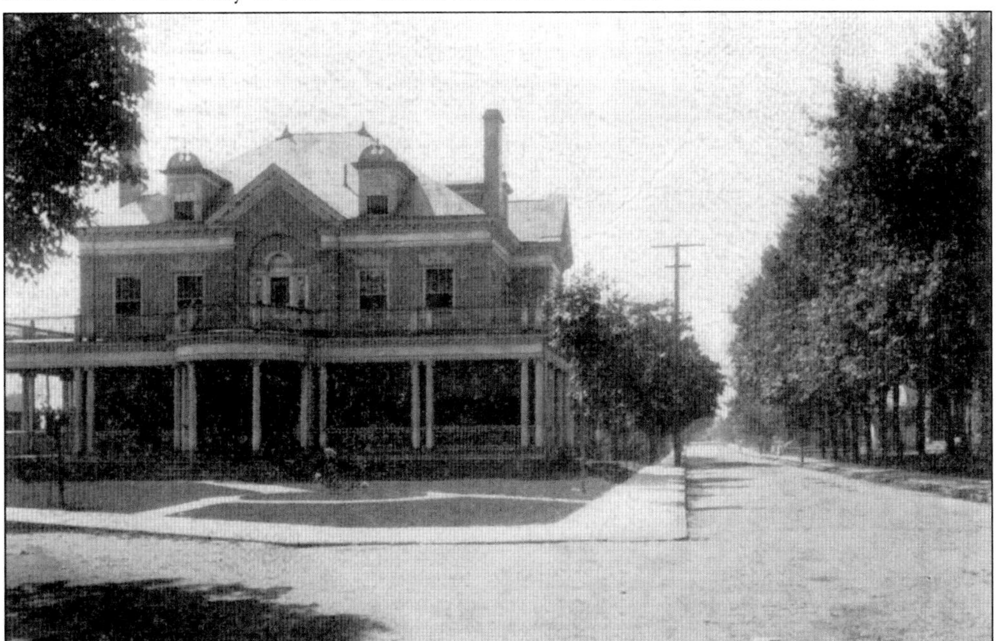

At the corner of Leavy and Second Streets is the home built by George Dimeling. This photograph was taken before the building became the American Legion and the war memorial was added to the front.

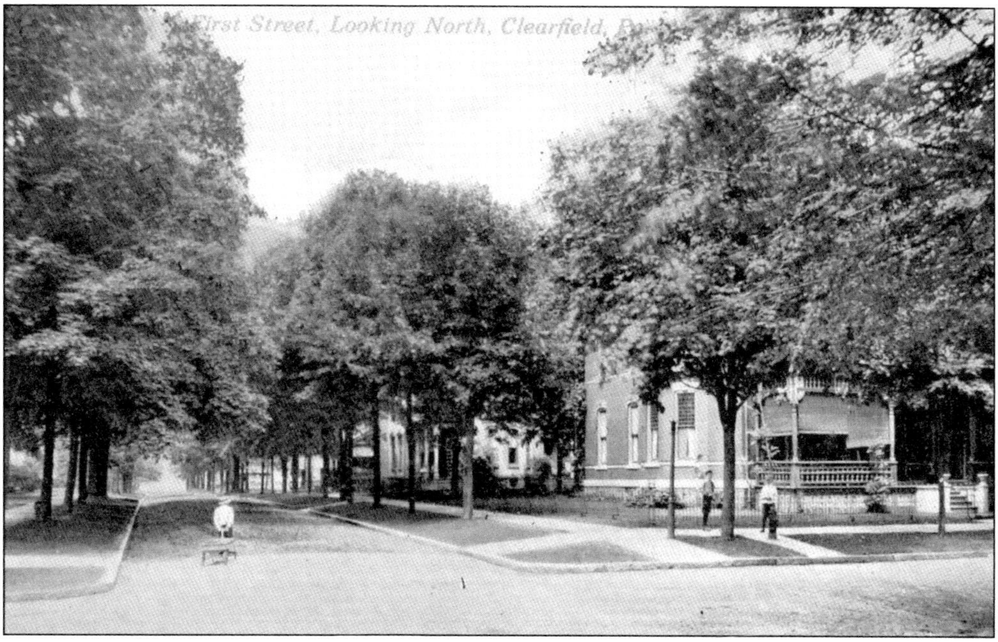

Shown here is the intersection of Front (then called First) and Market Streets. The home on the right was built in the 1870s. This spot is now a parking lot for Batcho Office Systems. (Courtesy Zalno collection.)

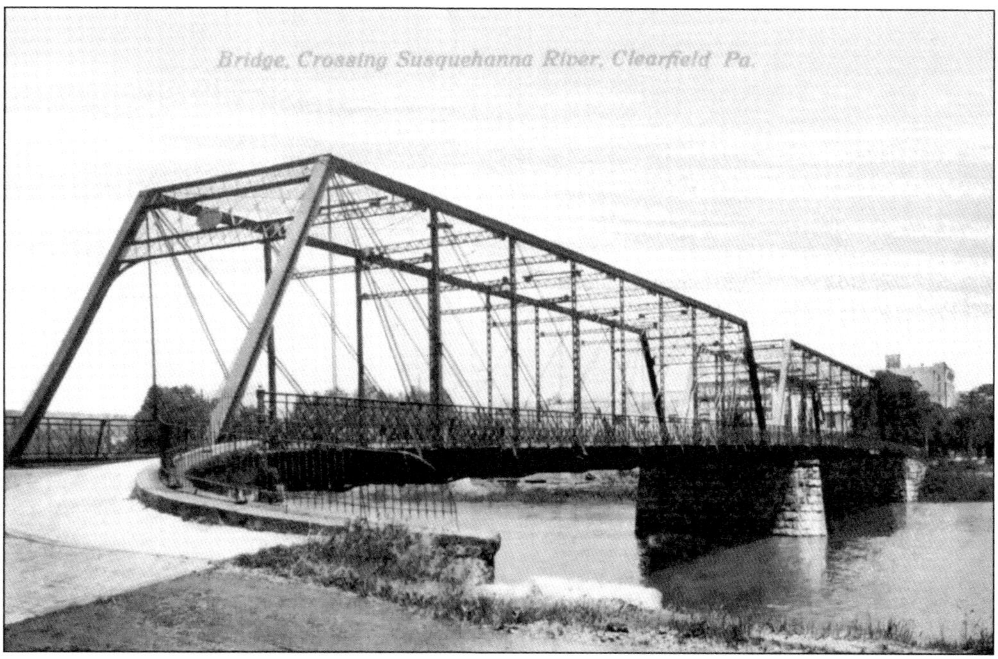

The Market Street Bridge is pictured here before it was rebuilt in 1937. The Dimeling is visible on the far right.

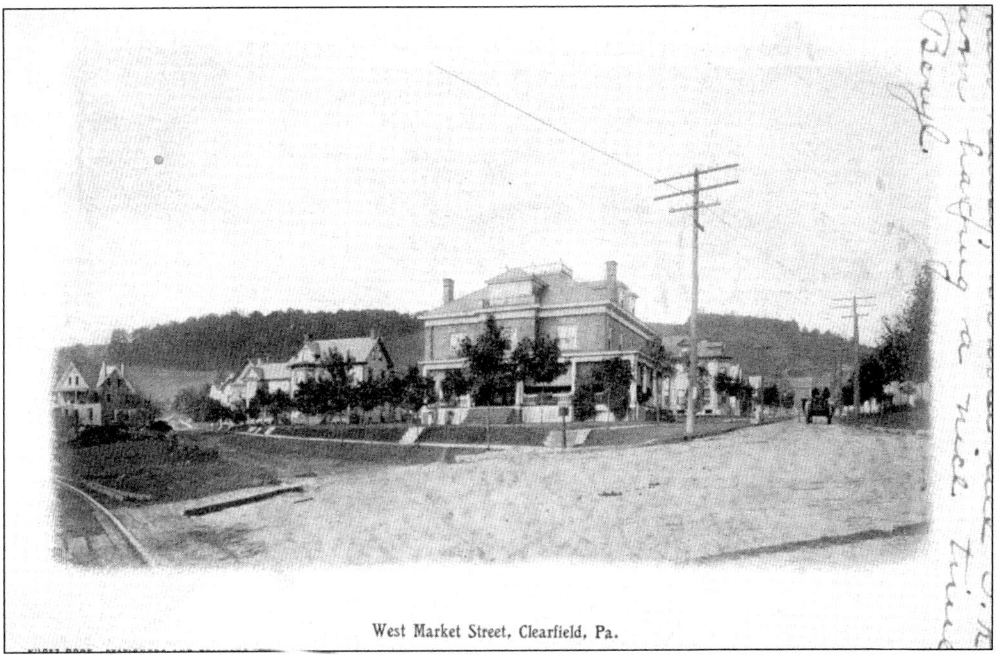

The intersection of West Market Street, Gulich Avenue, and Turnpike Avenue appeared this way in 1909. The house in the center was later converted into an apartment building. (Courtesy Zalno collection.)

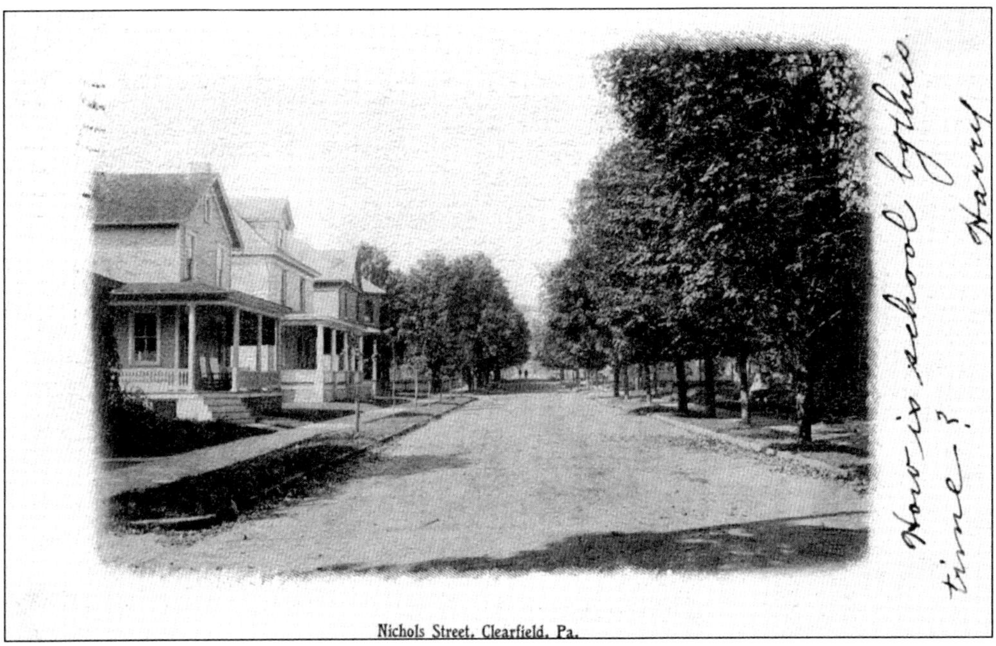

Shown here is Nichols Street in 1909. (Courtesy Zalno collection.)

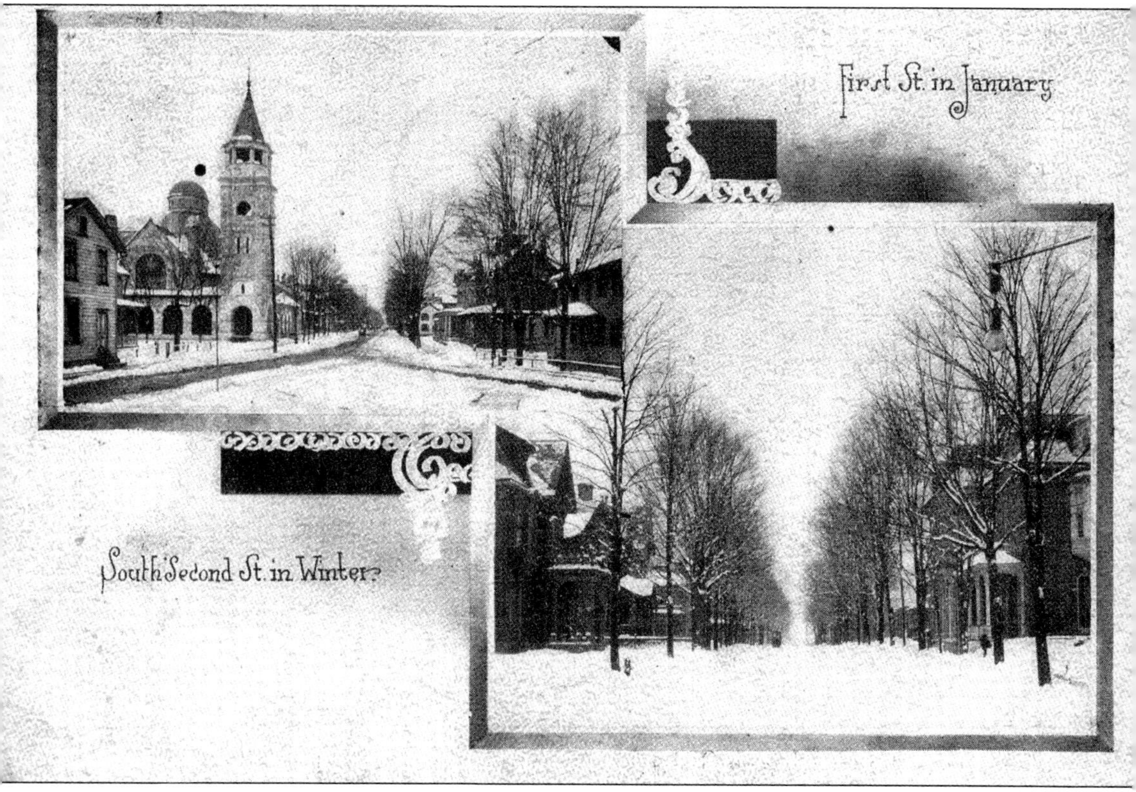

This 1910 combination postcard features winter scenes from both South Second and First (or Front) Streets. (Courtesy Zalno collection.)

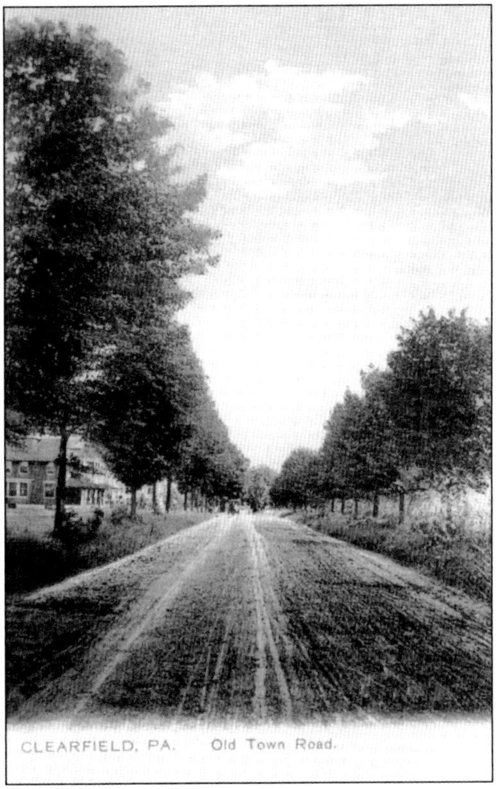

Shown here is Old Town Road in the early 1900s. The road's name may derive from the fact that, in the early 1800s, the Clearfield-Curwensville area was called "Old Town" by those in neighboring towns.

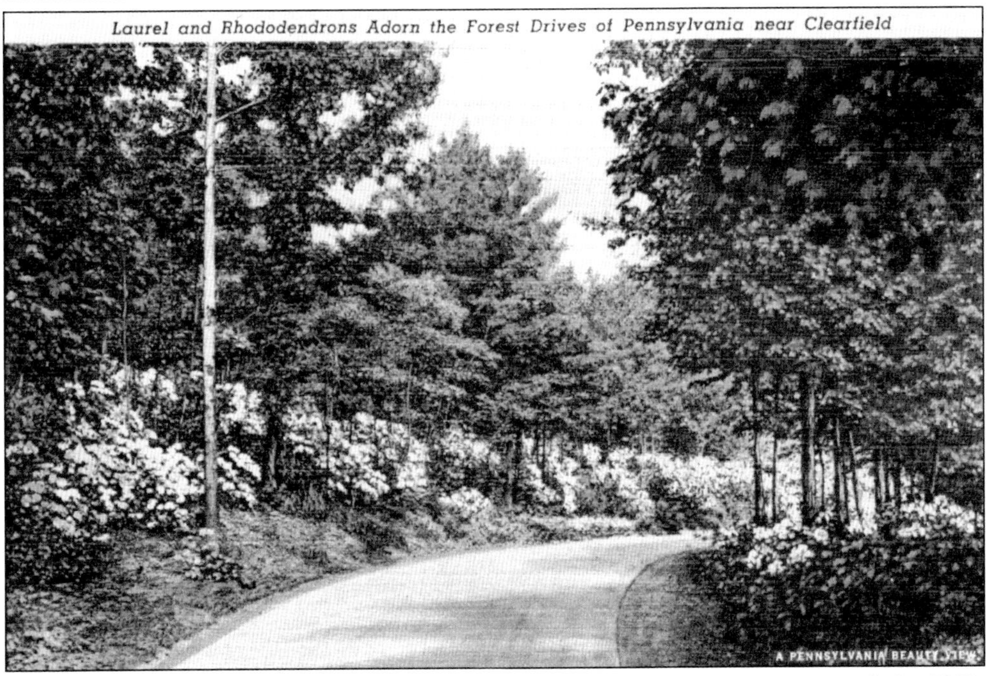

This card was sent out as a promotion for Clearfield Nature Appreciation Week in 1939. This celebration included tours by car or by foot of the mountain laurel in full bloom in the surrounding area. (Courtesy Zalno collection.)

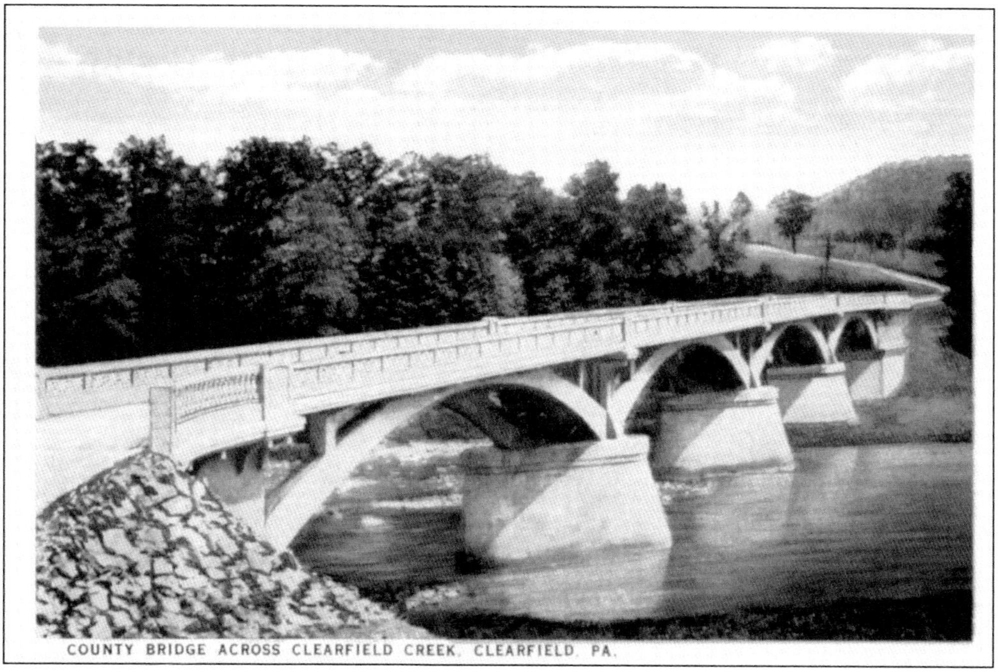

This bridge between Clearfield and Philipsburg crosses Clearfield Creek on Route 322 in Goldenrod. The postcard is from 1926.

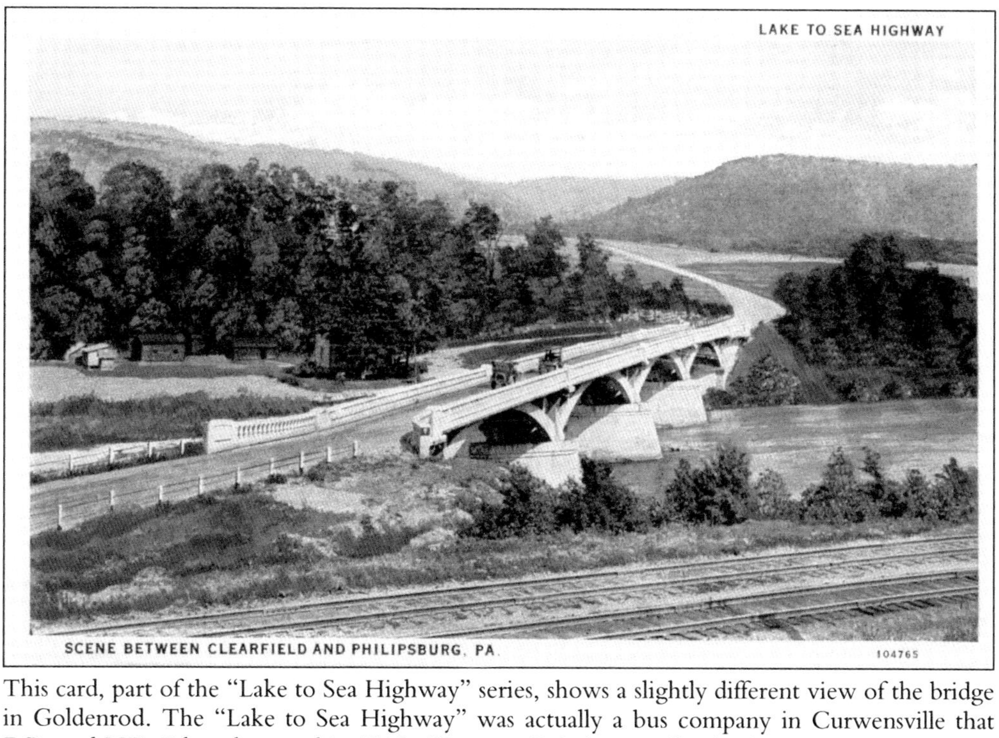

This card, part of the "Lake to Sea Highway" series, shows a slightly different view of the bridge in Goldenrod. The "Lake to Sea Highway" was actually a bus company in Curwensville that E.R. and J.W. Edwards started in 1918. (Courtesy Leitzinger collection.)

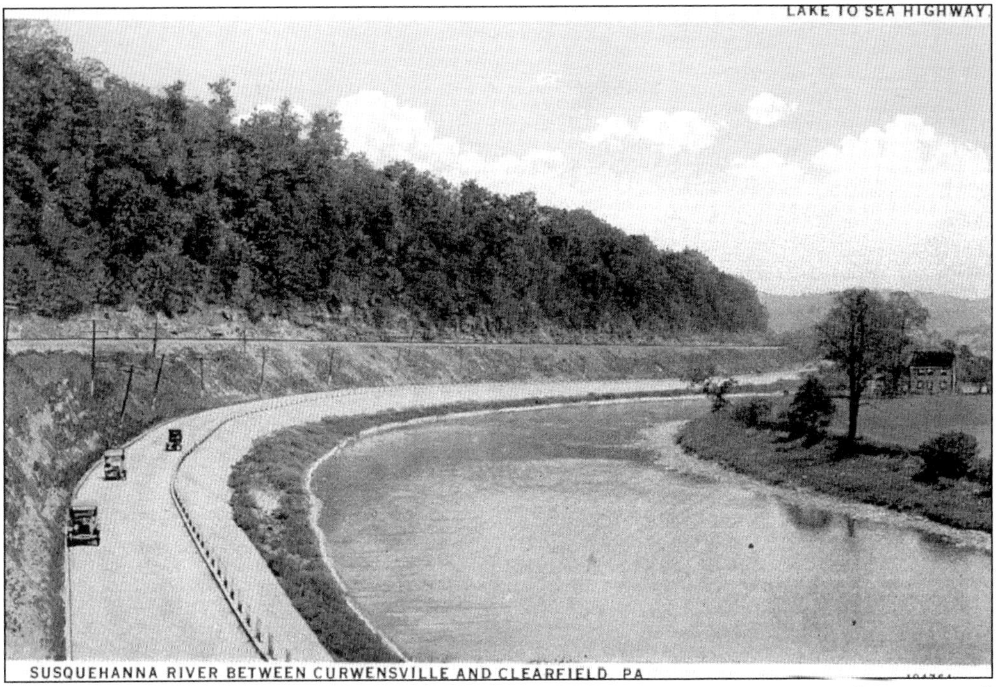

The area of Route 879 between Clearfield and Curwensville is known as "the narrows." (Courtesy Test collection.)

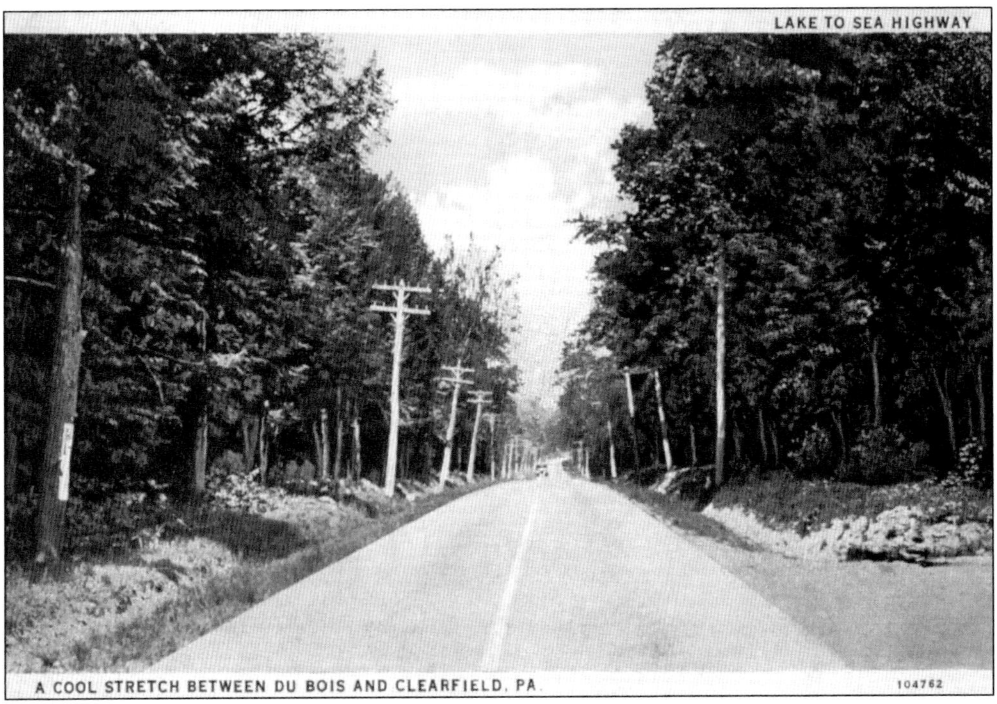

This "cool stretch between DuBois and Clearfield, PA" could be Route 322 north of Clearfield heading toward Rockton. The card is dated 1930. (Courtesy Leitzinger collection.)

Two

LANDMARKS

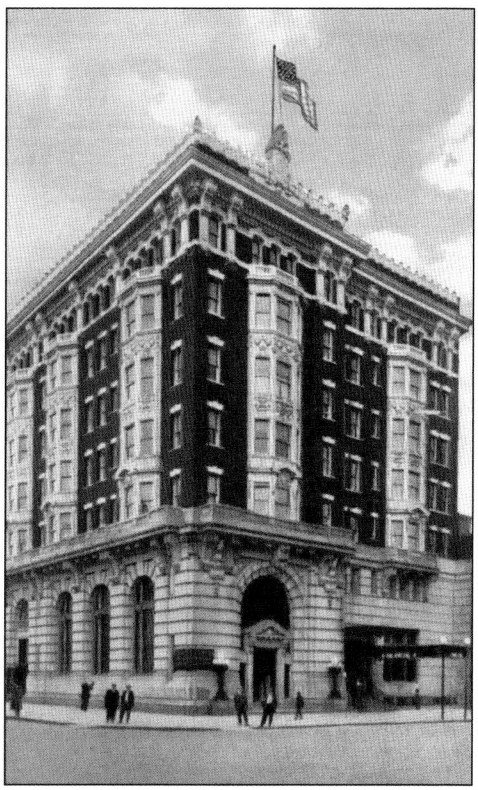

The historic Dimeling Hotel has stood on the corner of Market and Second Streets for almost 100 years. It was built in 1904 by Bezzer Bros. of Pittsburgh.

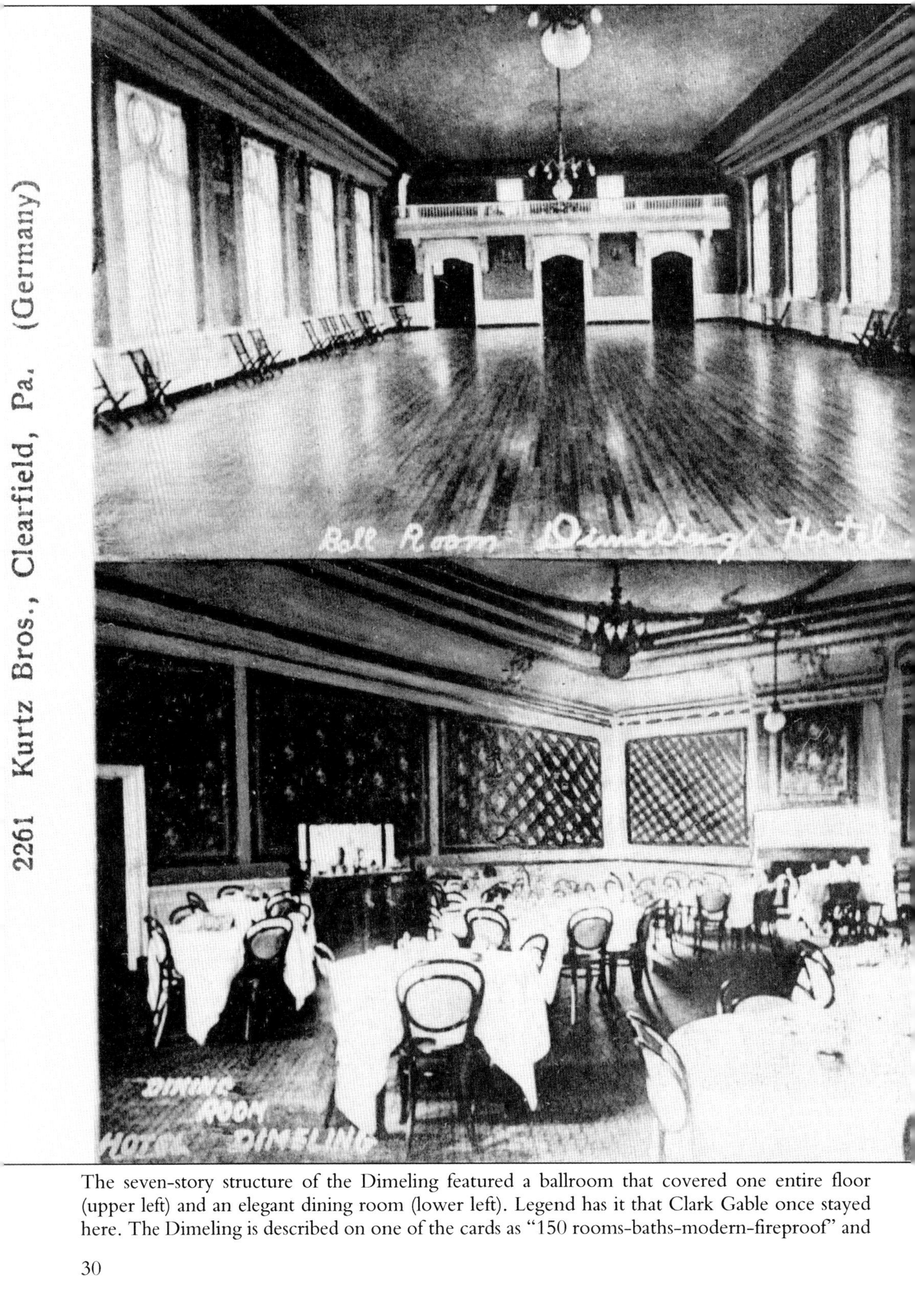

The seven-story structure of the Dimeling featured a ballroom that covered one entire floor (upper left) and an elegant dining room (lower left). Legend has it that Clark Gable once stayed here. The Dimeling is described on one of the cards as "150 rooms-baths-modern-fireproof" and

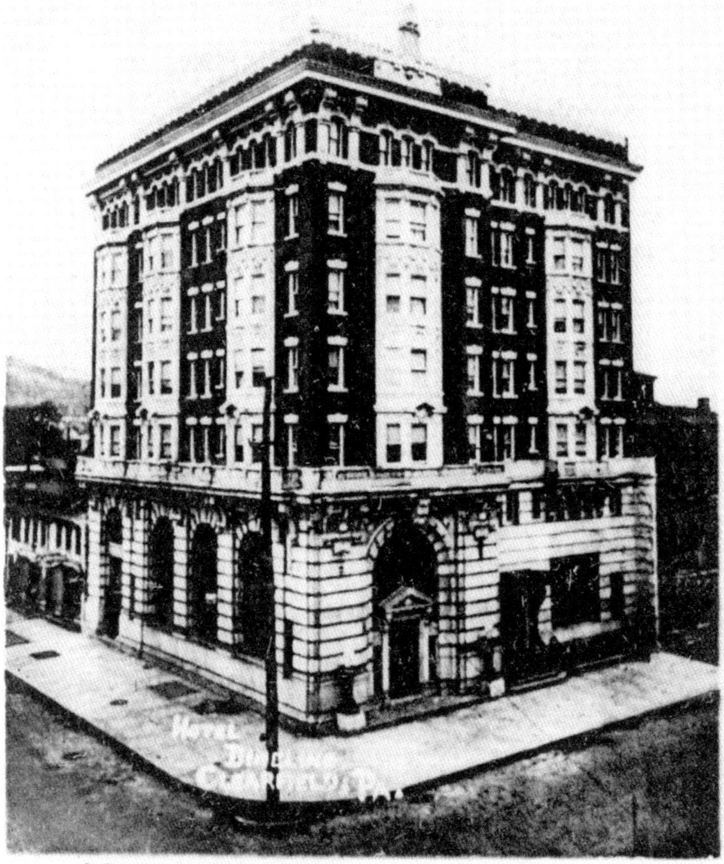

Hotel Dimeling, Clearfield, Pa.

"the finest hotel between Erie and Harrisburg." It has been converted into apartments and is now known as the Dimeling Senior Residence.

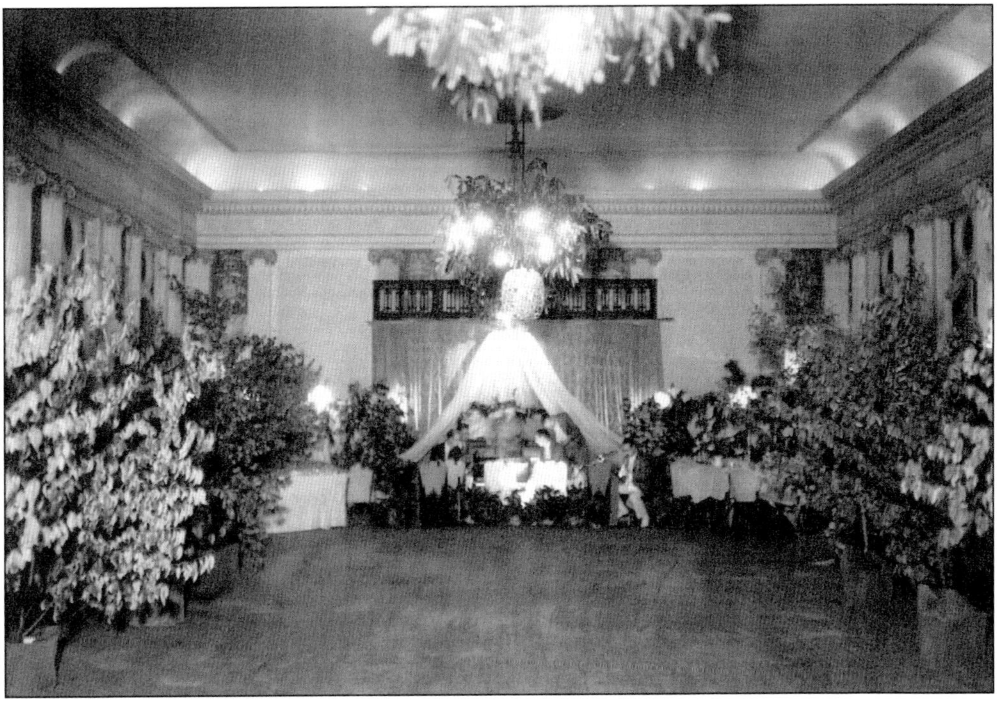

The Dimeling Ballroom was a center of activity for many years. Above, a band rehearses, and below, the tables are ready for an elegant banquet or a wedding reception. These photographs have been included in this collection to better illustrate the elegance of the Dimeling. (Courtesy Dimeling Senior Residence.)

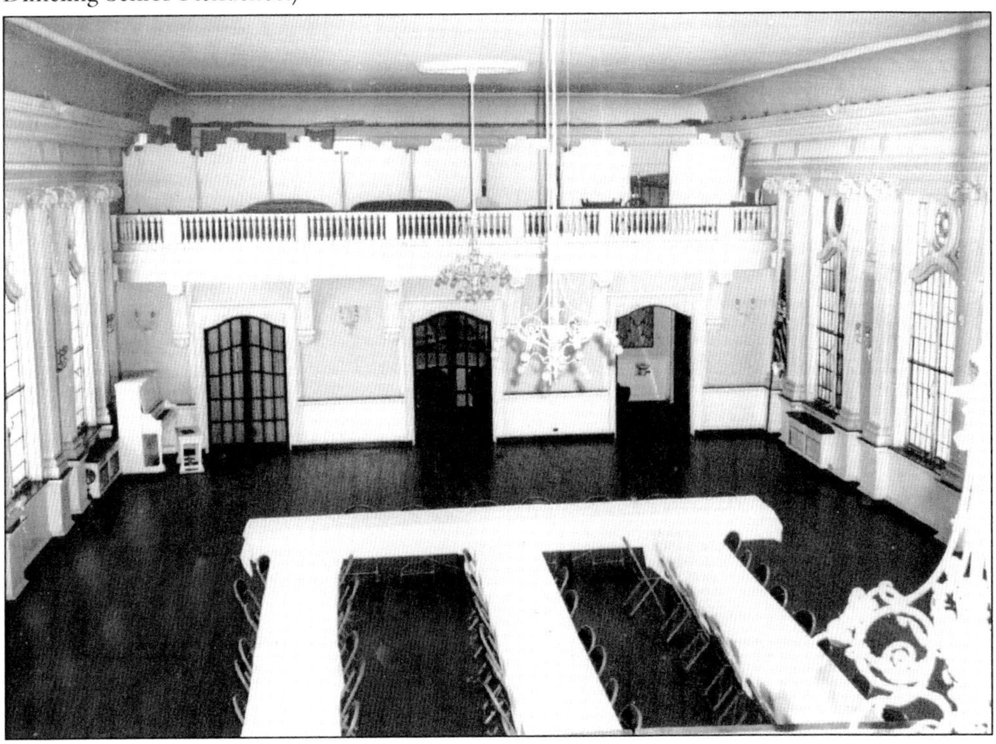

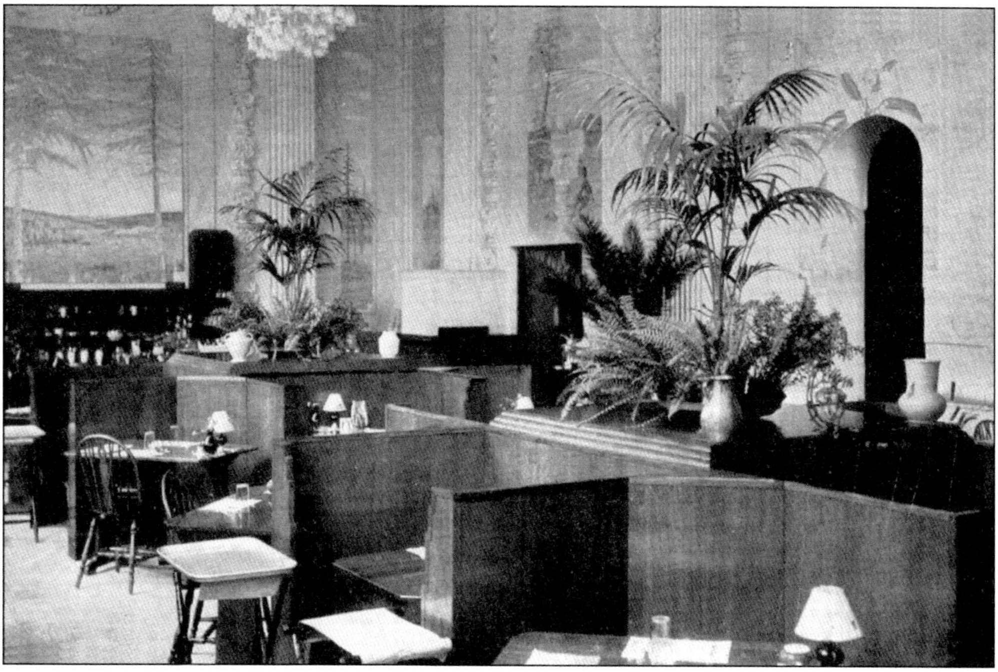

This postcard describes the Dimeling Coffee Shop as "one of Pennsylvania's most beautiful coffee shops. Wall murals depict early Indian life in the Clearfield vicinity."

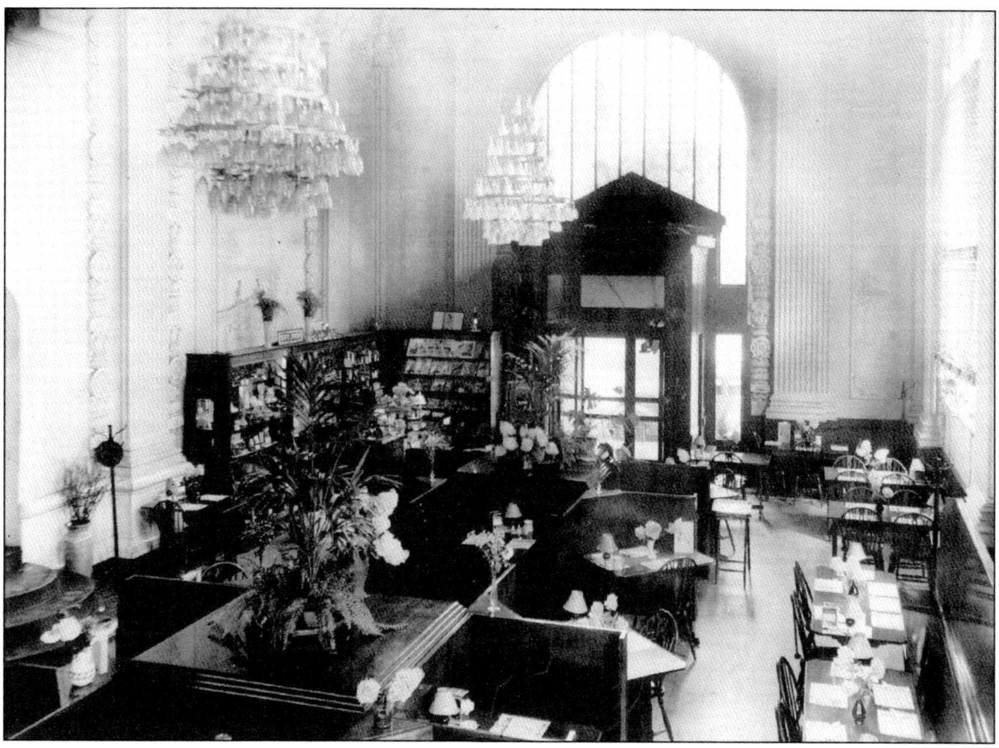

This wider view shows more of the Dimeling Coffee Shop. (Courtesy Dimeling Senior Residence.)

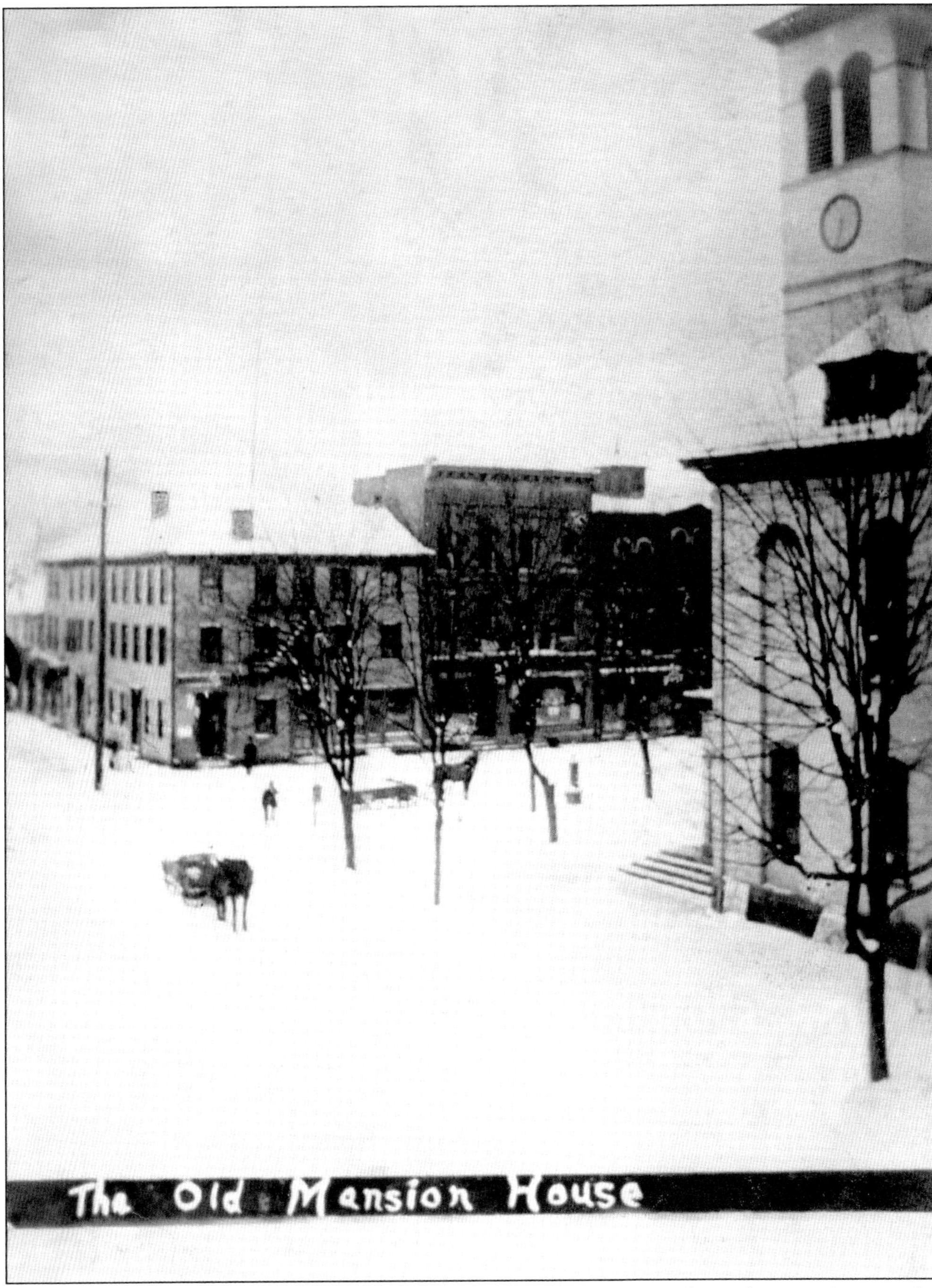

Yes, before the Dimeling, something did stand on the corner across from the courthouse. The Old Mansion House and the building next to it were both torn down in the early 1900s to make way for the Dimeling.

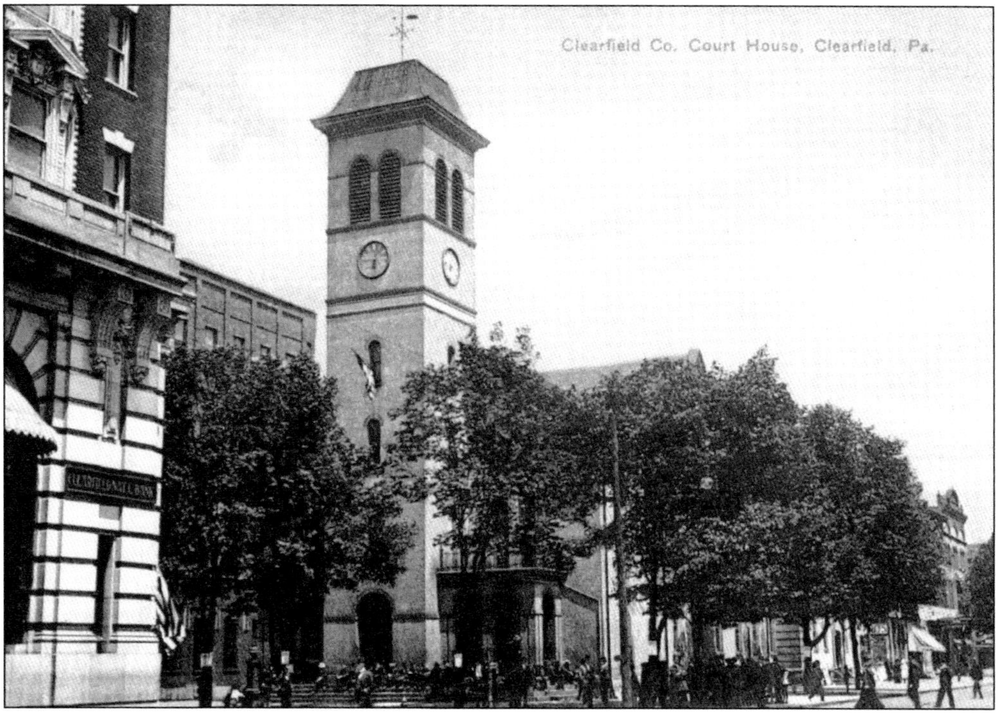

The second most popular subject for postcards is the Clearfield County Courthouse. The courthouse, which is still in use today, was built during the Civil War. The original building was only 60 by 96 feet. However, a 51- by 75-foot addition was completed in 1884. Those renovations included a steam heating system. As the county grew, so did the need for more space. The problem was first settled by placing offices in various buildings across the street. A debate over whether to build another addition or a new courthouse raged for many years before an annex was built in 1996.

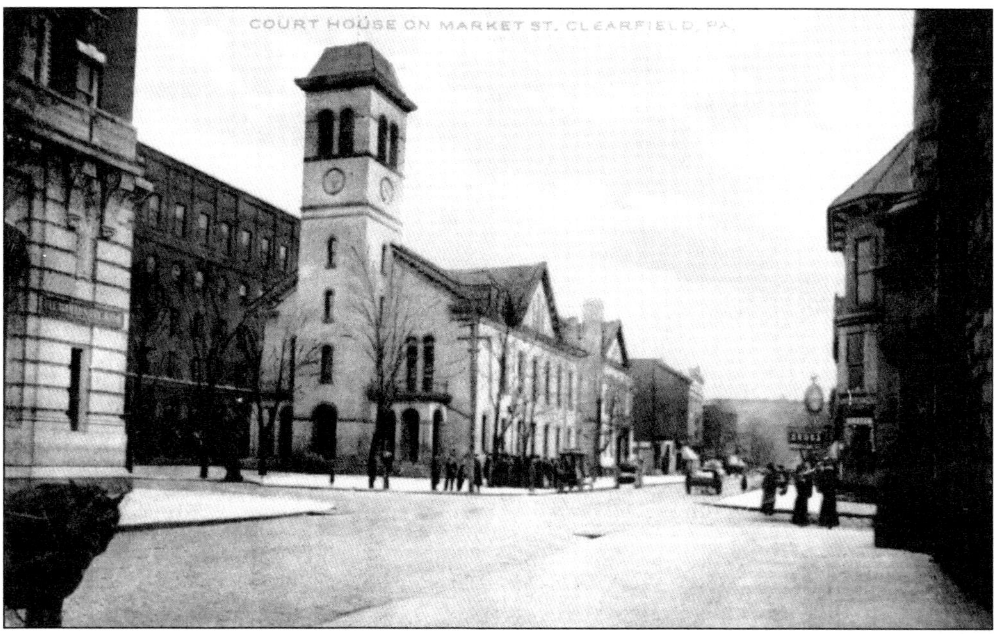

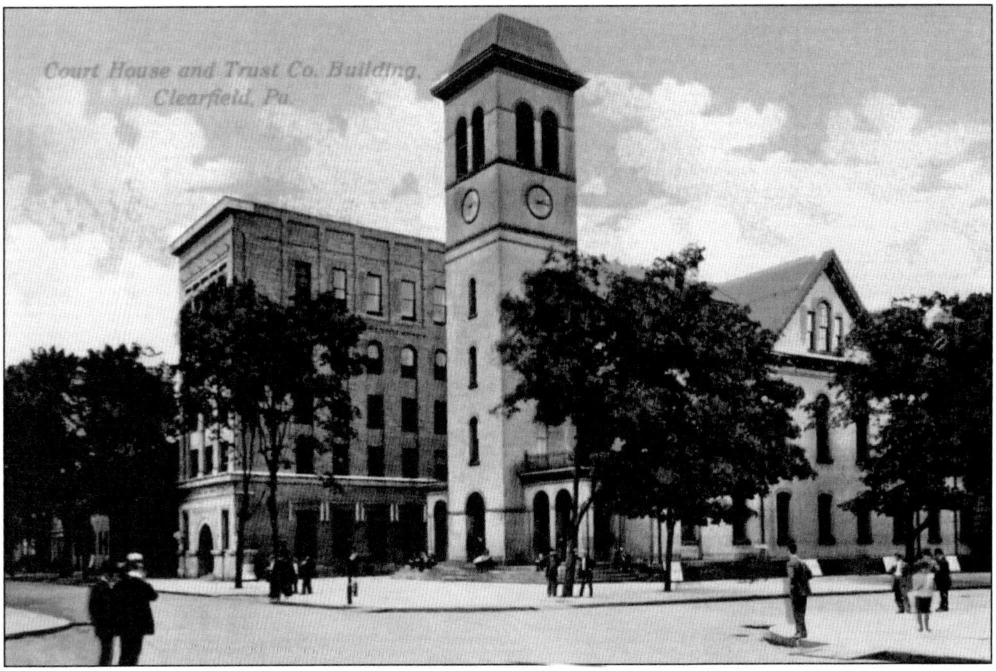

The Clearfield County Courthouse is shown from a different angle. In these pictures, one can also see its longtime neighbor, the Clearfield Bank & Trust Company building.

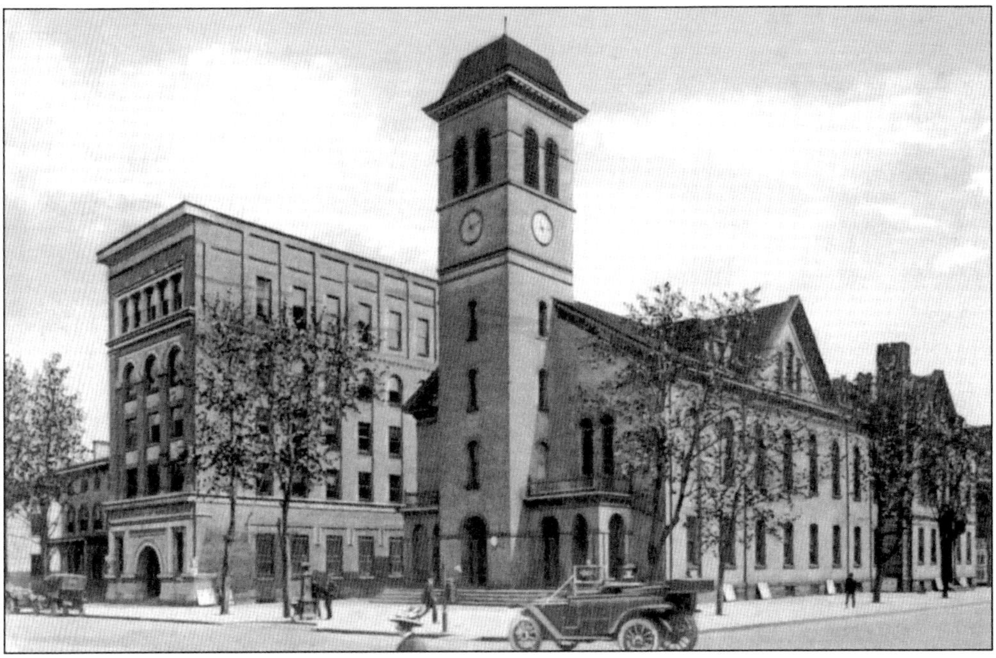

The Clearfield Bank & Trust Company building was completed in 1903.

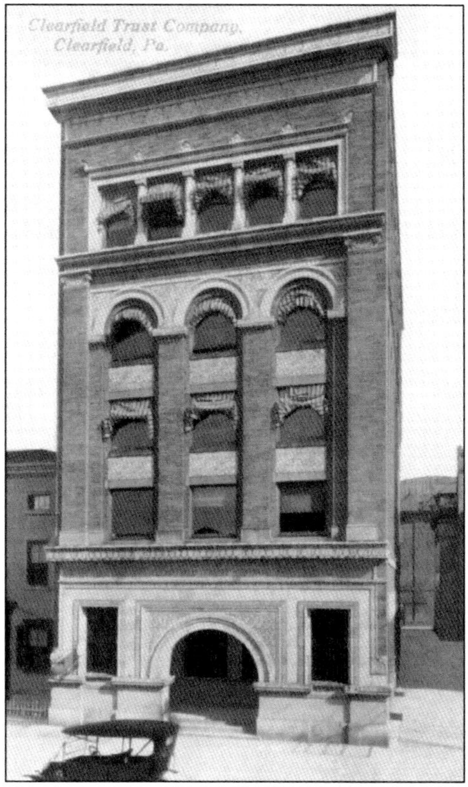

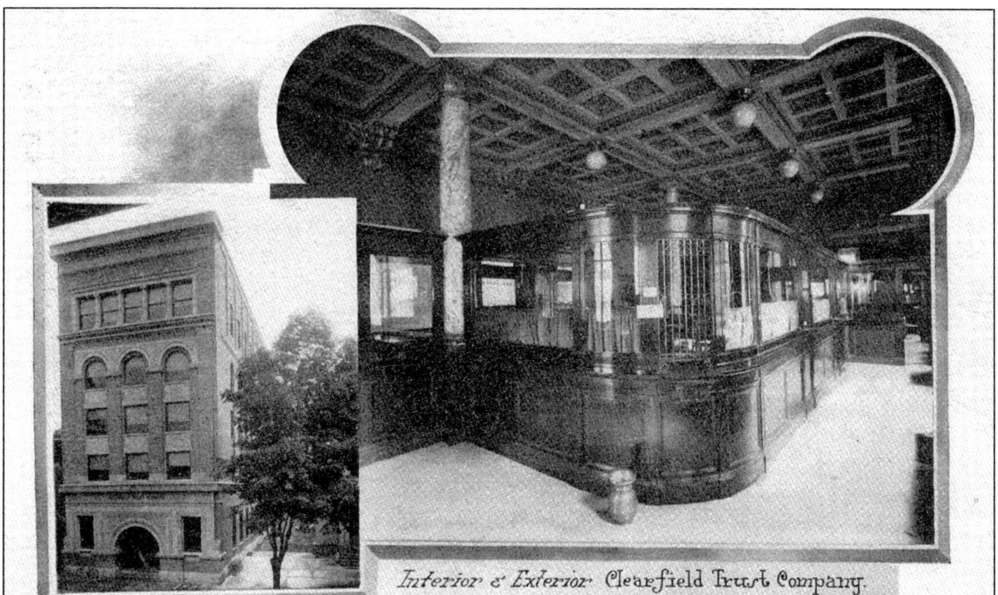

This 1913 card features not just the exterior but an interesting interior view of what was then the Clearfield Trust Company. (Courtesy Zalno collection.)

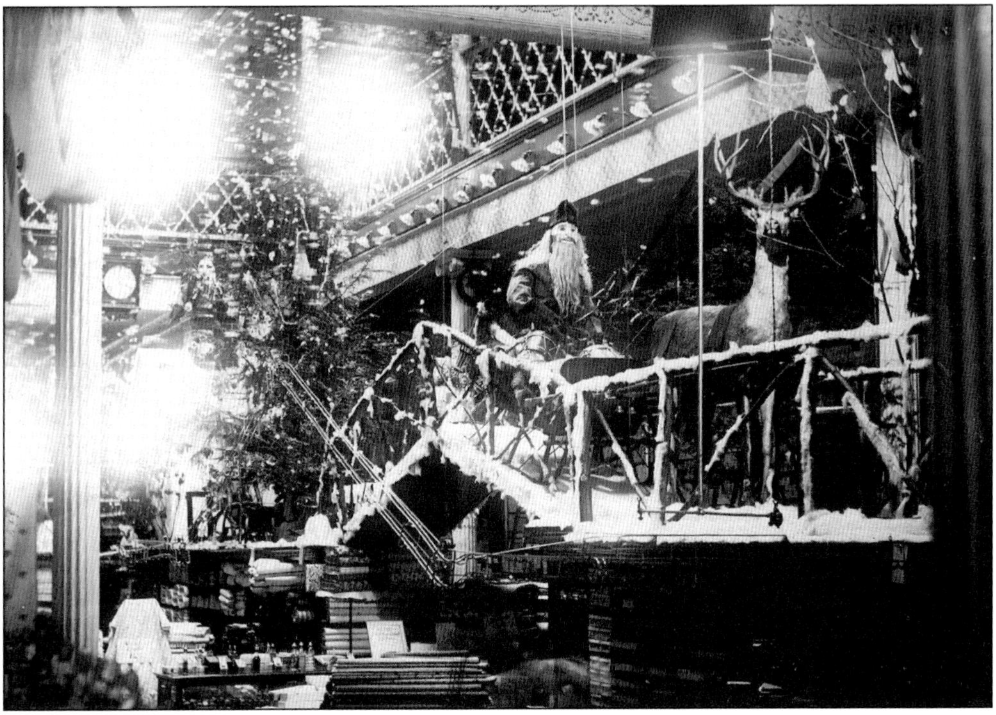

The Leitzinger Bros. Department Store remained a part of downtown Clearfield for more than 100 years. Here is one of its famous Christmas displays.

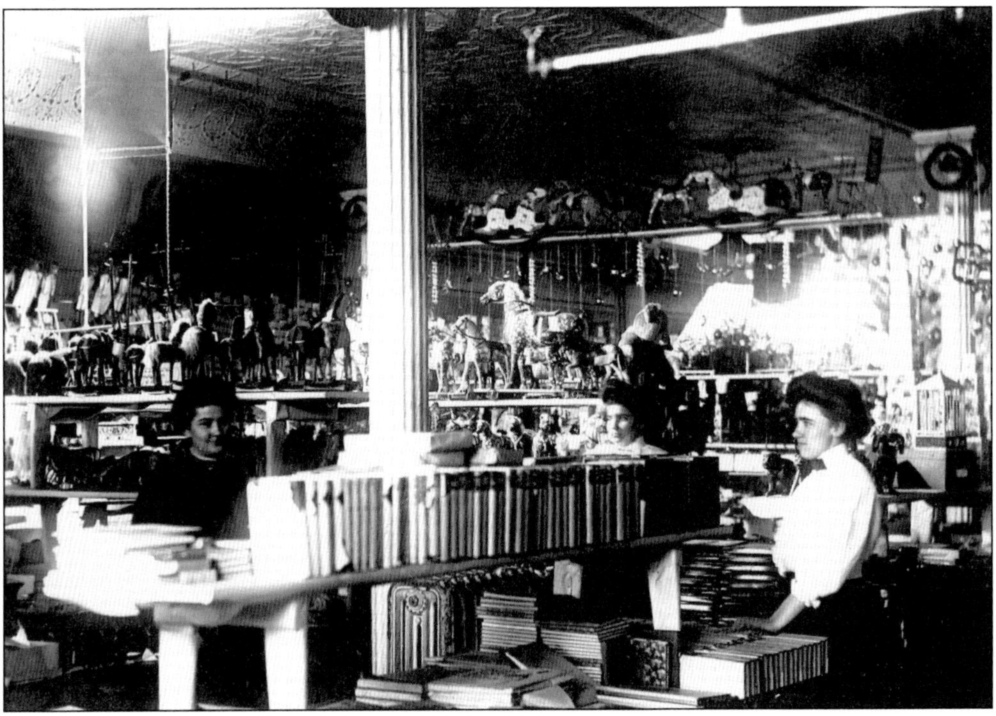

This view shows the interior of the Leitzinger Bros. Department Store. It is described as "one of the holiday scenes in Leitzinger Bros. store, December 1907." (Courtesy Leitzinger collection.)

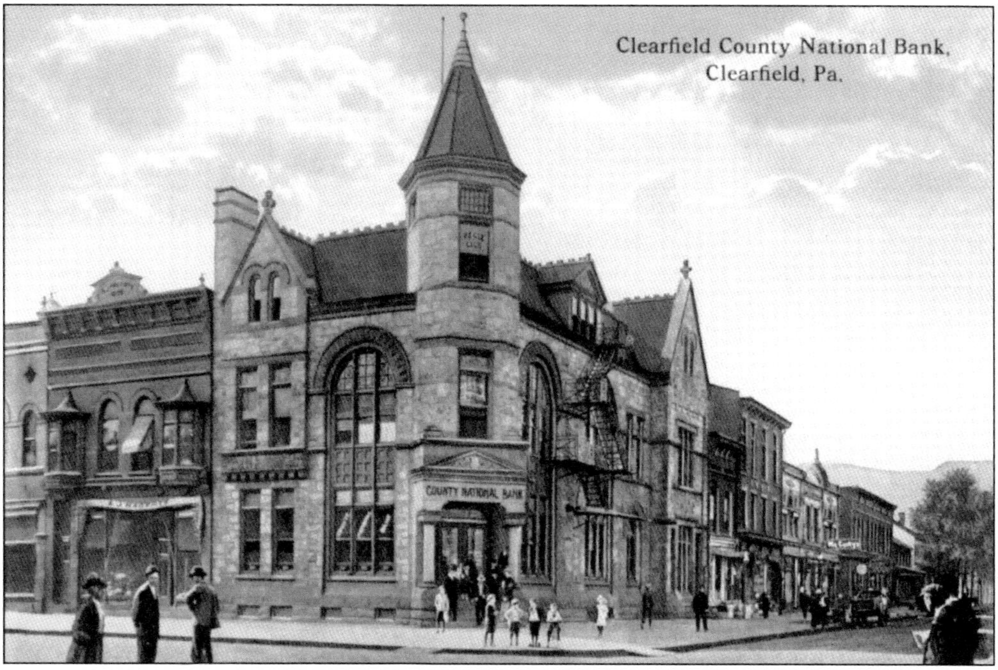

The third landmark at the corner of Market and Second Streets is the County National Bank building, constructed in 1890. To the left of the building is A.J. Hagerty's Dry Goods and Millinery Shop. Today, this is part of the County National Bank building.

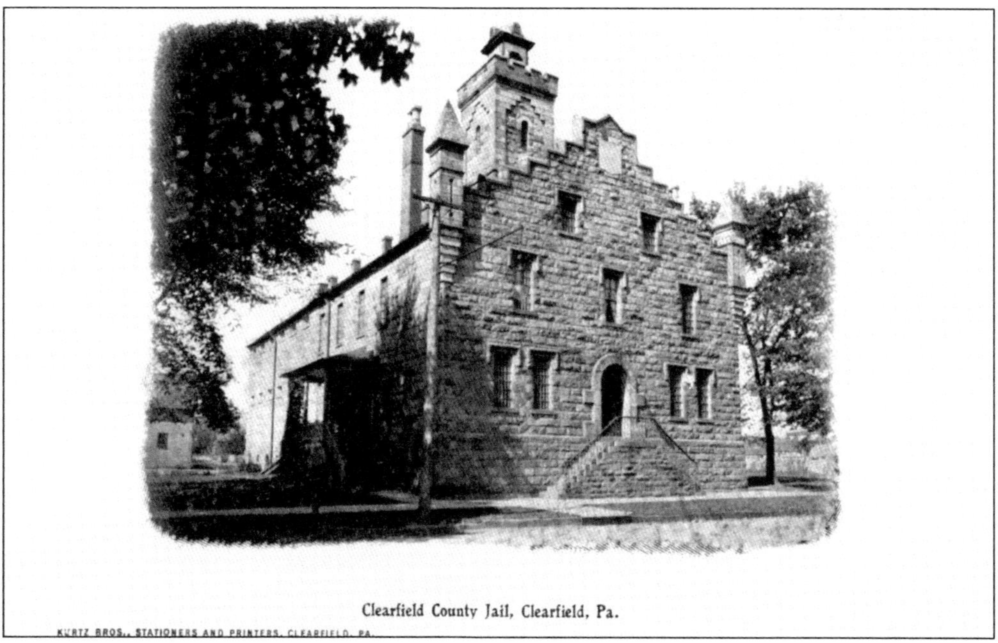

This interesting building is the old Clearfield County Jail. For more than 100 years, prisoners were kept here. Today, the building is home to Land and Mapping Services. (Courtesy Zalno collection.)

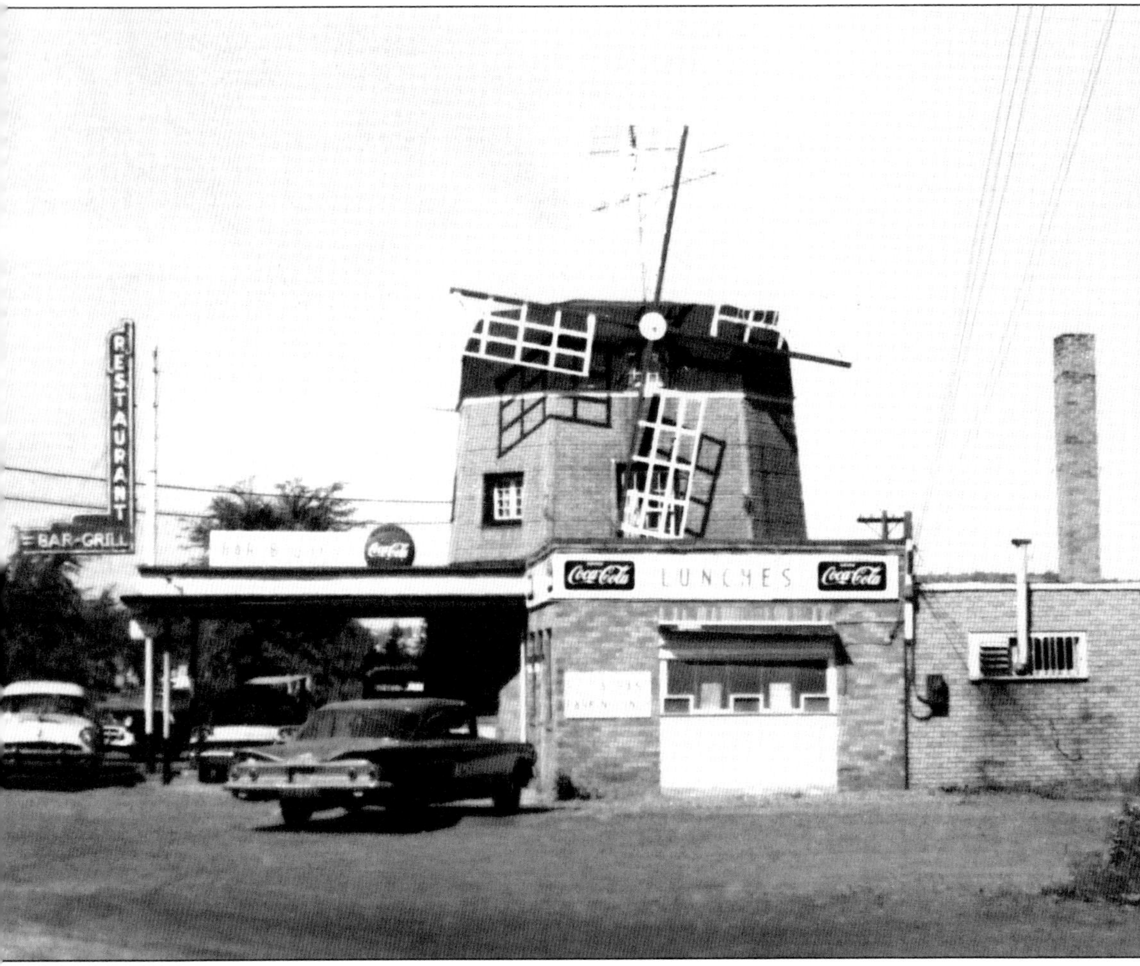

The Windmill Restaurant and gas station was located on Old Town Road. During the summer of 1933, Eleanor Roosevelt ate lunch here, dining on a toasted cheese sandwich, a piece of apple pie, and a cup of black coffee. Instead of an entourage, she traveled with only a female companion thought to be a secretary. Although not a postcard, this photograph and story are worthy of inclusion in any history of the area.

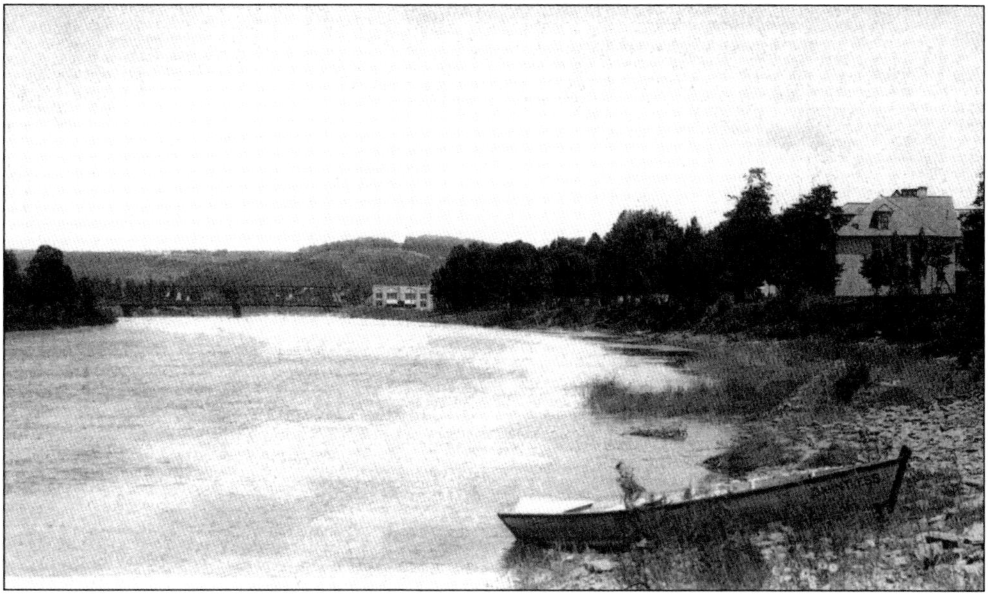

The most scenic landmark of Clearfield is the west branch of the Susquehanna. That is the Market Street Bridge in the background. (Courtesy Zalno collection.)

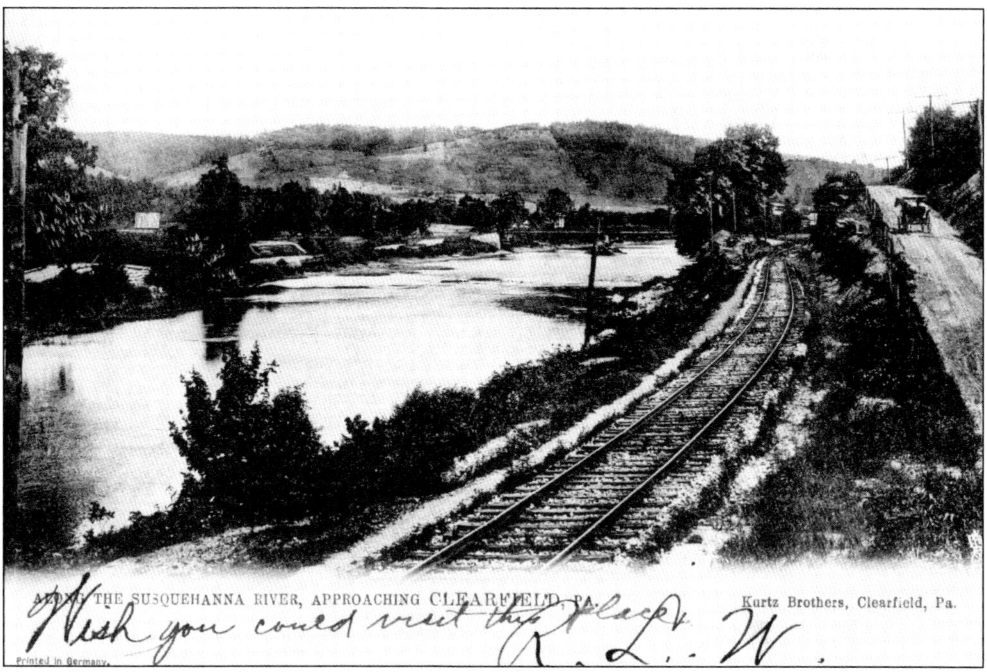

This is a view along the river between Hyde and Clearfield. Today, the road runs next to the river and the railroad is on the right. (Courtesy Zalno collection.)

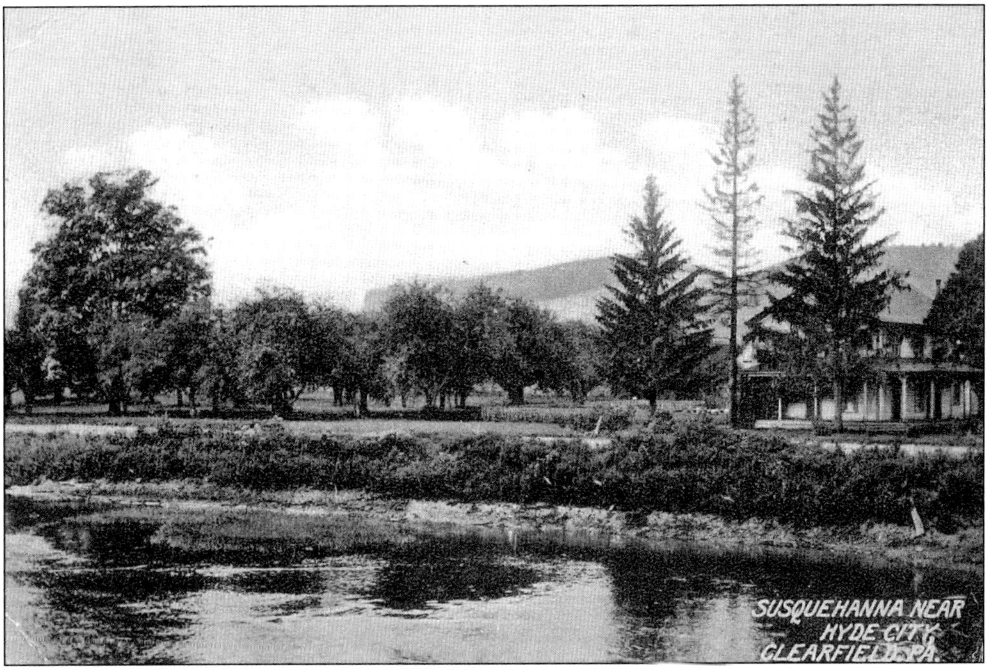

Shown here is the river near Hyde as it appeared in 1908. (Courtesy Zalno collection.)

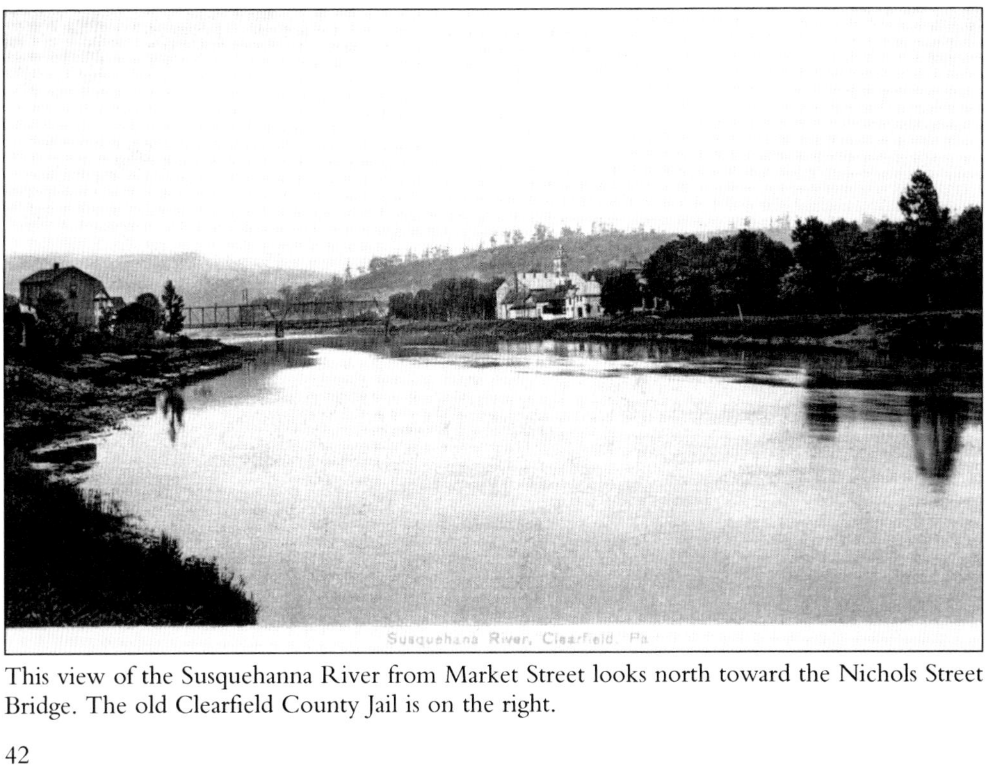

This view of the Susquehanna River from Market Street looks north toward the Nichols Street Bridge. The old Clearfield County Jail is on the right.

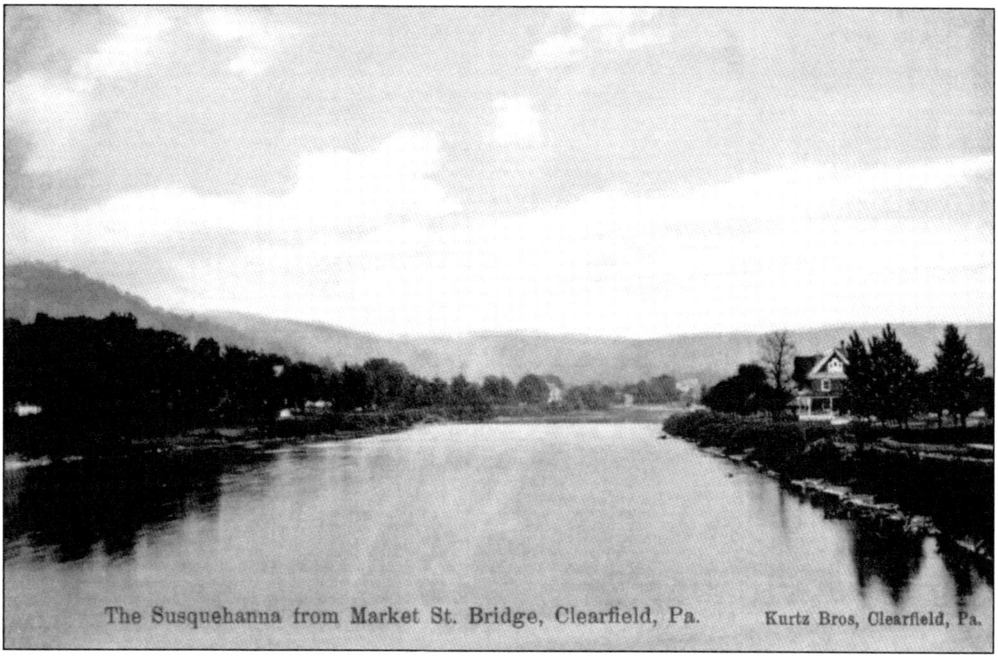

From the Market Street Bridge, looking south, this view shows the west branch of the Susquehanna River.

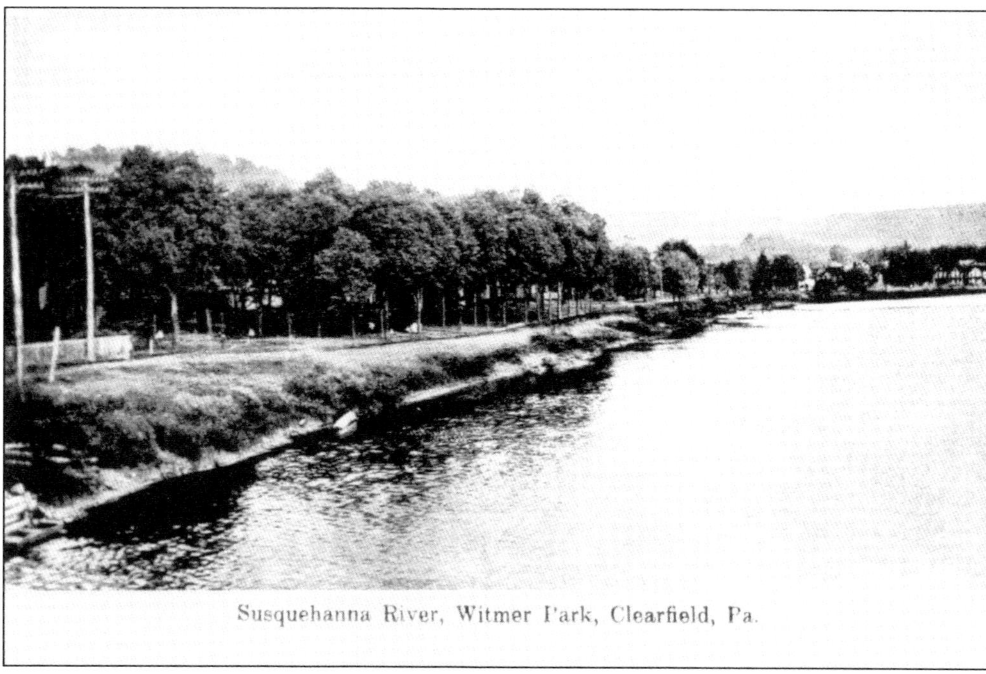

Pictured here is Upper Witmer Park, probably from the Market Street Bridge as well.

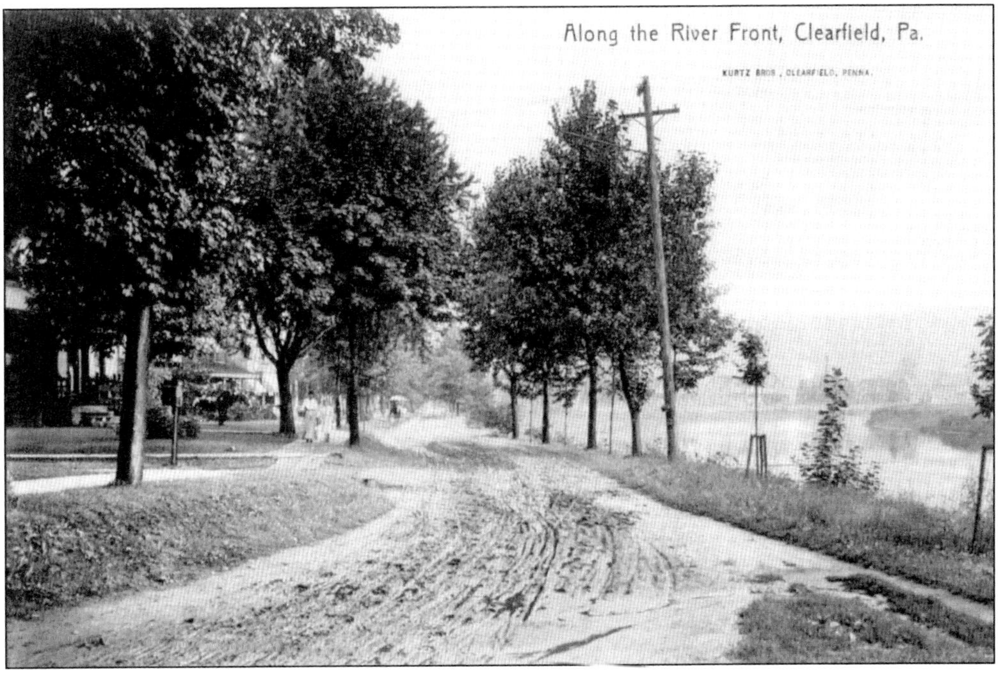

This path runs along the riverfront in Upper Witmer Park, near Front Street. Buses once traveled this way from the junior high school. The path still exists today.

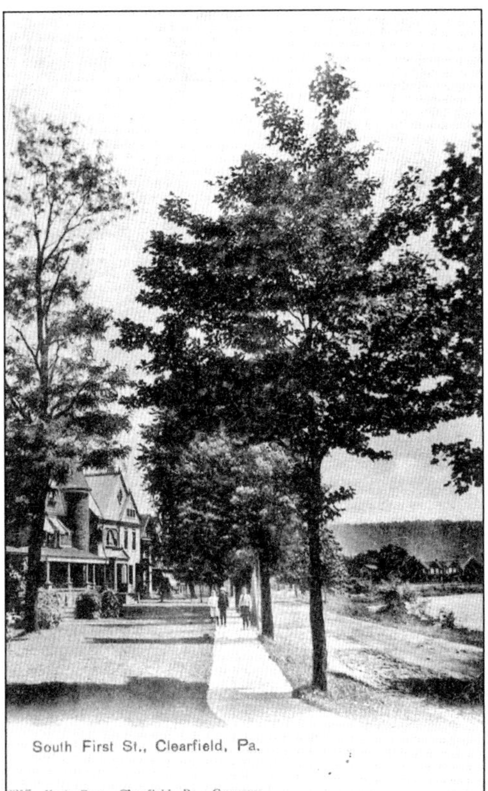

Shown here in 1912 is South First (or Front) Street in the same area as above. The path from the park is to the right of the children. (Courtesy Zalno collection.)

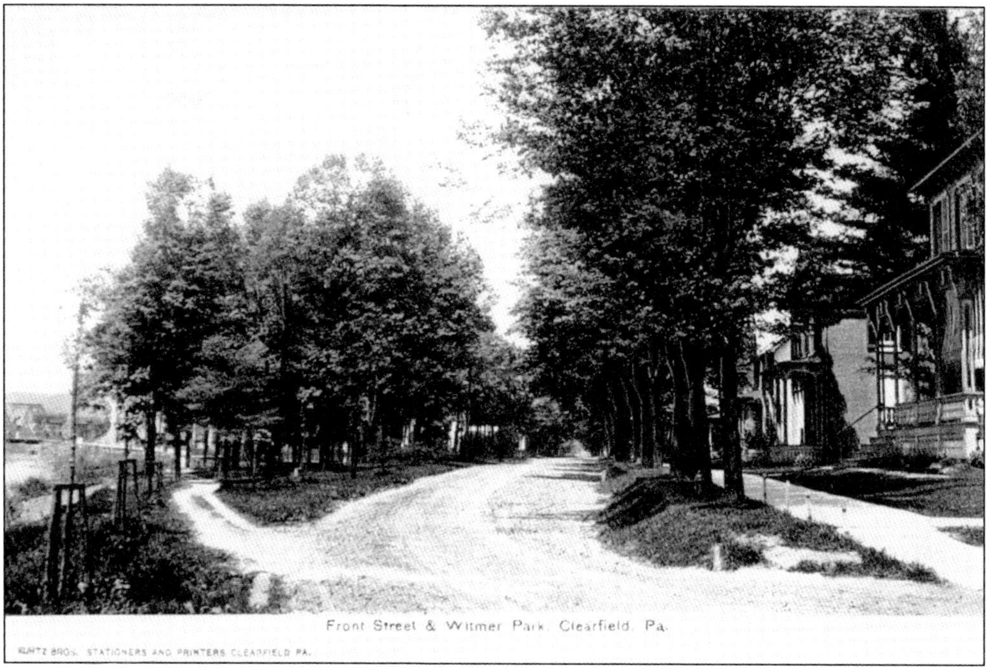

This postcard photograph, taken in 1909, shows an opposite angle of Upper Witmer Park and the path.

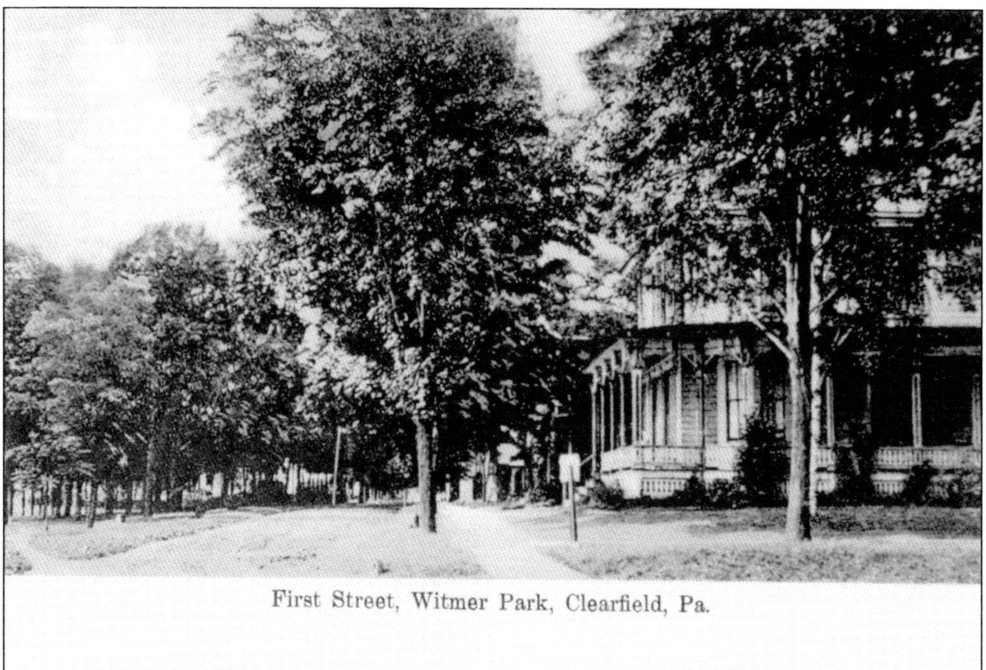

This card, as with many others, existed in two variations. One was black and white and the other a tinted blue. It pictures Upper Witmer Park from Walnut Street. To the right is the A.K. Wright home, which today harbors the offices of Dr. Jon Wood and Dr. David Bell.

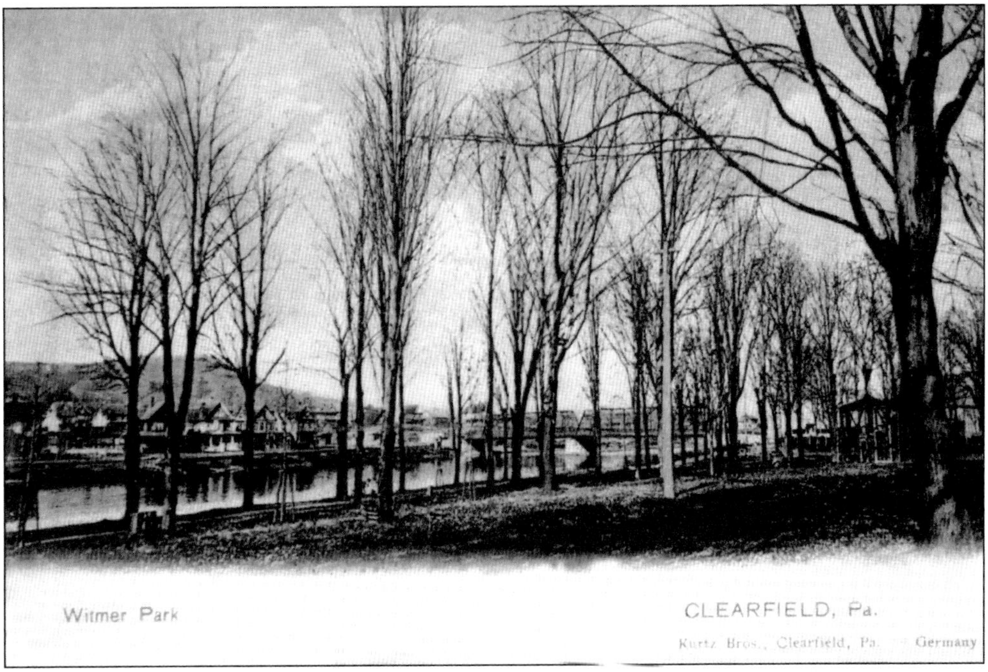

Witmer Park has been a part of the town since the beginning. When Clearfield County was first being set up, Abraham Witmer donated land for a courthouse, a jail, a market house, and an academy, as well as for general public use. The public lots became Upper and Lower Witmer Park.

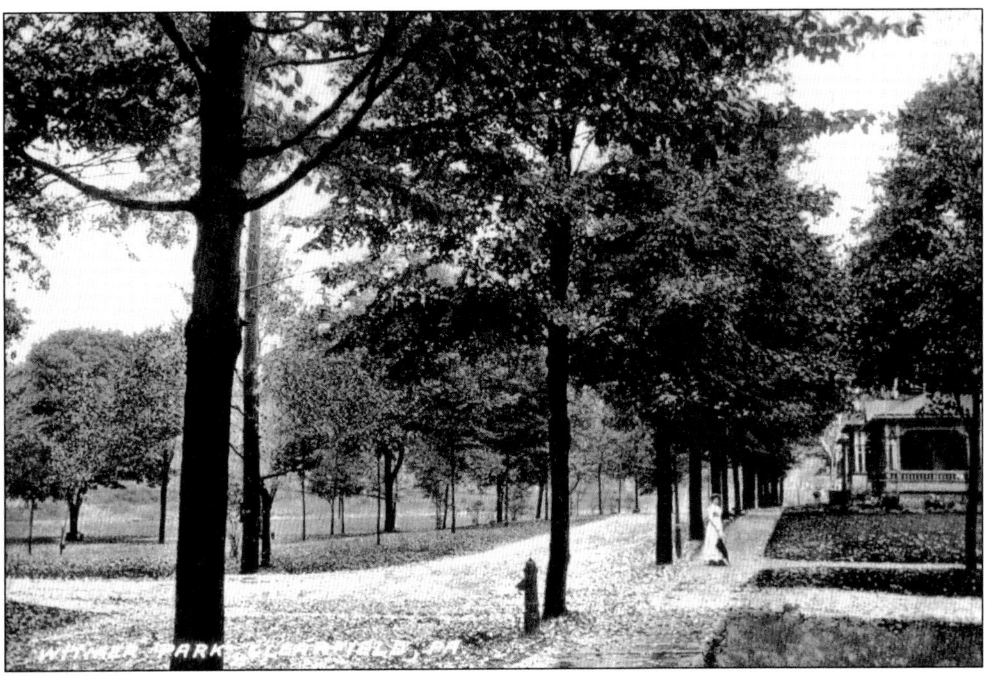

This view shows Lower Witmer Park from Locust Street.

Three

Disasters

KURTZ BROS., CLEARFIELD, PA. Wreck of Electric Light Plant and Smith's Mill after the Explosion.

At 8:15 on the morning of November 25, 1906, the town was rocked by the sound of an explosion. A boiler at the Central Pennsylvania Light and Power Company exploded, destroying both the electric plant and the neighboring Smith's Grist Mill (the area on Leavy Avenue where Mitchell Milling is now located). The explosion also damaged several nearby homes and blew a brick onto the bed of a little girl who had gotten up just a few minutes earlier.

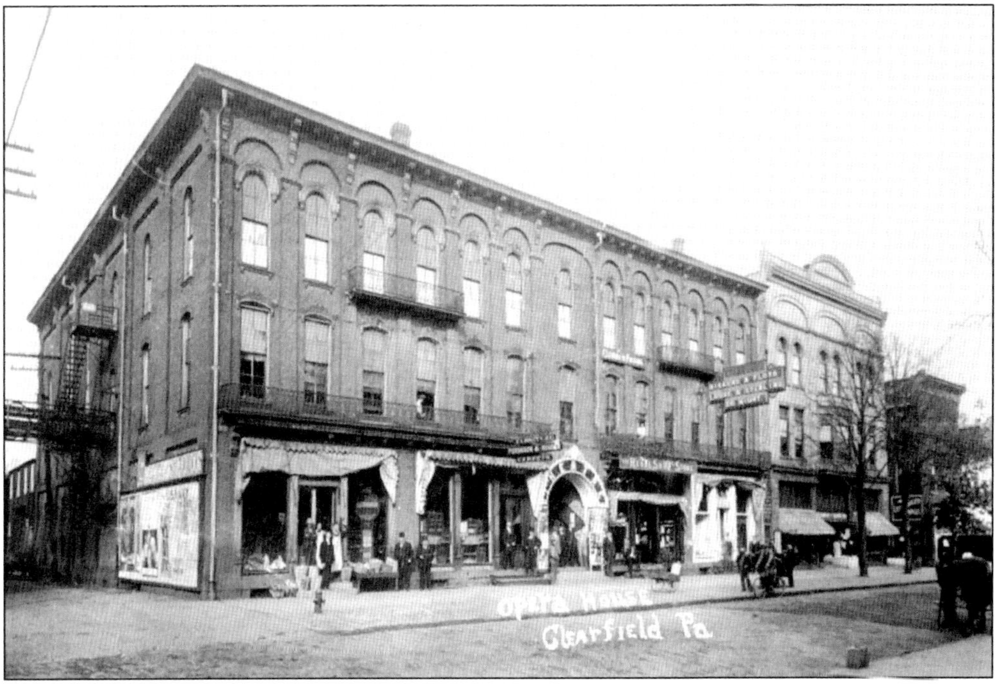

The Pie Opera House was built in 1873. The building also housed the Regal five-and-dime store (to the right of the horseshoe-type entrance to the opera house). The store was owned by Charles T. Kurtz, who sold it in 1903 to devote his full time to operating Kurtz Bros. To the right is the Leitzinger Bros. building, which at this time was only three floors.

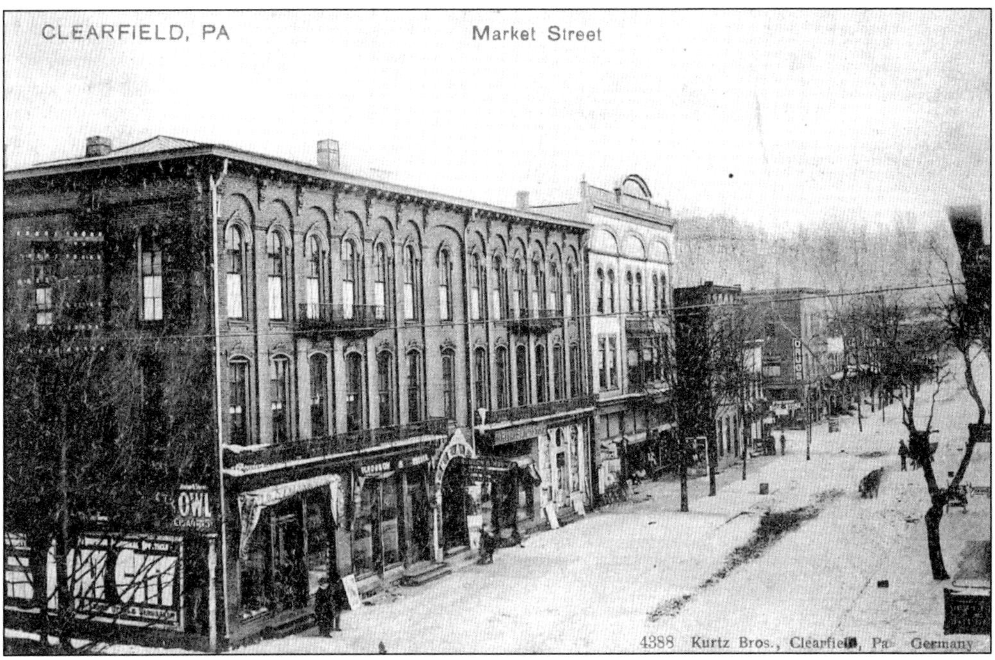

This angle of the opera house, from 1907, shows more of Market Street, including the Hotel Bloom, which is next to Leitzinger's. (Courtesy Zalno collection.)

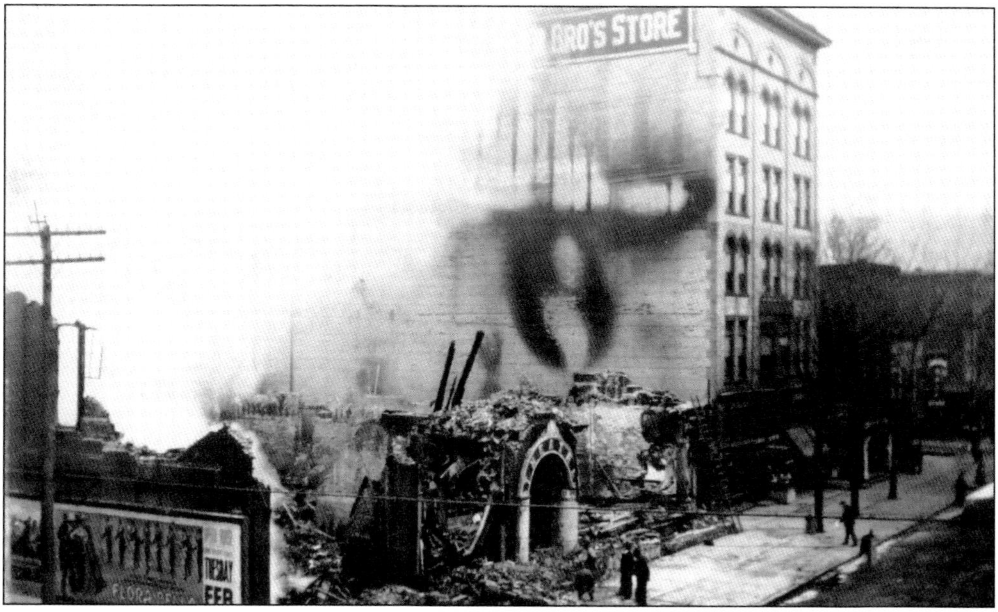

On February 27, 1917, the Pie Opera House caught fire, and the entire building was destroyed. Note that the Leitzinger Bros. building is now its full five stories.

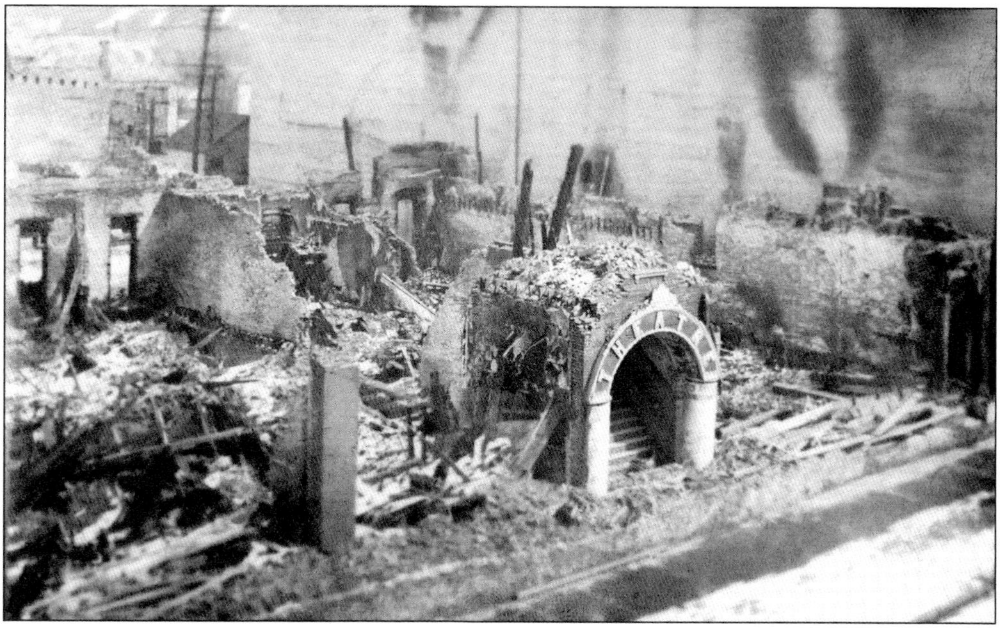

The aftermath of the opera house fire can be seen in this closer view. The postmark on the back of this card is dated March 27, 1917, just one month after the disaster.

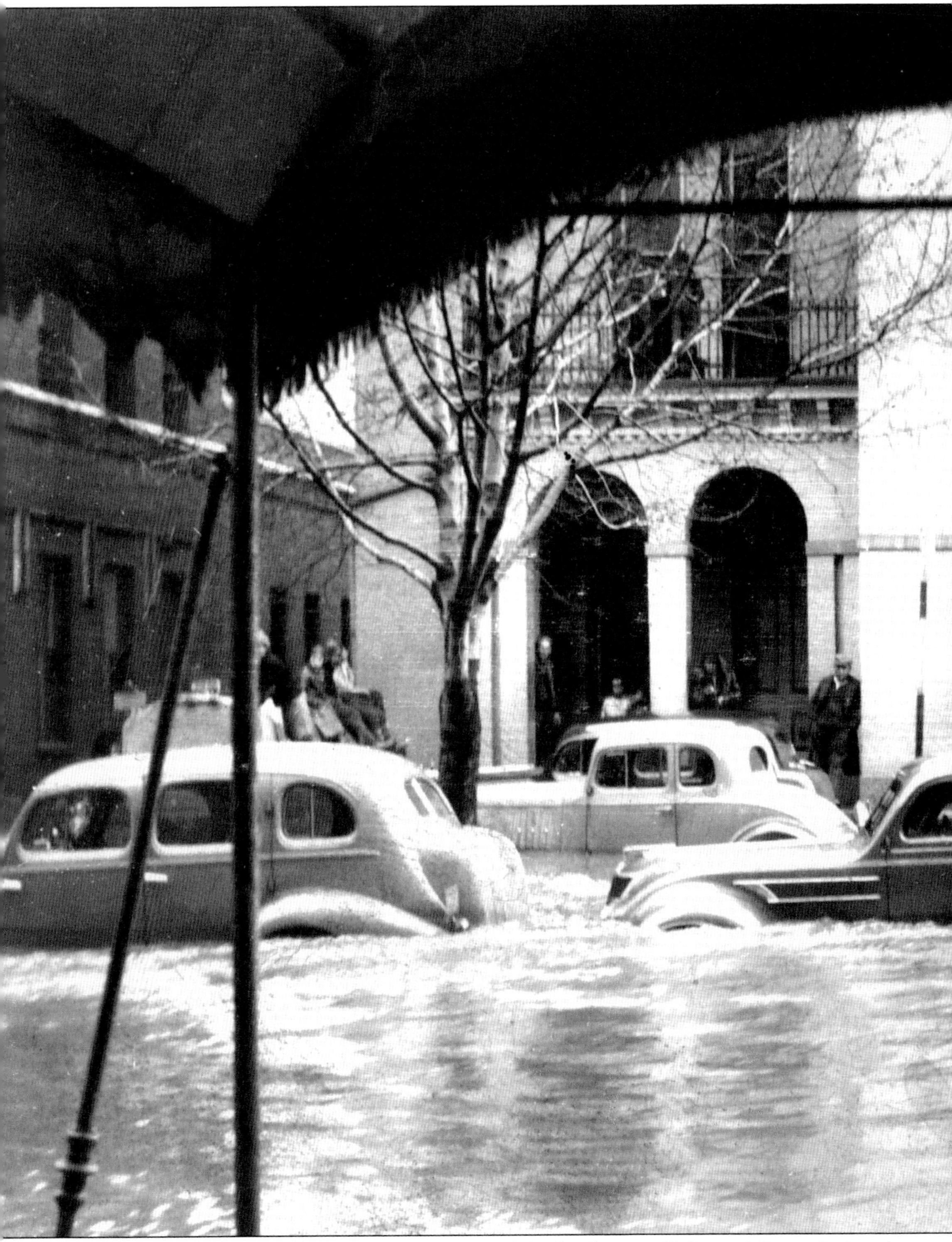

People huddle in the safety of the courthouse while floodwaters fill Second Street during the St. Patrick's Day flood of 1936. This photograph was taken from the lobby of the Dimeling Hotel

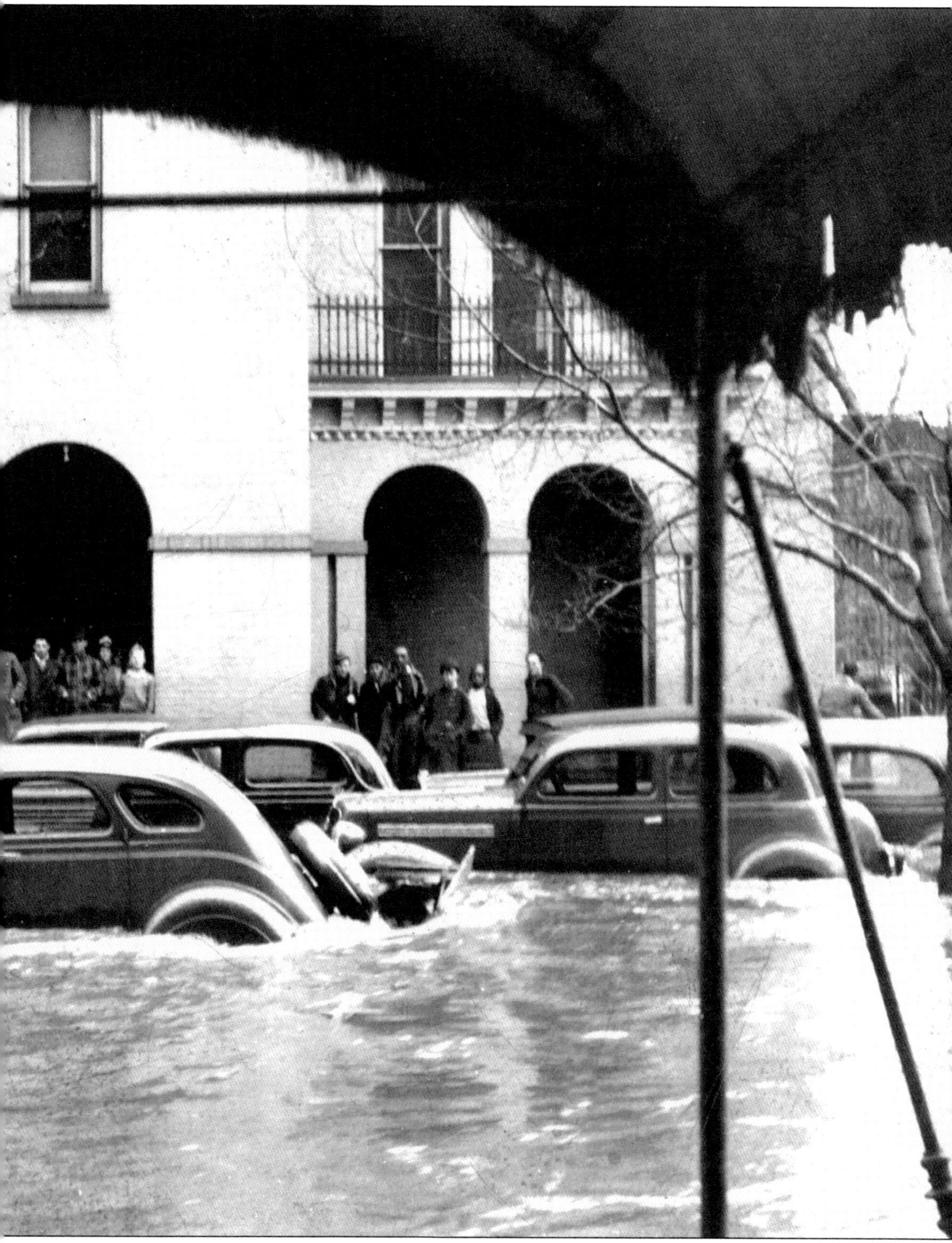

across the street. (Courtesy Leitzinger collection.)

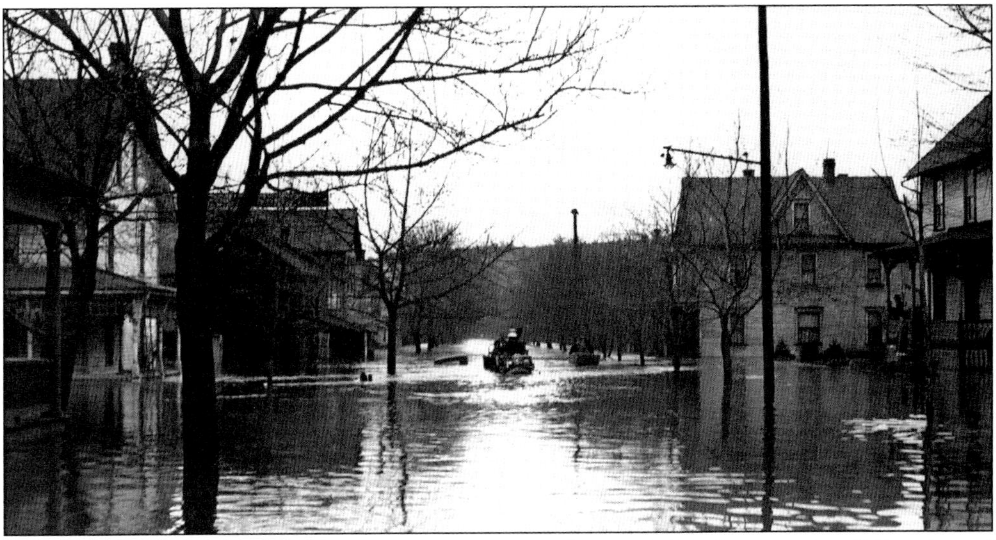

A boat makes its way down the road in this March 18, 1936 photograph of Fourth and Cherry Streets.

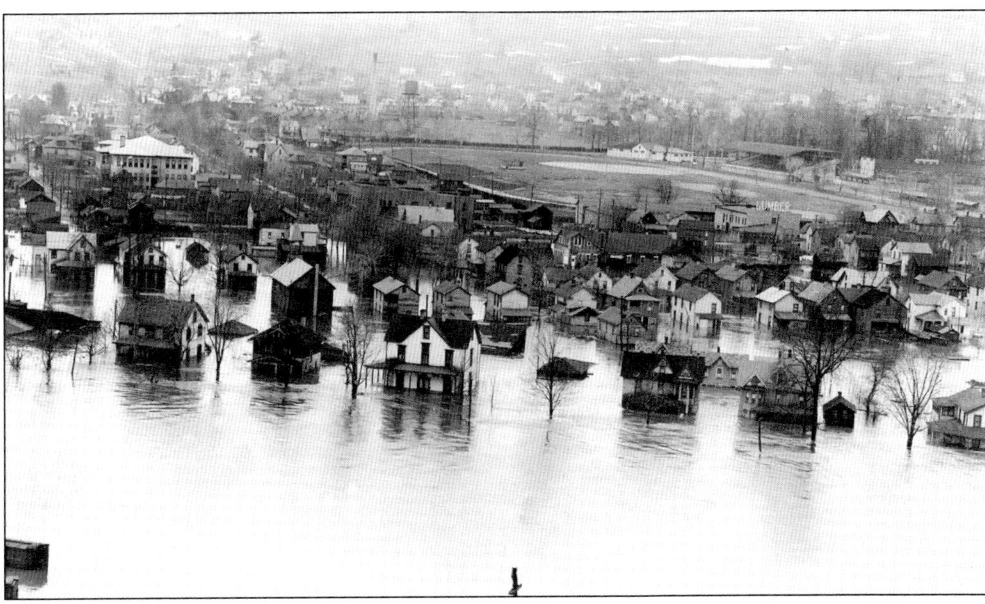

Water fills the West Side of Clearfield. The Driving Park can be seen in the upper right corner, and the Third Ward School is on the left.

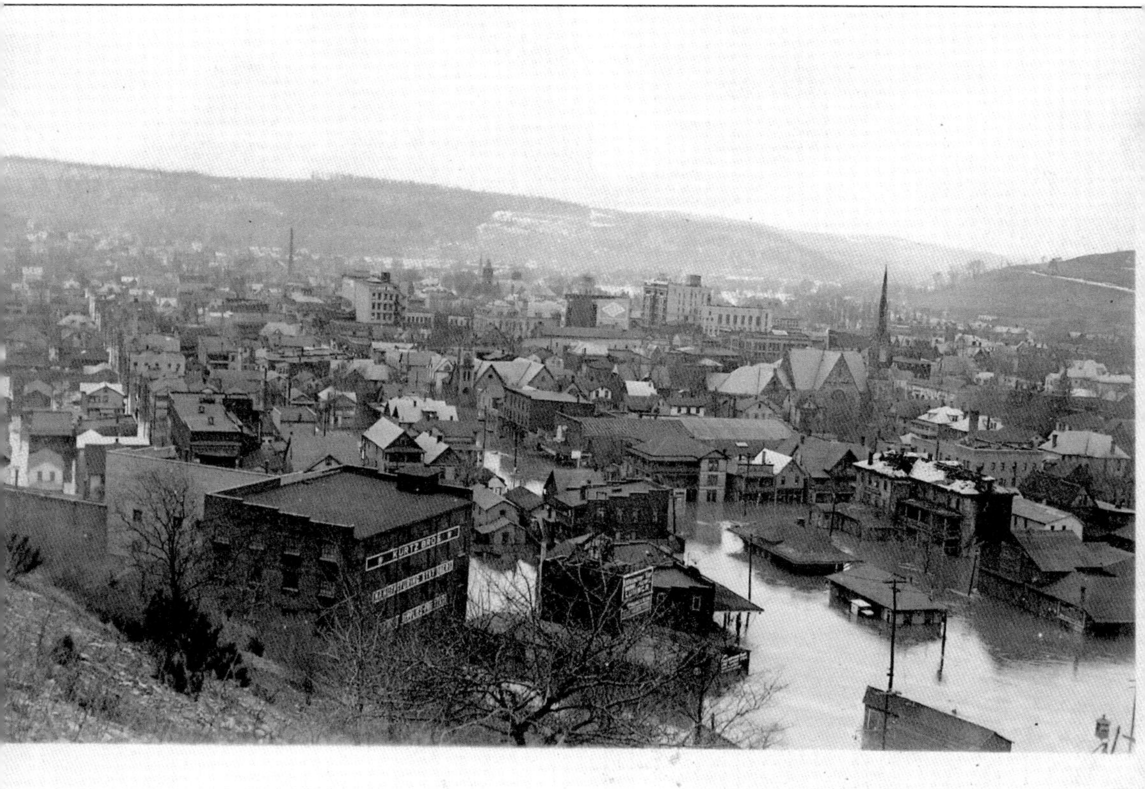

This image provides another look at the floodwaters of 1936 from a hill near Kurtz Bros. (Courtesy Zalno collection.)

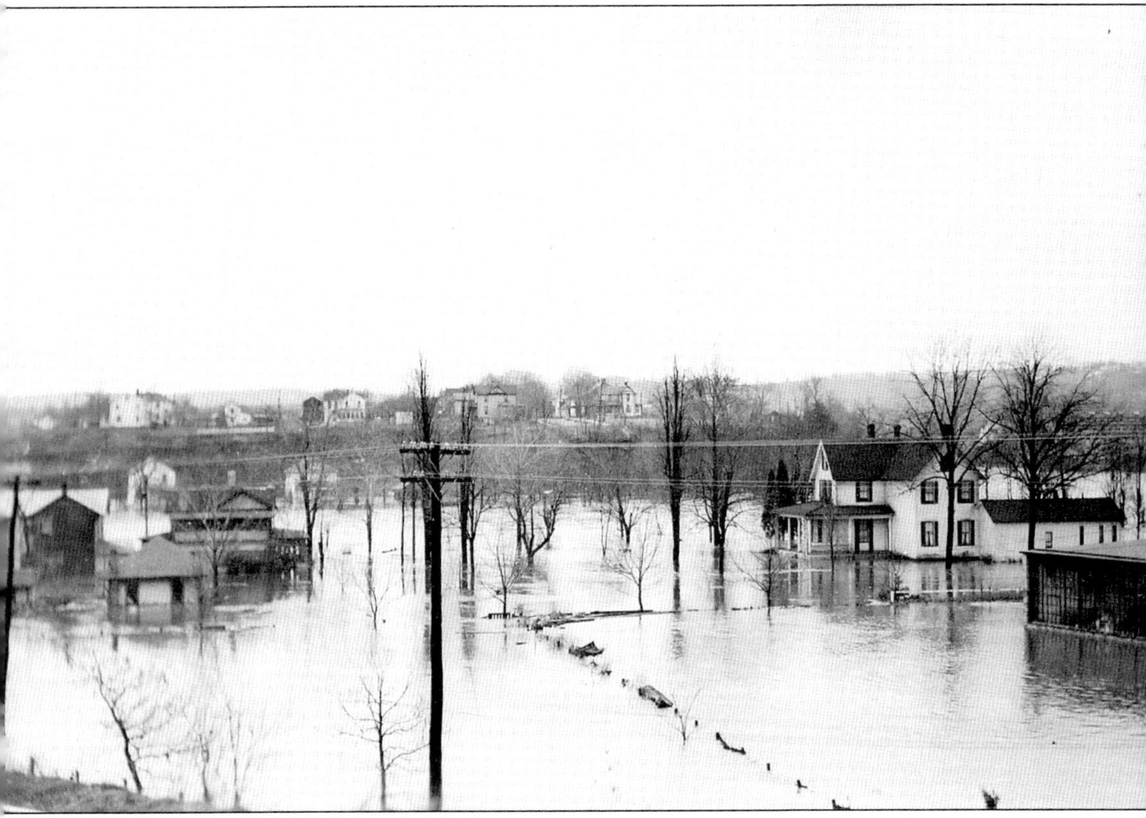

Shown here is Curwensville during the 1936 flood. (Courtesy Test collection.)

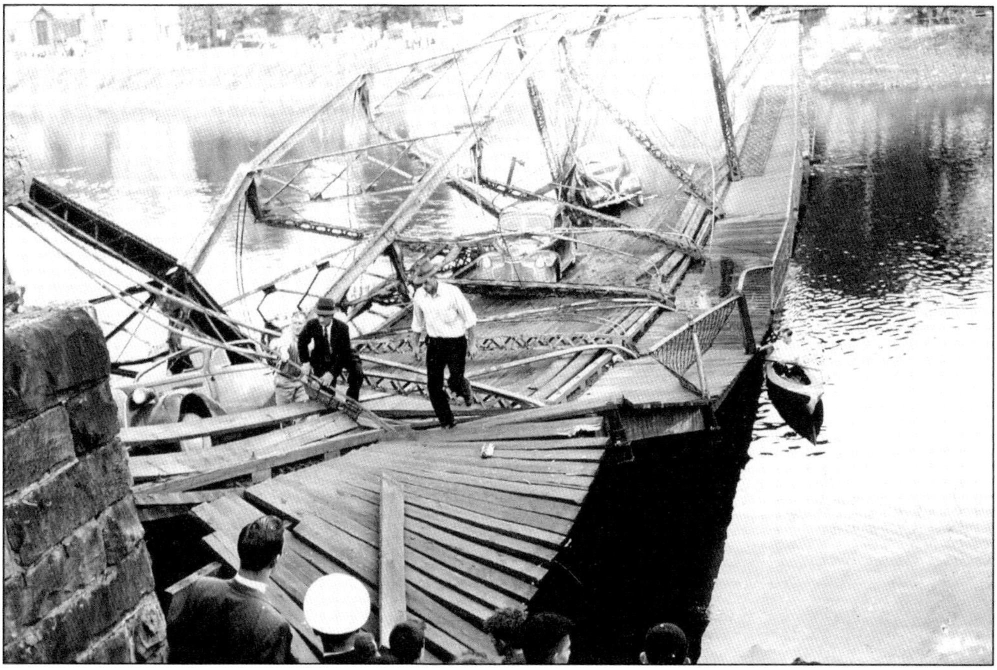

On June 3, 1944, a portion of the Nichols Street Bridge collapsed after a six-ton truck hauling a 14-ton tractor struck a girder on the western end. Three cars and three pedestrians were on the bridge at the time. Only one person was seriously injured.

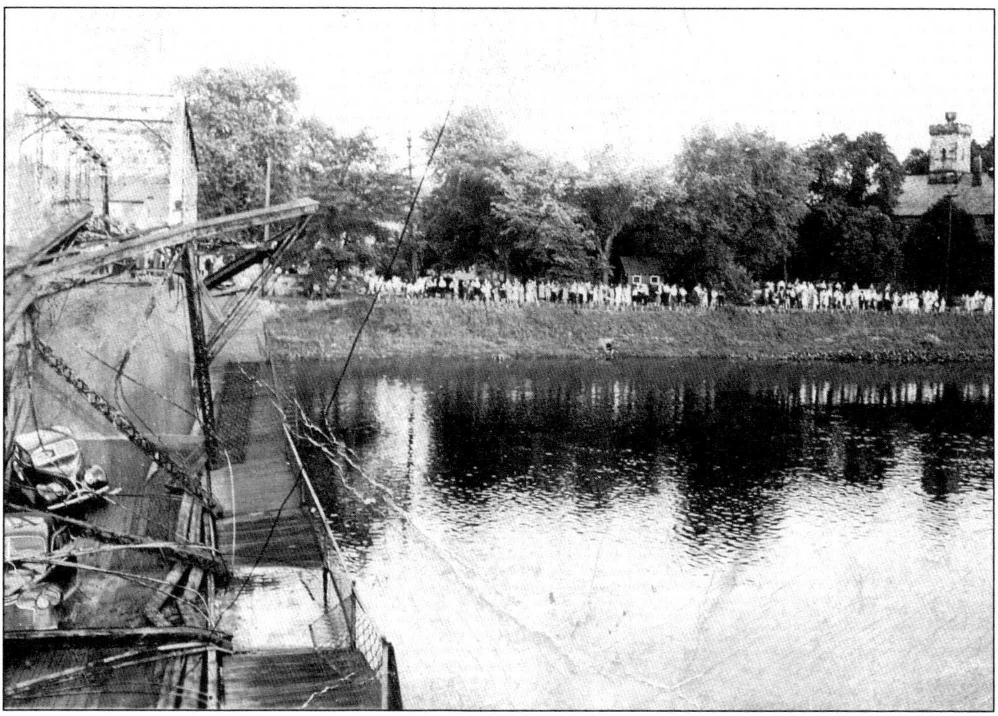

A crowd watches the tragedy from the riverbank near the Clearfield County Jail.

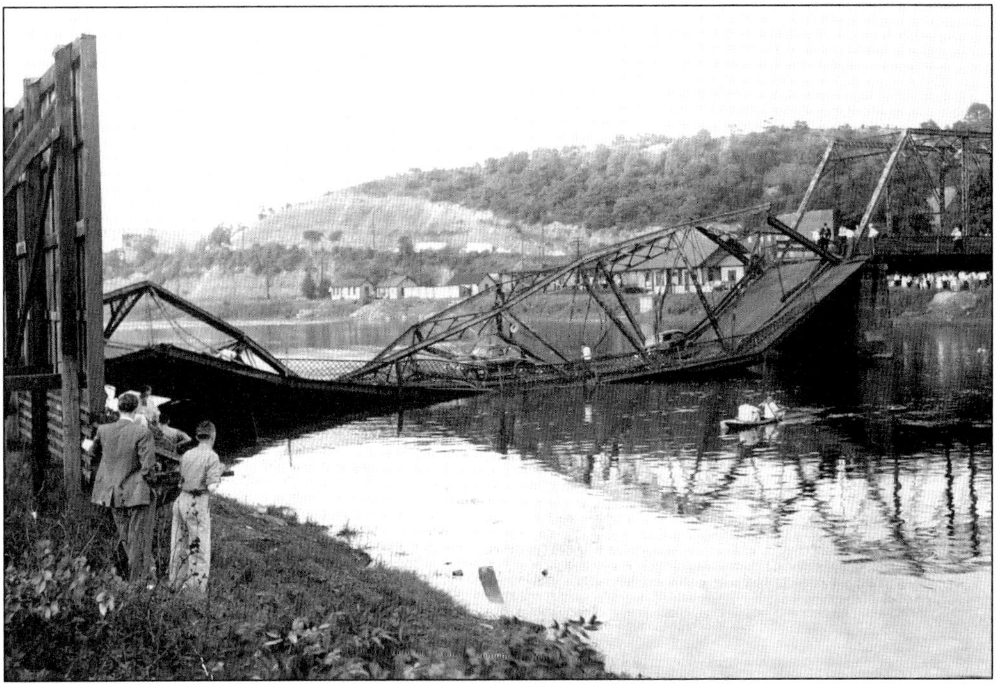

Pictured here is a full view of the Nichols Street Bridge. After waiting for 10 to 15 minutes, the driver who caused the collapse left the scene. He was later apprehended near Leitzinger Spring and fined $50 for transporting equipment more than 96 inches in length without a permit.

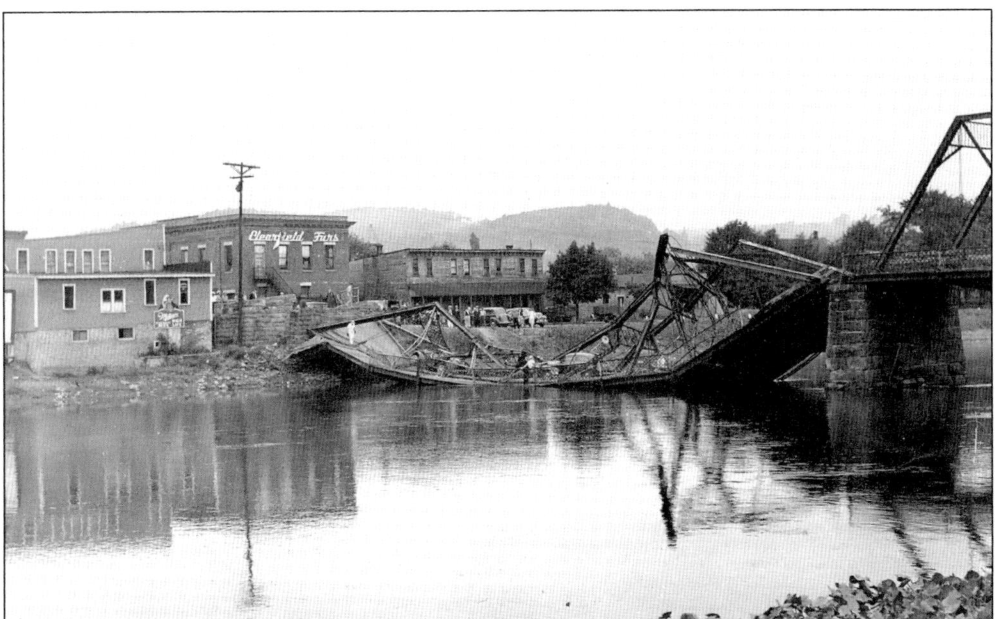

This photograph shows another angle of the Nichols Street Bridge collapse. The bridge was not replaced until after World War II due to a shortage of steel. (Courtesy Test collection.)

Four

Community

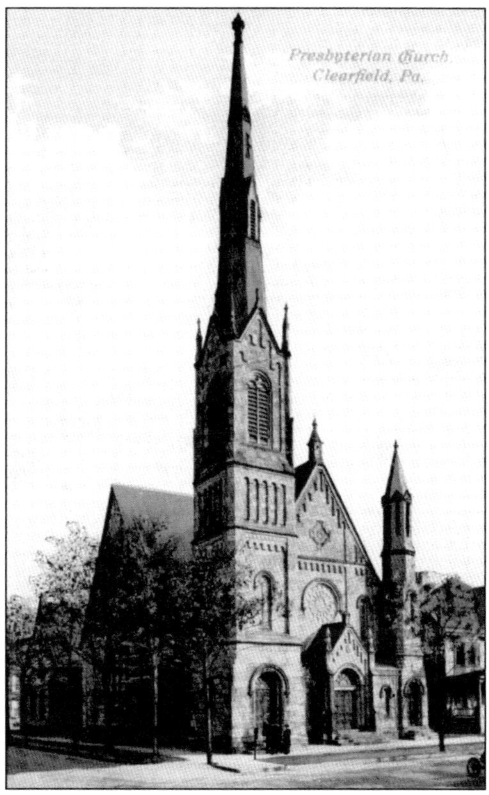

A common subject for area postcards is churches, and Clearfield certainly has its share of beautiful ones. Here is the Presbyterian church, which features a 150-foot steeple. Built on the site of the first wooden Presbyterian church in Clearfield, it was dedicated in 1869.

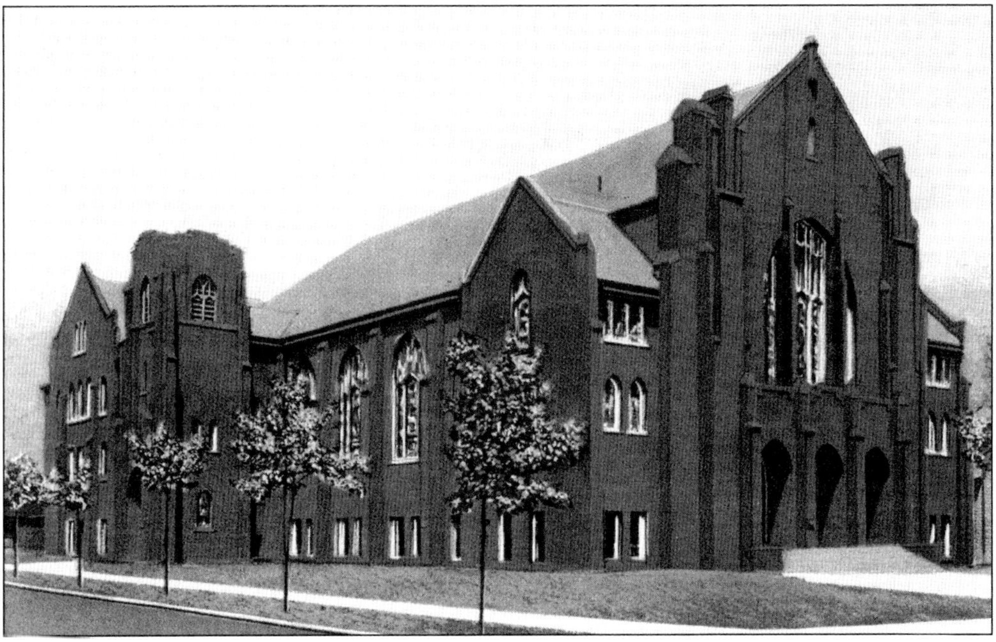

One of the biggest churches is the West Side Methodist Church, which was built in 1872.

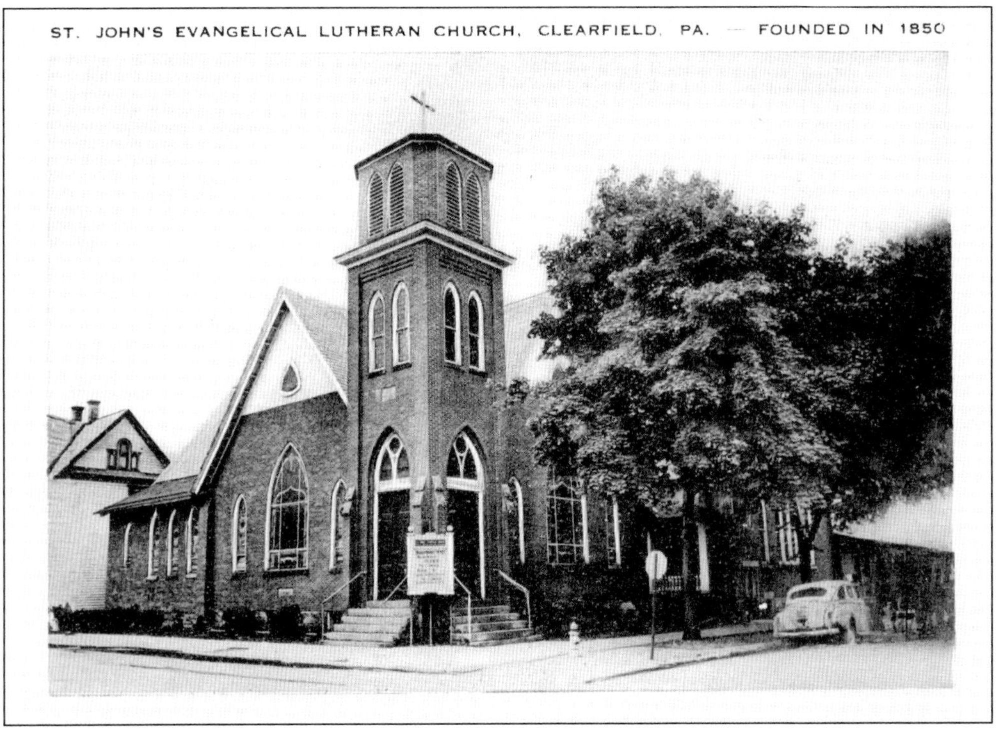

Founded in 1850, the current St. John Lutheran Church was dedicated on November 10, 1889. In the 1970s, it was also home to the St. John Studio Theatre. (Courtesy Zalno collection.)

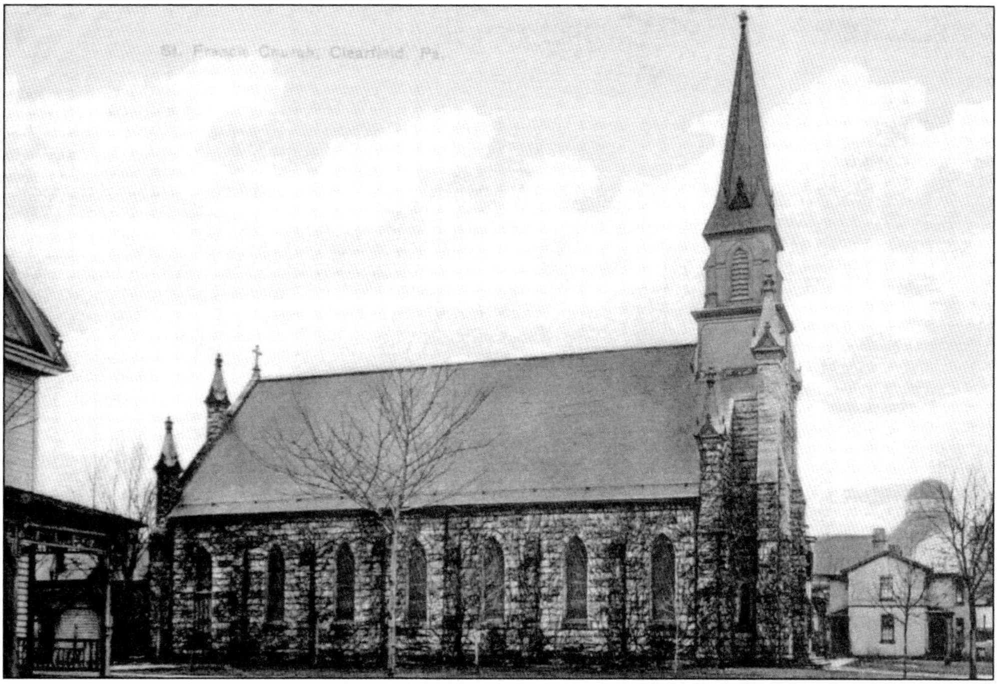

The St. Francis Church was built on the site of the old Catholic cemetery. The cornerstone was laid in July 1886, and the church was dedicated in 1889. This postcard is dated 1915.

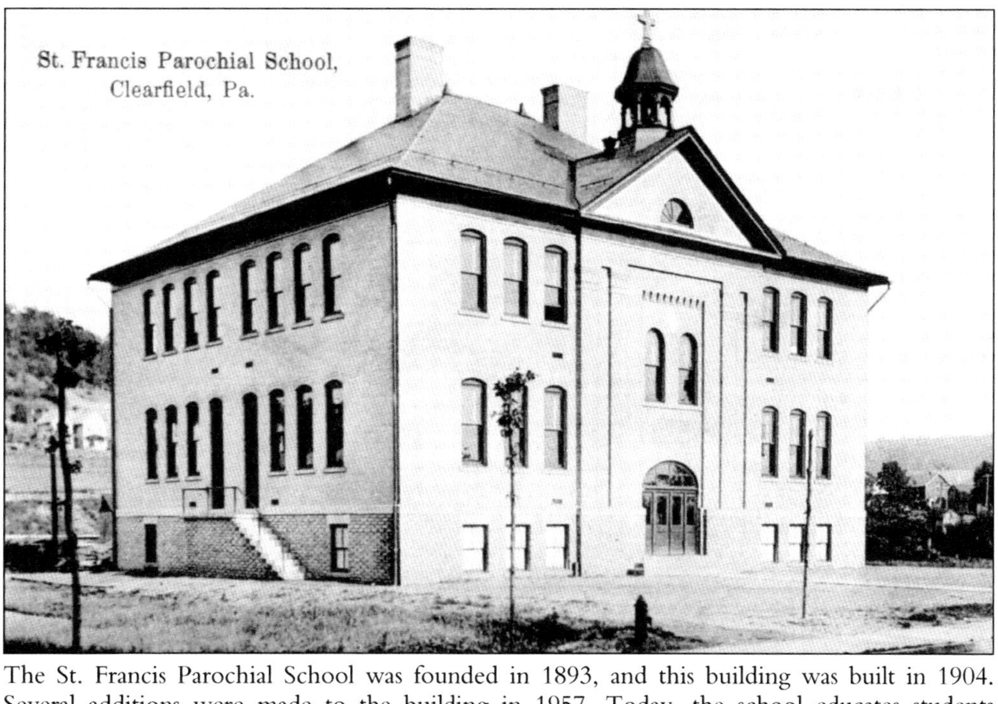

The St. Francis Parochial School was founded in 1893, and this building was built in 1904. Several additions were made to the building in 1957. Today, the school educates students through the eighth grade.

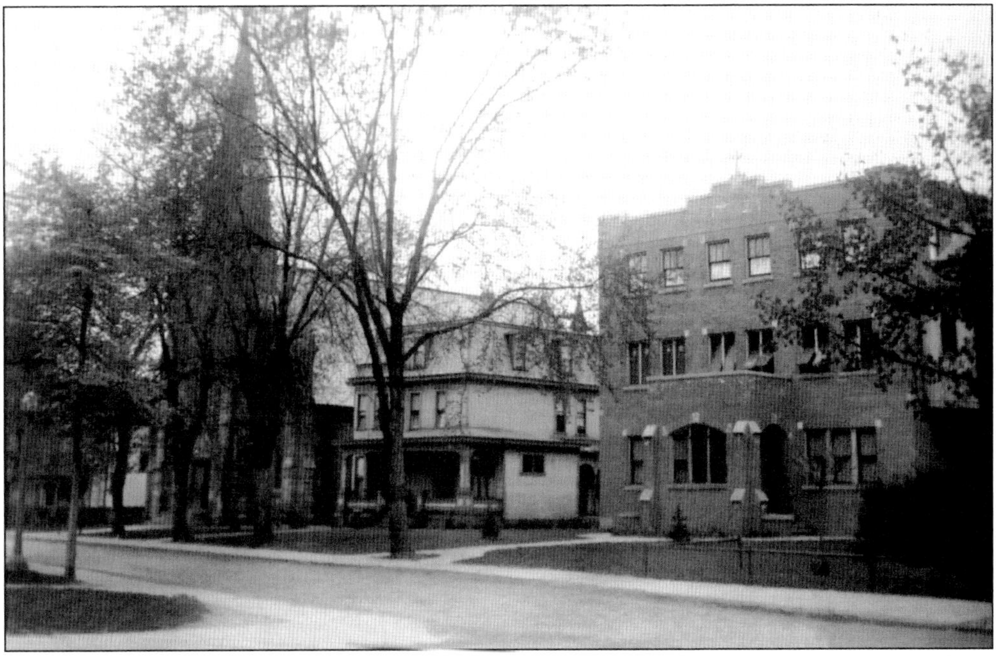

Next to the St. Francis Church (far left) stands the St. Francis rectory, and on the right is the convent.

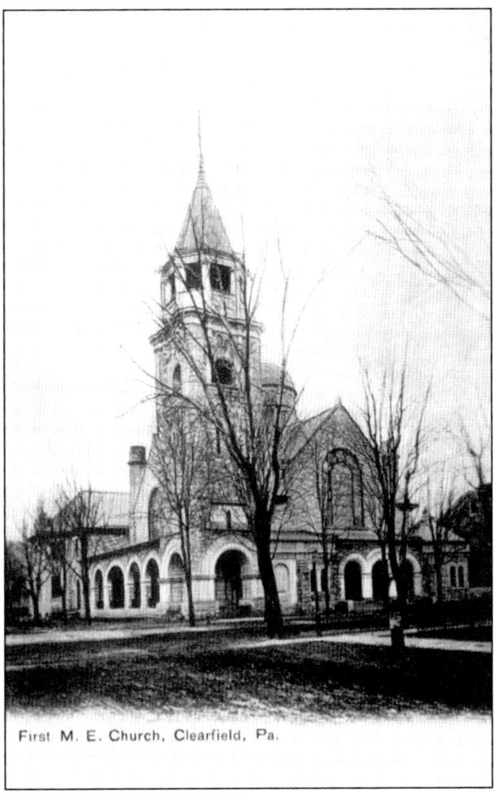

Built in 1904, the Trinity Methodist Church was destroyed by a fire on December 21, 1968. The church was rebuilt in 1971.

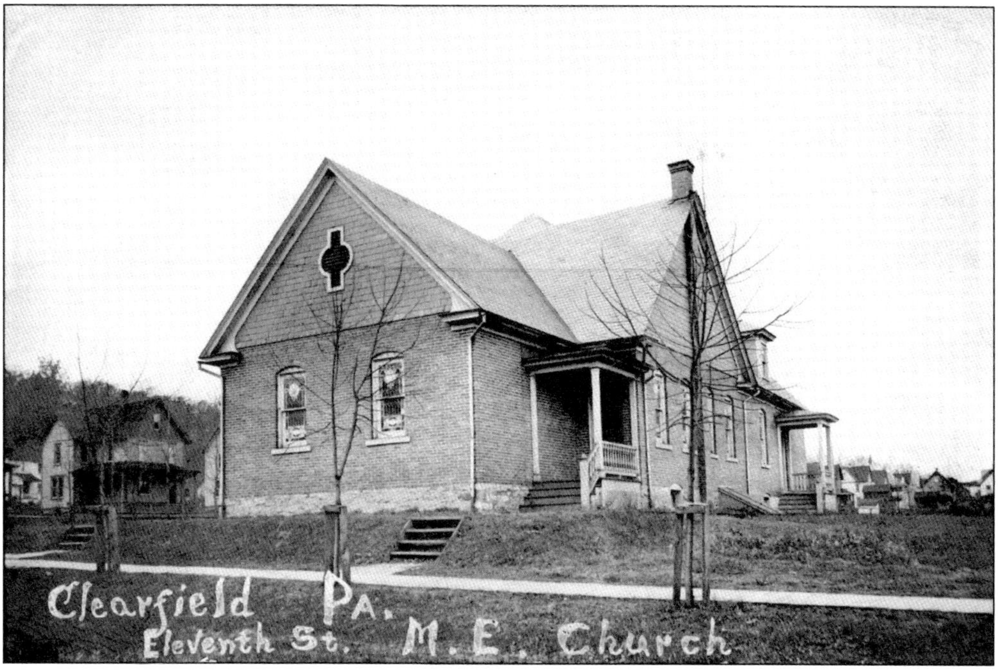

The Methodist Episcopal church is now the Emmanuel United Methodist Church in the East End. (Courtesy Leitzinger collection.)

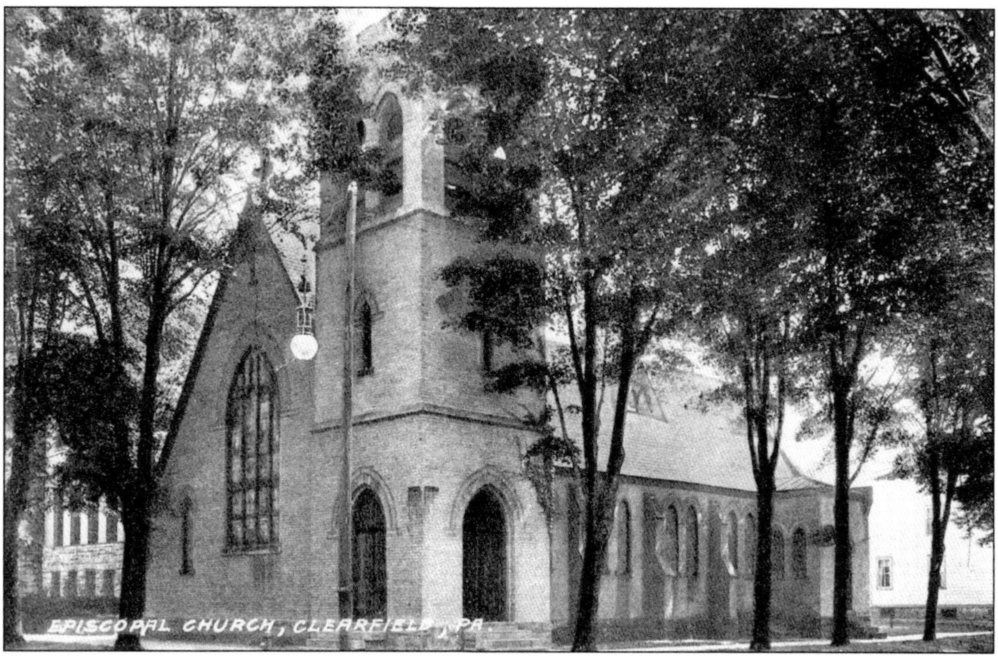

The Episcopal church was established in 1850, and this building was constructed in 1895. Currently, the church is known as St. Andrew's Episcopal. (Courtesy Leitzinger collection.)

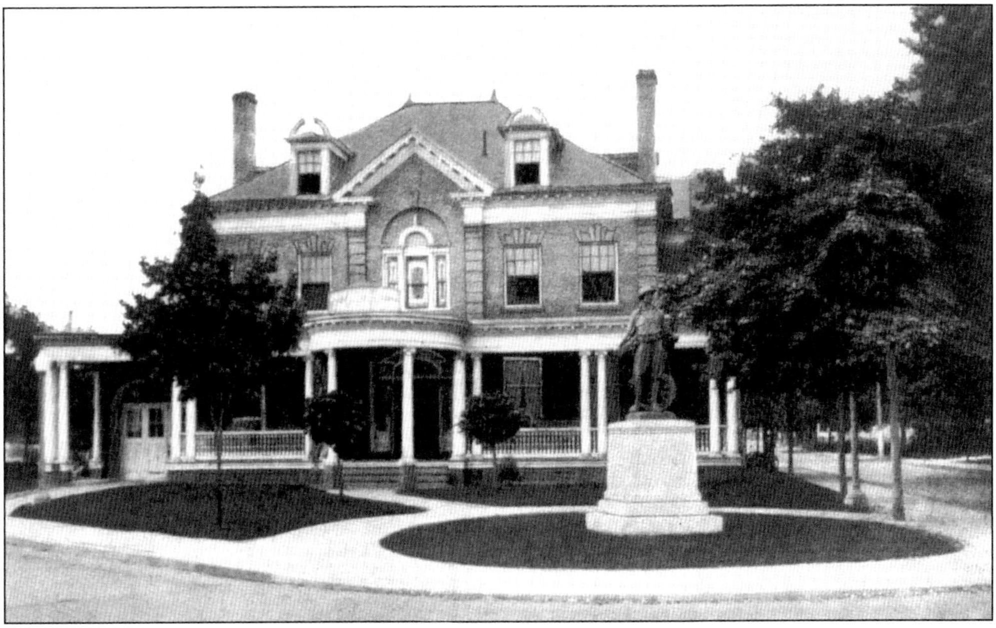

The American Legion moved into this location, which was built by George Dimeling, in 1924. The war memorial, in the foreground, was originally dedicated to those who served in the Civil War, Spanish-American War, and both world wars. In 1957, it was rededicated to include Korean War veterans and, in 1977, to include Vietnam veterans as well.

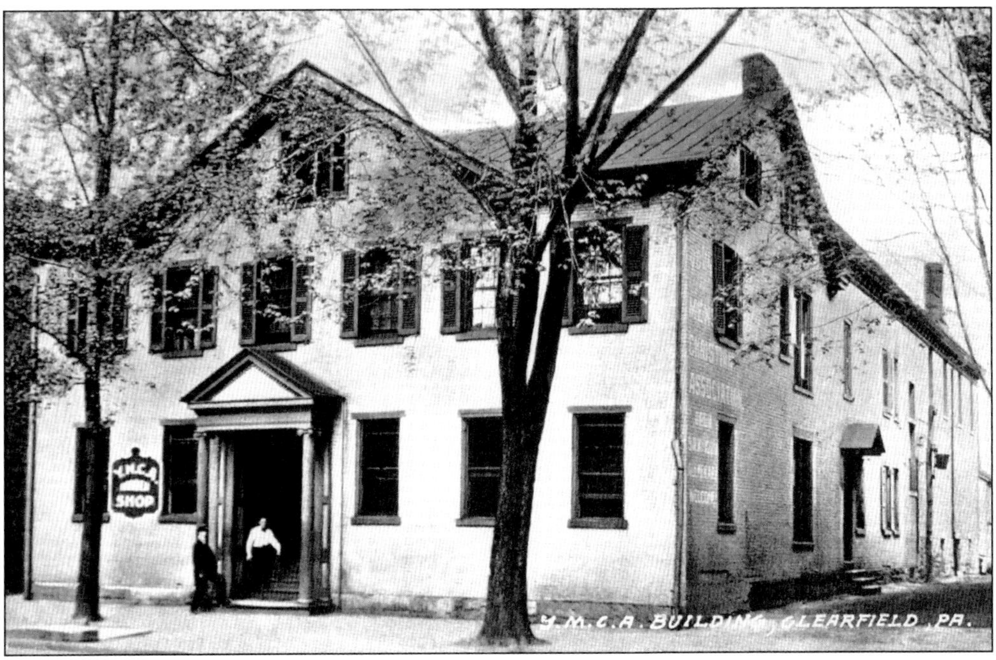

The old YMCA building, shown here in 1910, burned in the late 1950s. The current YMCA is built on this same location on Second Street.

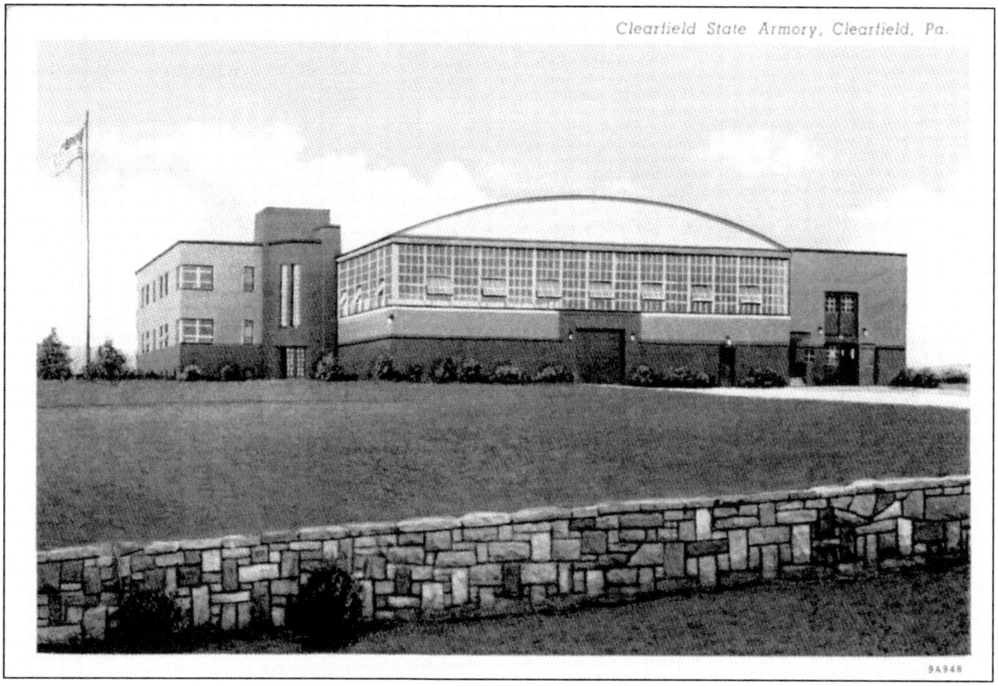

The Clearfield State Armory houses the local Pennsylvania National Guard unit. Although it was remodeled in the late 1930s, part of the original building still exists, including stables where the unit, once a cavalry, kept their horses.

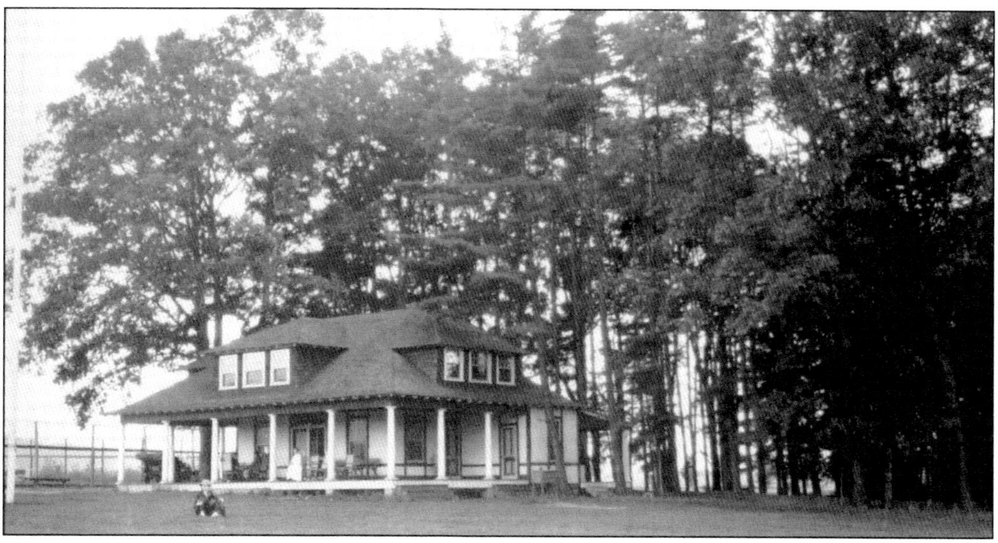
The Clearfield-Curwensville Country Club was founded in 1906. Originally it was a four-hole course, but today the club offers nine holes. This card is from 1917.

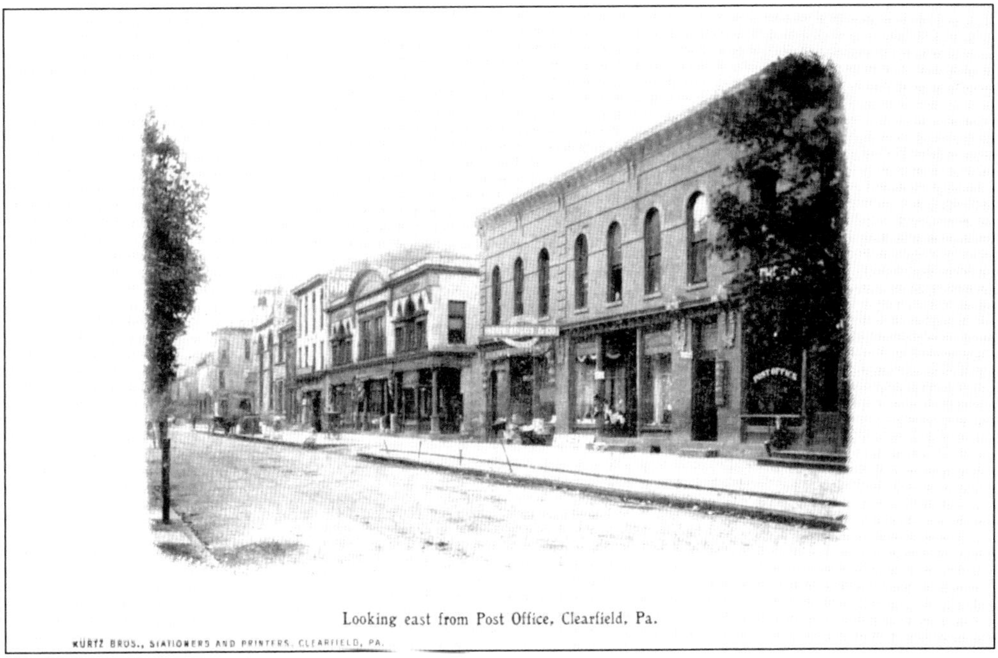

In the early 1900s, the post office (far right) was located on Market Street in the shop currently housing B & E Coins, near the Ritz Theater. Note the County National Bank building on the corner on the far left.

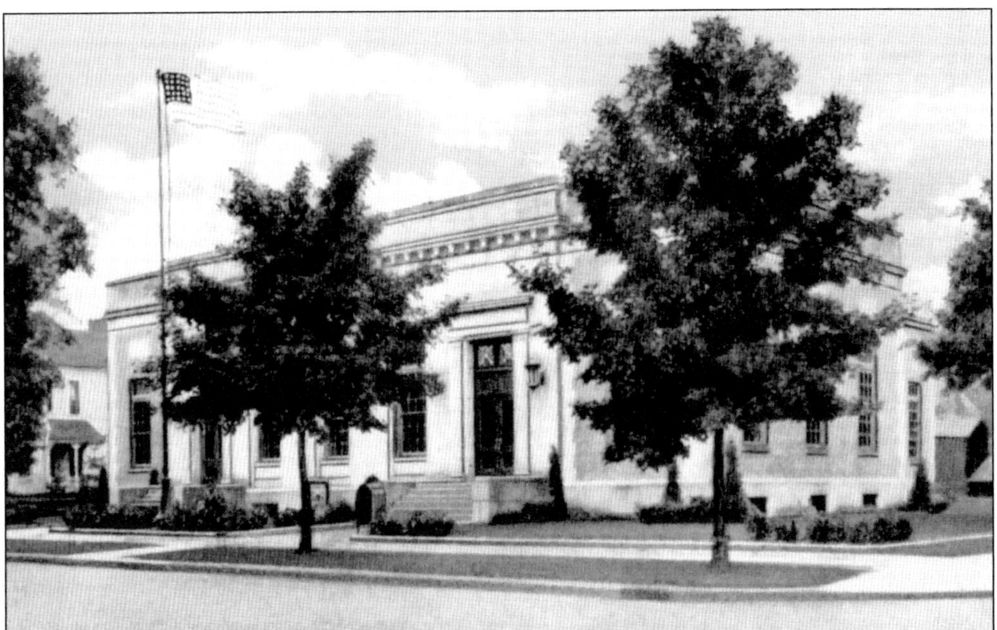

The current post office building on Second Street was built in 1936 from local stone. James A. Wetmore served as the acting supervising architect.

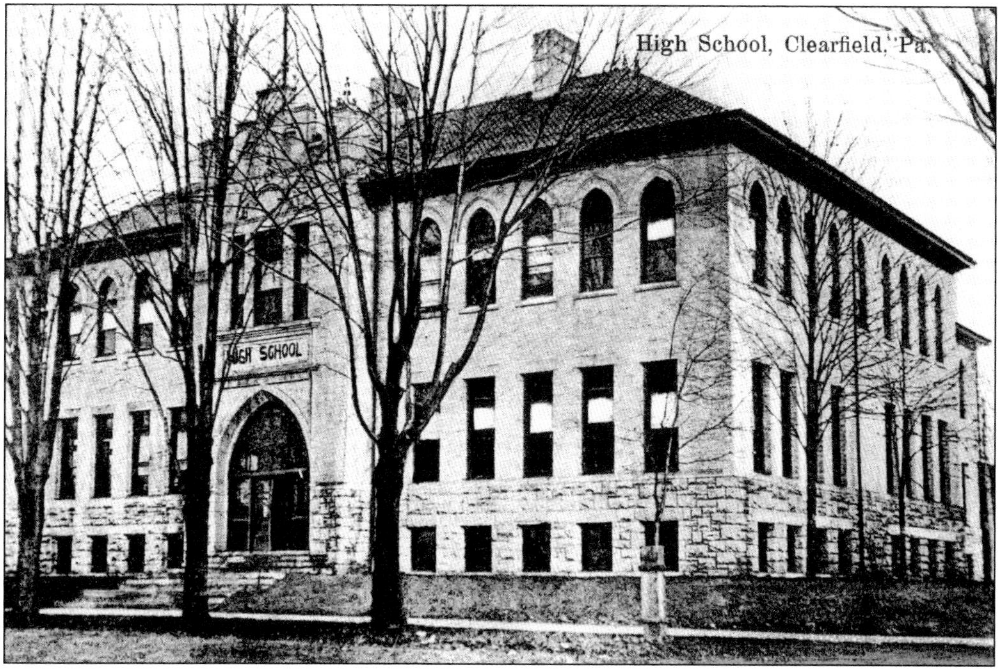

This Clearfield High School was built in 1902. An addition in 1924 included an auditorium, gymnasium, and eight classrooms. The high school was the subject of many postcards.

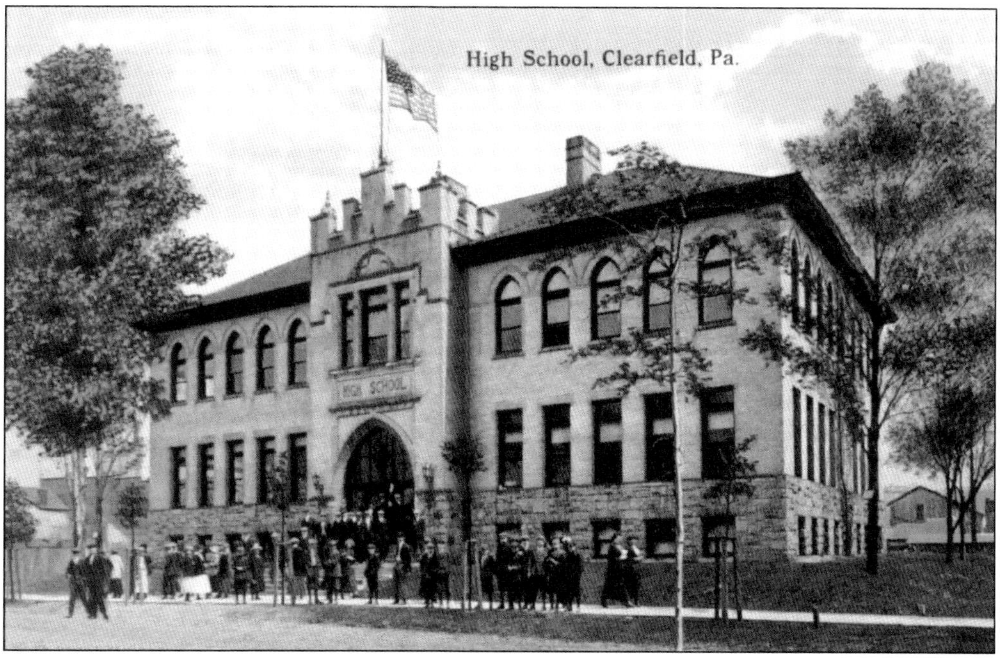

This Clearfield High School postcard, dating from *c.* 1915, is a colorized and enhanced version. Note that the trees in the front have been removed.

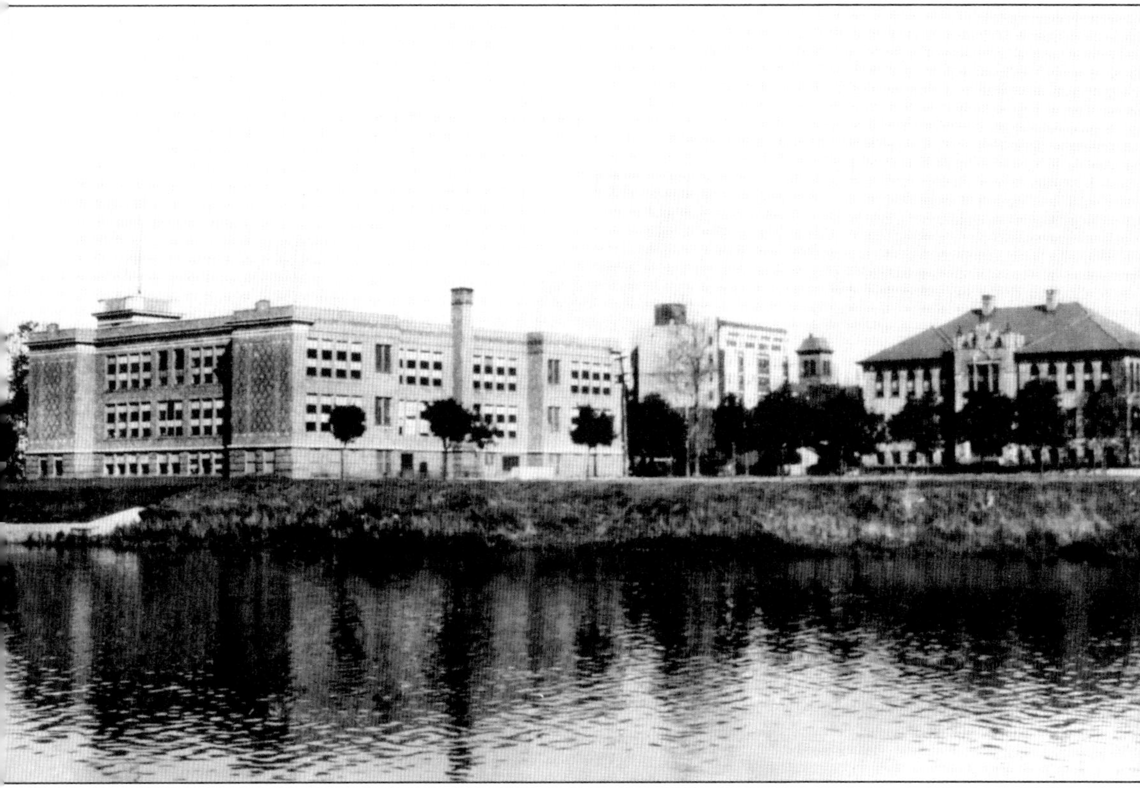

When the new high school (left) was built in 1915, the old one (right) became the junior high school. The Dimeling Hotel and the top of the Clearfield County Courthouse (center) can also be seen in this photograph.

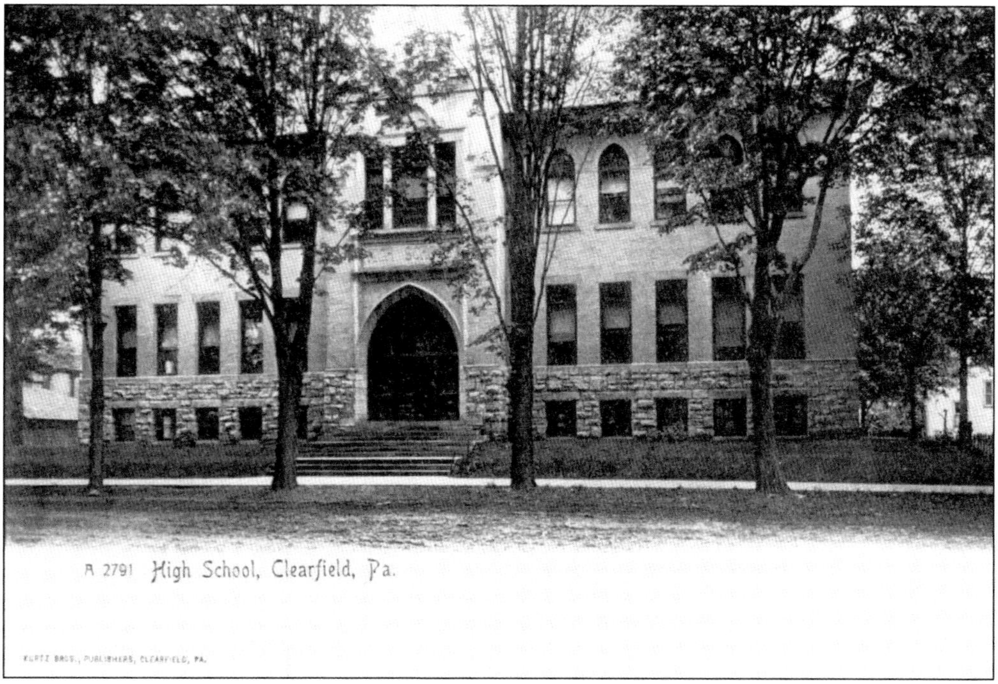

The Front and Market Street building (below) served as the high school until the 1960s, when the Mill Road School was built. It eventually became part of the junior high school and was known as the "West" building, while the older building (above) was known as the "East" building. For years, junior high students traveled back and forth across the street to their classes. Both schools were closed in 1975 and later torn down. Today, their locations are home to the Clearfield Borough Building and the Shaw Public Library.

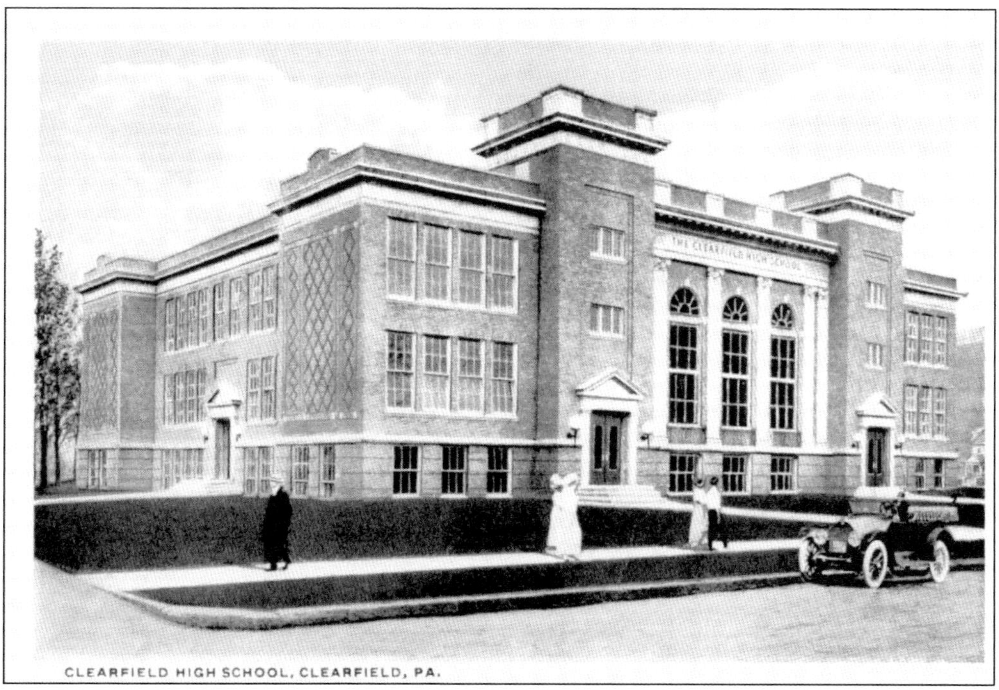

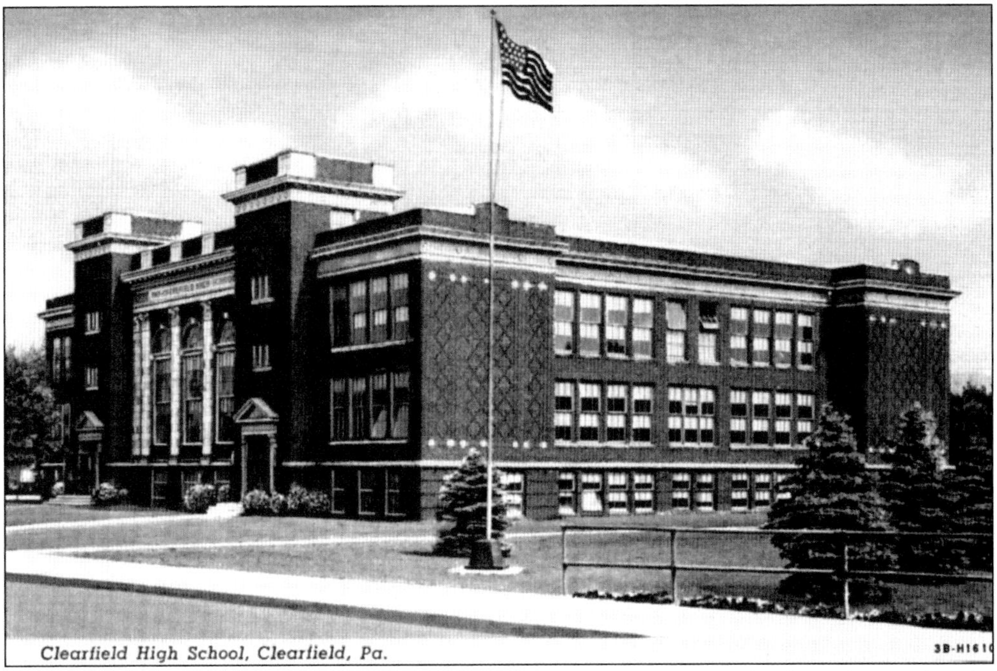

Here is another view of the high school from 1951. The area around the flagpole is today the location of the Bison Wall, which lists many of the graduates of Clearfield area schools. (Courtesy Zalno collection.)

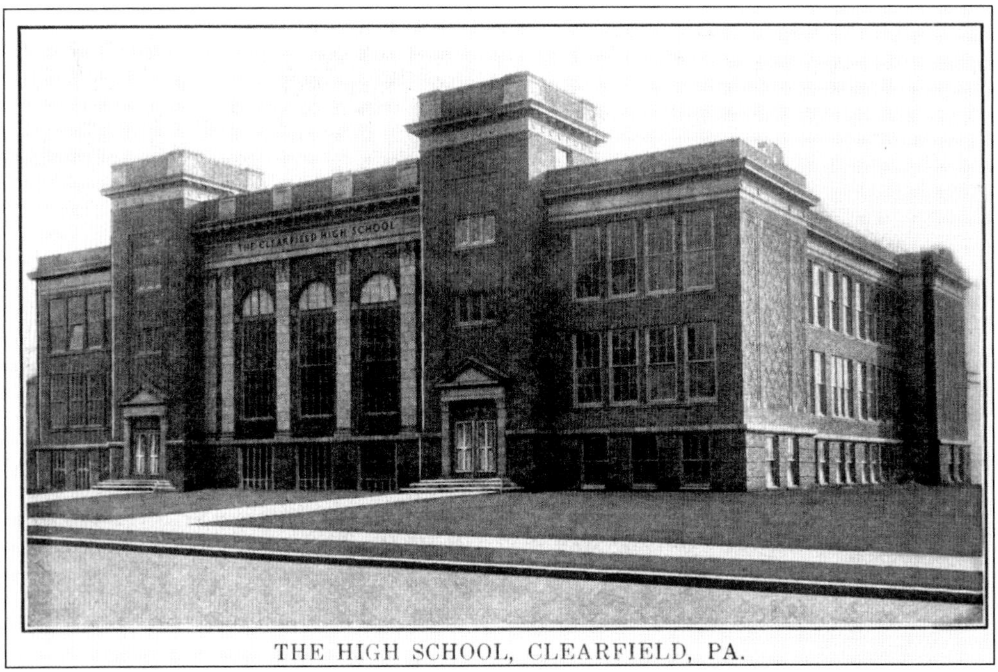

This angle shows a clear view of the side of the school that faced Market Street. (Courtesy Zalno collection.)

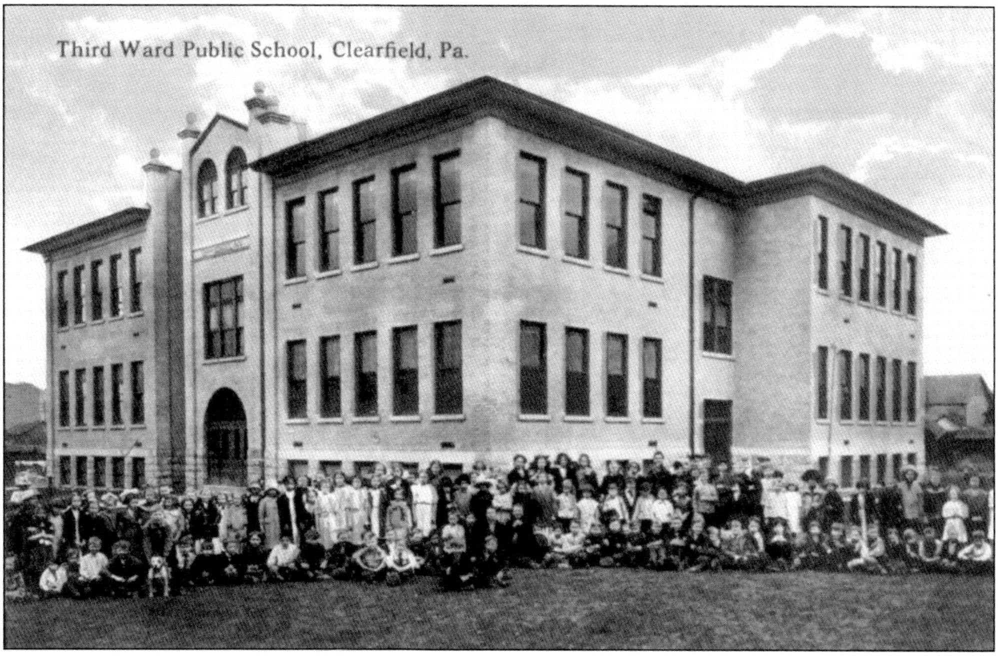

The Third Ward School, located at Weaver and Merrill Streets, was built in 1908. It featured a large auditorium, an office, and a clinic room.

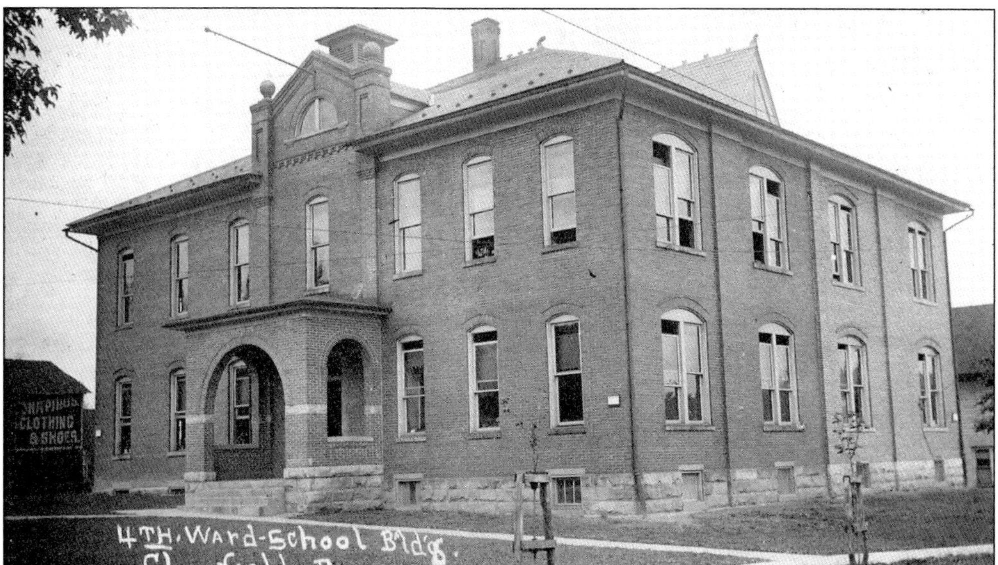

Built in 1896, the Fourth Ward School is located at Dorey and Seventh Streets. An addition of four rooms was completed in 1908. The building was eventually converted into apartments. (Courtesy Zalno collection.)

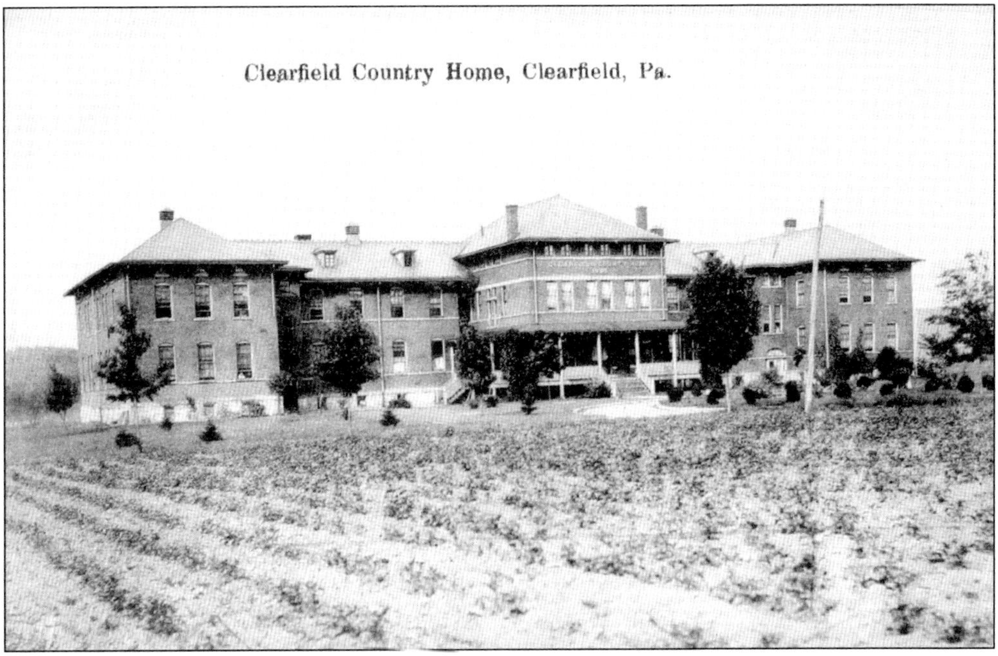

The Clearfield County Home, misidentified here as the "Clearfield Country Home," was built in 1895. It is now used as a government building and is known as the Multi-Service Center.

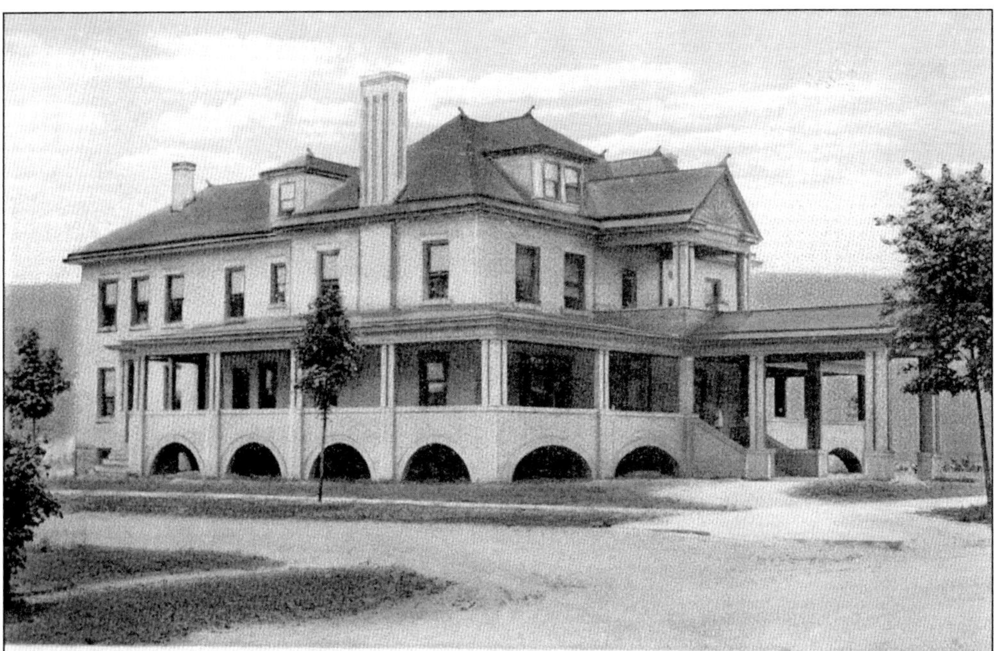

The children's home was used as a makeshift hospital during the Spanish flu epidemic of October 1918. So many people were ill that the board of health issued quarantine restrictions that lasted until January 1919. (Courtesy Zalno collection.)

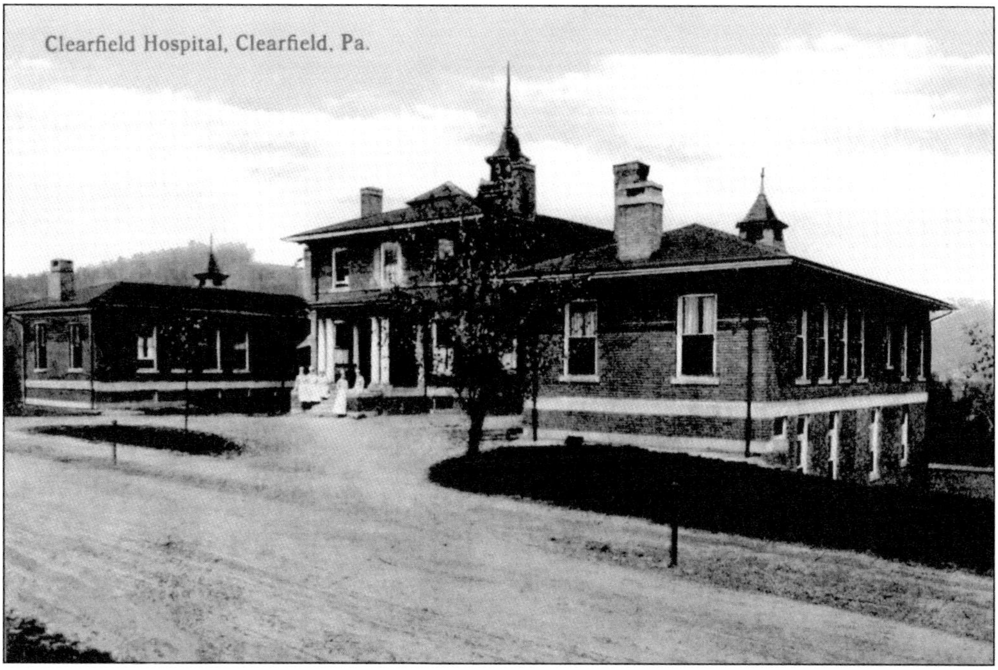

For more than 100 years, the Clearfield Hospital has served this area. The hospital moved into these buildings in 1906. The land on Turnpike Avenue was donated by the Mossop sisters in memory of their deceased brother Fred, who had been a director at the hospital's first location on South Second Street. He had served as director at the River Road location as well.

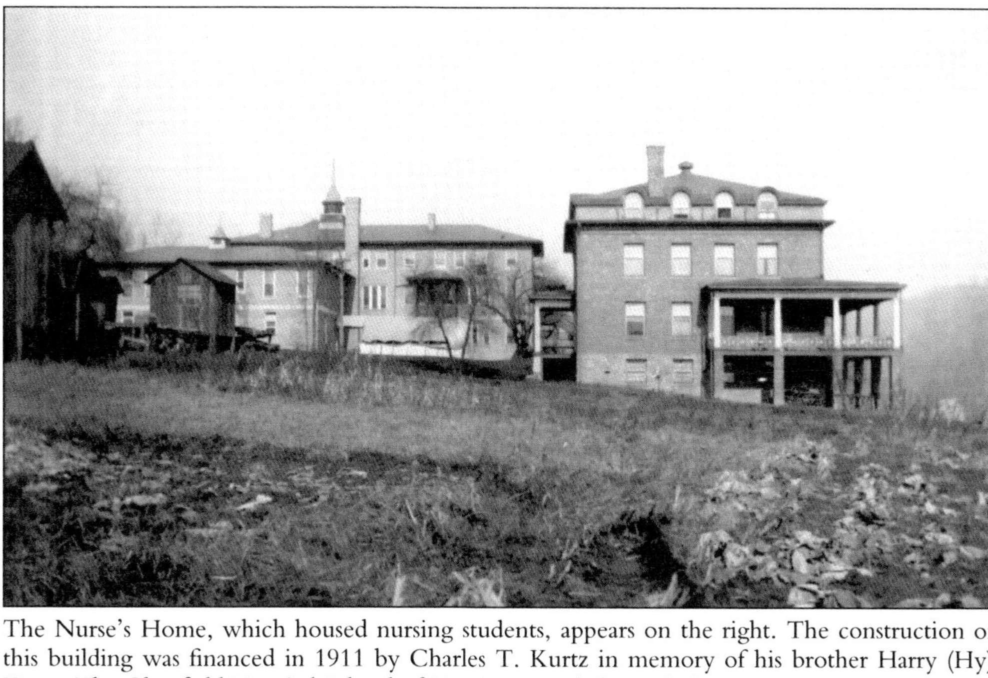

The Nurse's Home, which housed nursing students, appears on the right. The construction of this building was financed in 1911 by Charles T. Kurtz in memory of his brother Harry (Hy) Kurtz. The Clearfield Hospital School of Nursing awarded 875 diplomas in its 62 years. It closed in 1969.

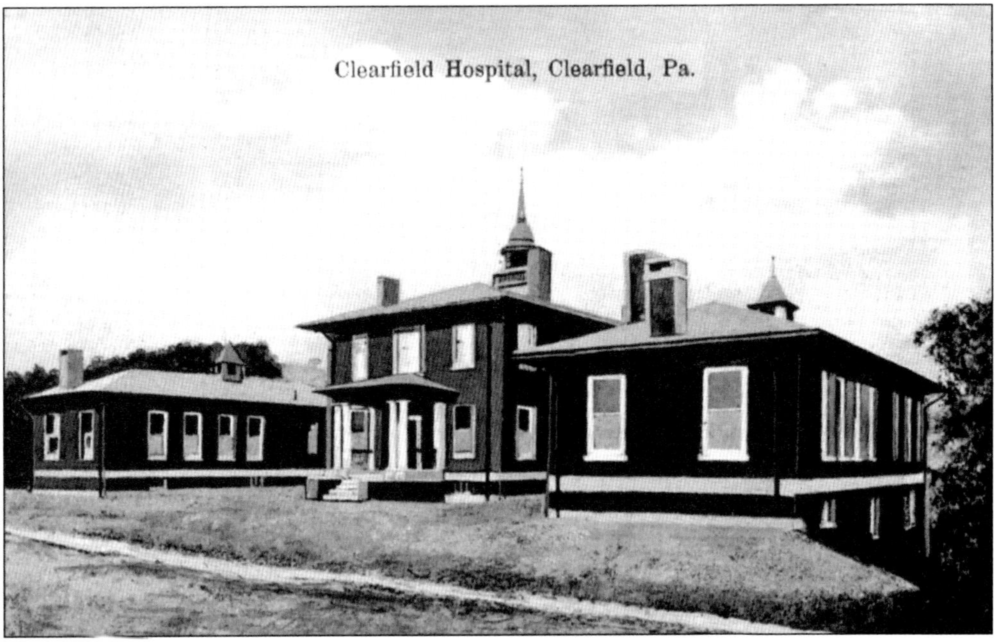

This postcard shows the Clearfield Hospital at its first location on Turnpike Avenue. The building had a 30-bed capacity when it opened on July 3, 1906.

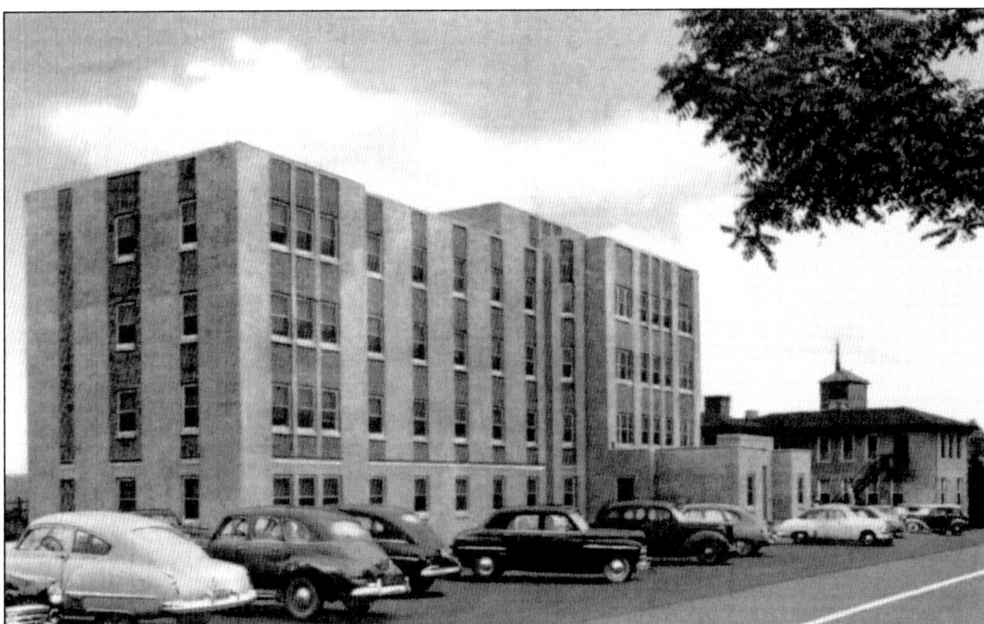

The current Clearfield Hospital building was constructed in several stages. The first stage began in 1949. The second was completed in 1966, and the third in 1972.

Five

Curwensville

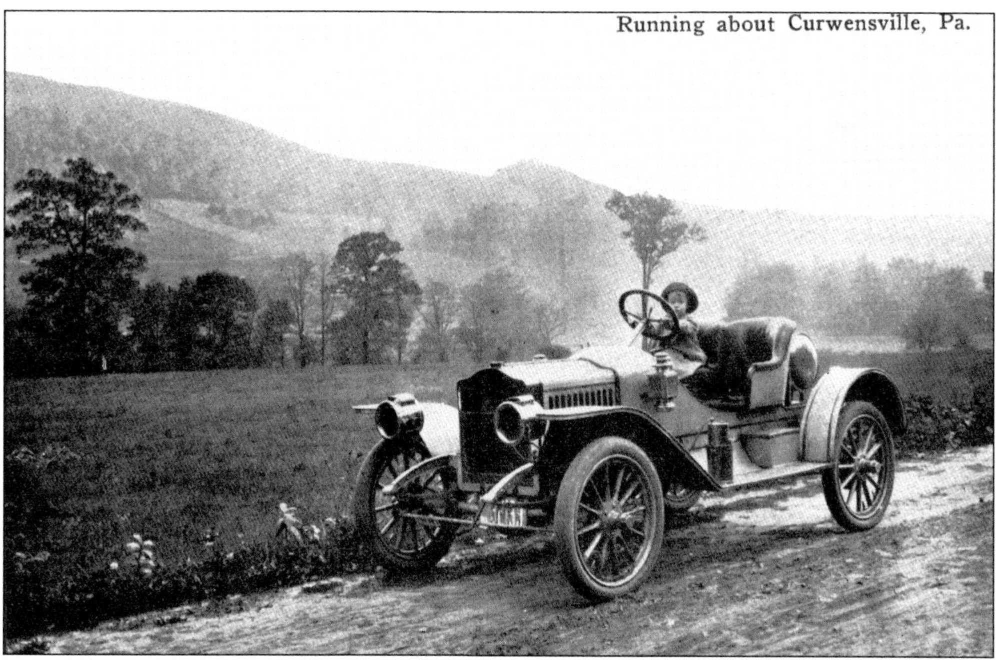

A lot of people were "running about Curwensville" in the early part of the 20th century. Thanks to Way's Stationery Store, we have the postcards to prove it. Mr. Way sent many of his own and other people's photographs to his postcard company in Germany, which then turned them into entertaining postcards. These cards, in addition to the standard street and building views, illustrate the history of Curwensville in the early 1900s.

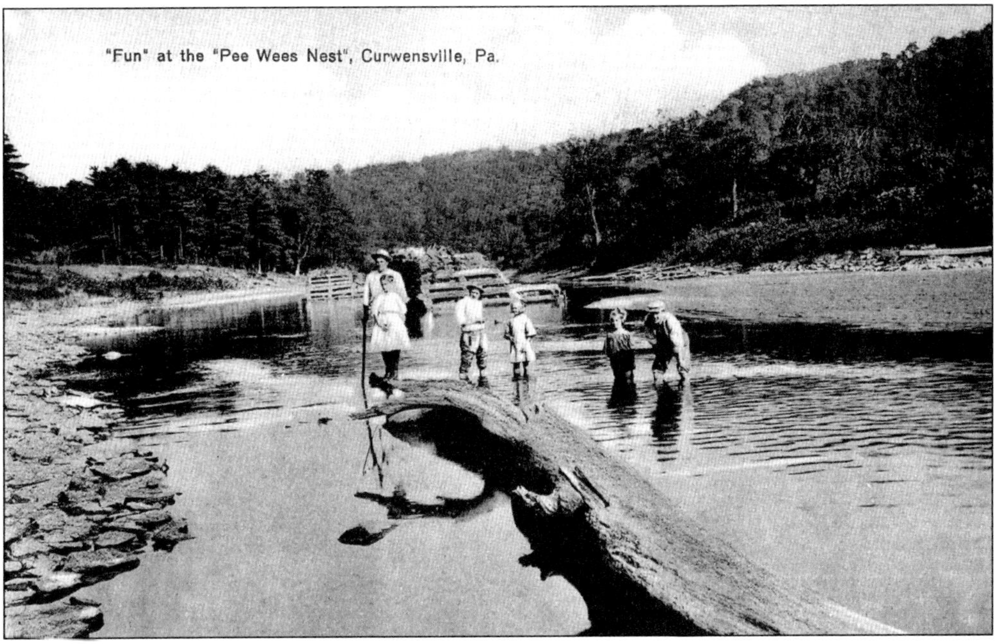

"Pee Wee's Nest," now known as Irvin Park, was given to Curwensville by Elizabeth and Hugh M. Irvin in 1921.The name Pee Wee's Nest came from the small birds that roosted there. The park is the setting for the annual Curwensville Days celebration.

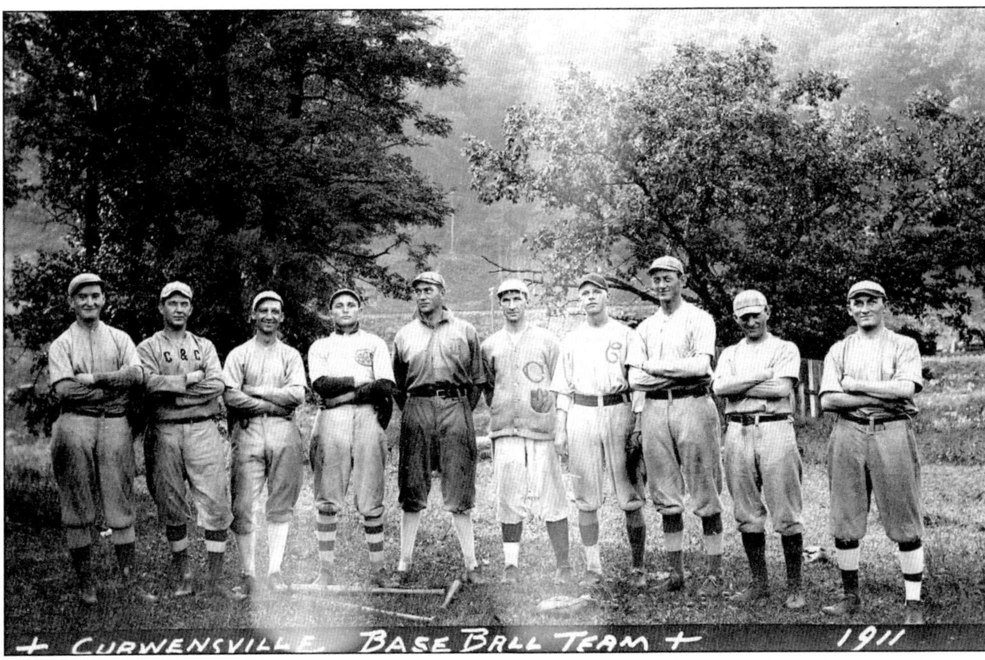

A baseball team poses in 1911, most likely near the old ball ground in Irvin Park. The regulation-size baseball diamond was lost in the construction of the Curwensville Dam. (Courtesy Test collection.)

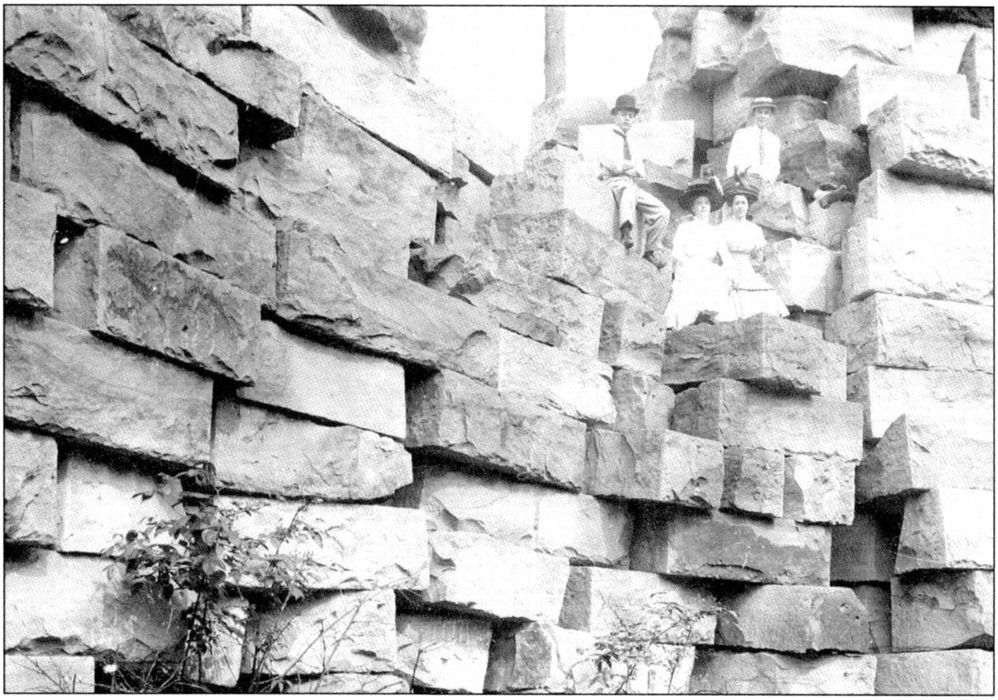

Curwensville was once known for its fine stone quarries. At one point, three were operating outside of town. The current Curwensville Post Office, built in 1938, was the last building constructed with local stone. This scenic portrait shows the Snyder Stone Quarry near Chestnut Ridge. (Courtesy Test collection.)

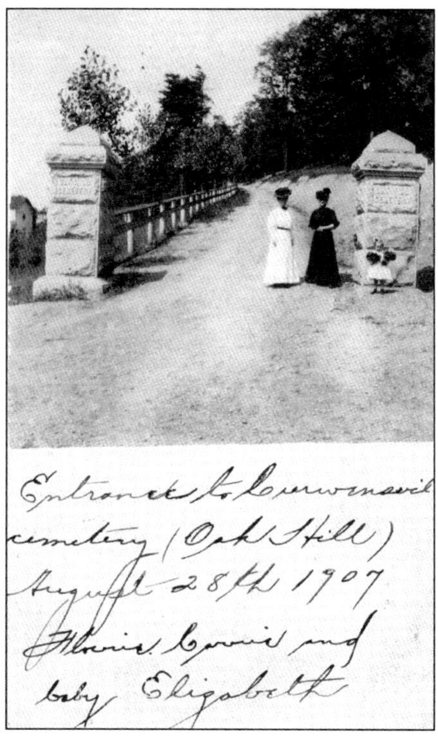

Since the early 1830s, people have used Oak Hill Cemetery as the final resting place for their loved ones. Here, a few visitors pose at the entrance. (Courtesy Zalno collection.)

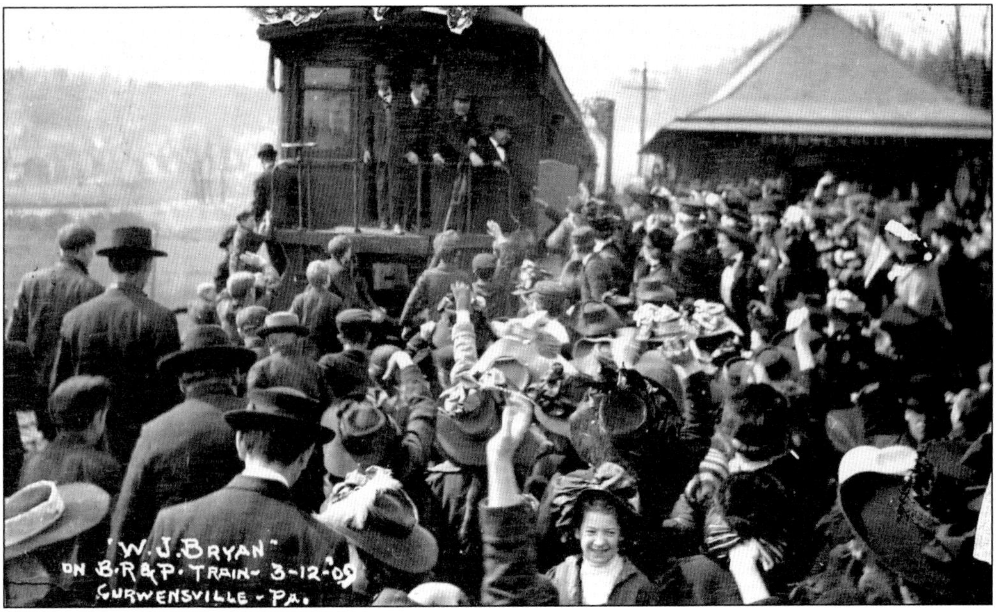

In March 1909, William Jennings Bryan, on the train above, passed through Curwensville. Bryan was known as a "silver tongued orator" and was a presidential candidate in 1896, 1900, and 1908. He was also well known for being an attorney in the Scopes trial, which debated the issue of teaching evolution in public schools. During an earlier visit to Clearfield and Philipsburg, Bryan spoke from the porch of the Kerr home, now the Clearfield County Historical Society. Below, the crowd lingers as the train pulls away. (Courtesy Test collection.)

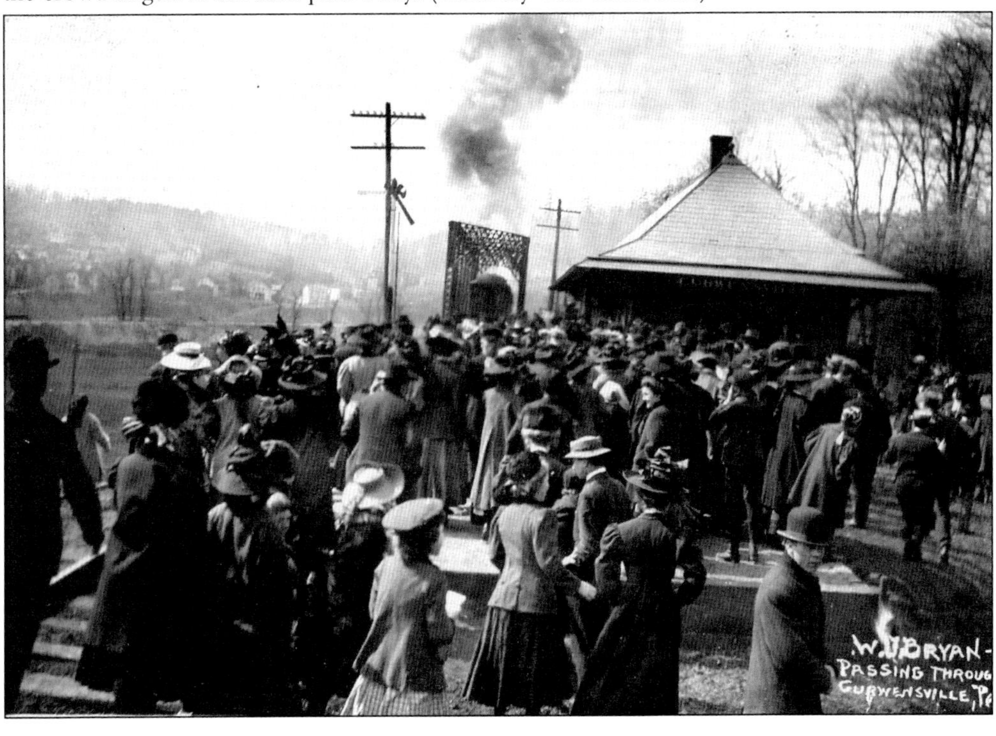

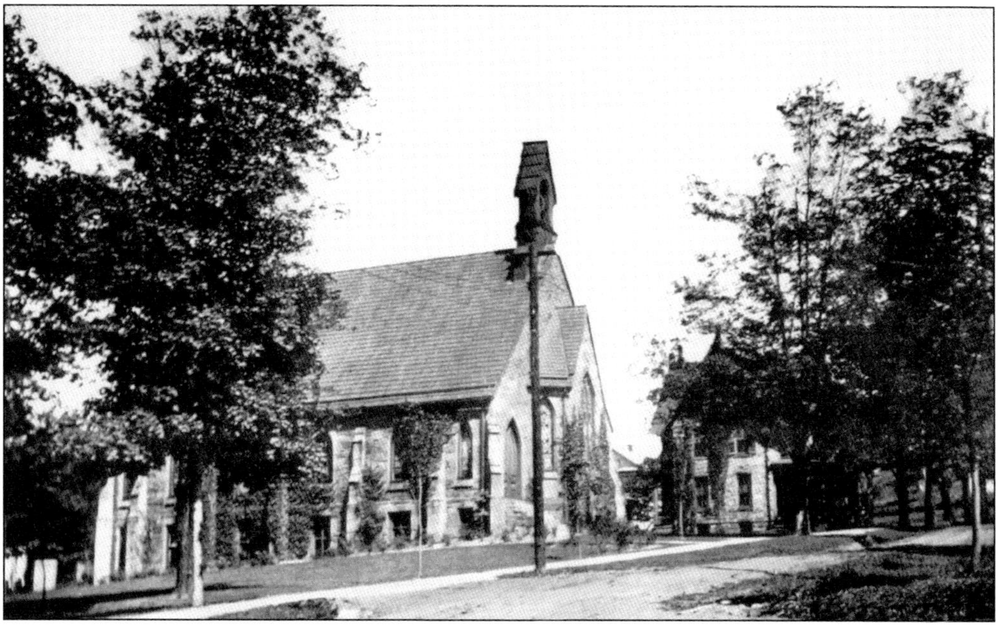

The Curwensville Presbyterian Church, built of native stone, was dedicated in 1869. It was patterned after the Chapel of Flowers in Scotland. The church was enlarged in 1903 and was renovated after being damaged by fire in 1937.

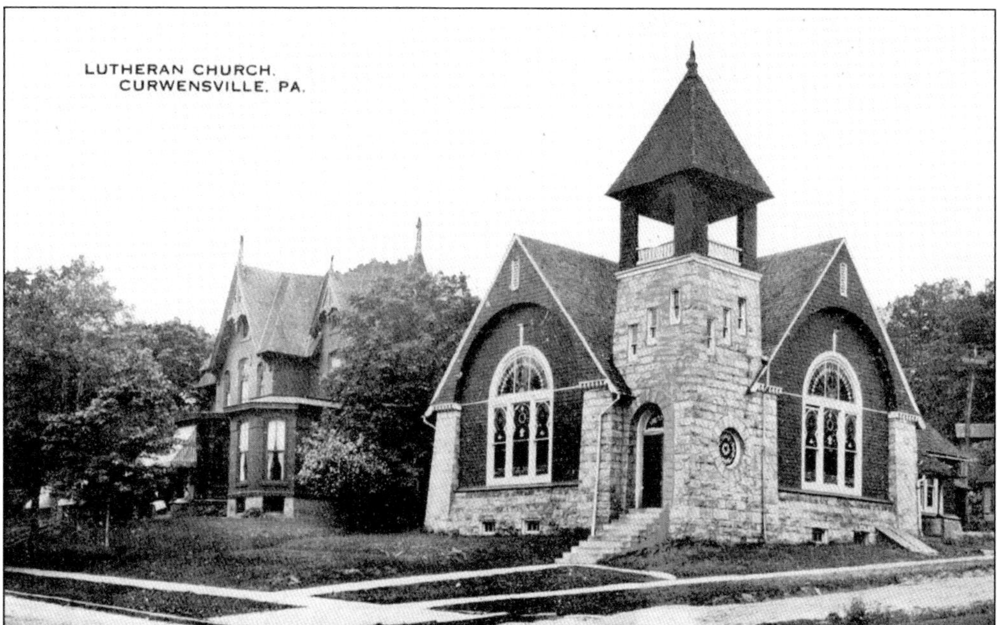

The cornerstone for the Lutheran church was laid in September 1899, and the church was dedicated in 1901. It is now the Grace Lutheran Church. (Courtesy Zalno collection.)

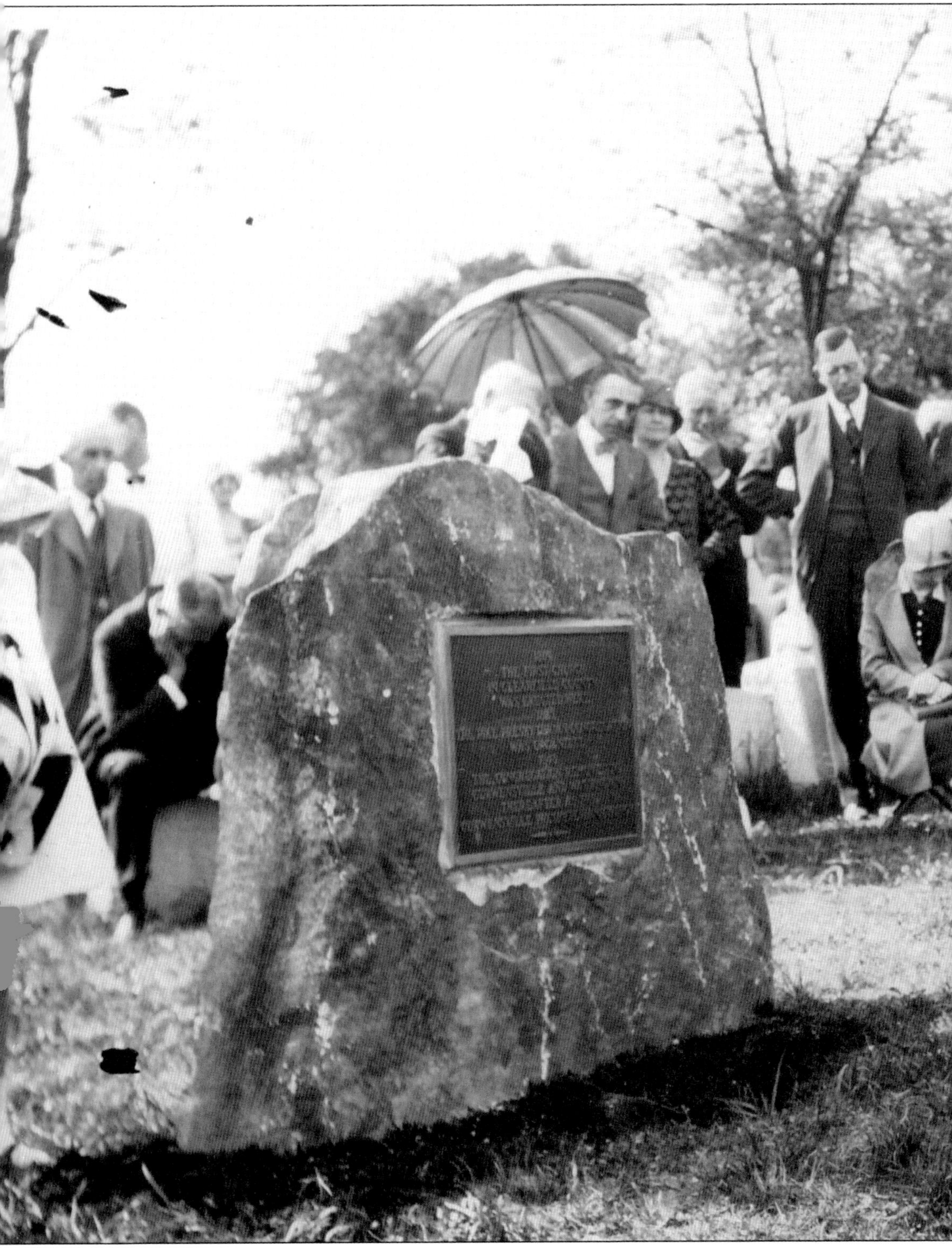

On June 9, 1929, Reverend Herron leads a prayer at the dedication of a monument in memory of the first church in Clearfield County. The Pike Presbyterian Church was built in 1809 in what

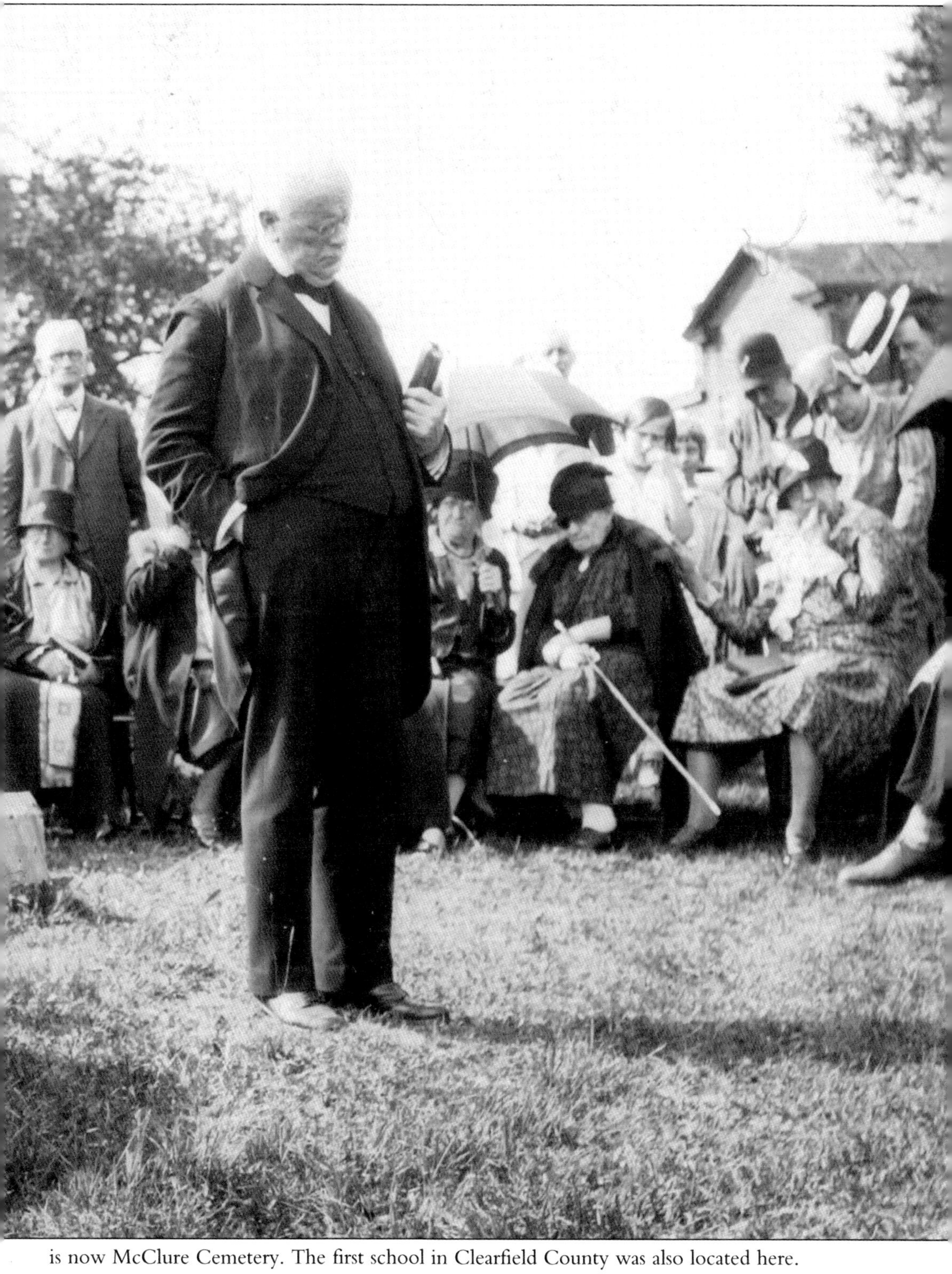

is now McClure Cemetery. The first school in Clearfield County was also located here.

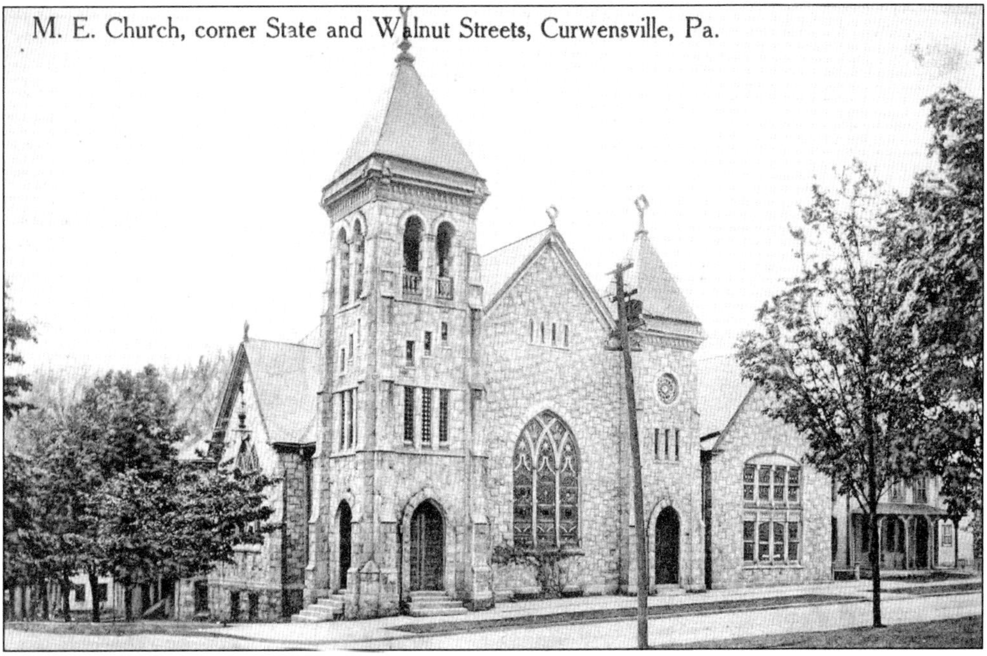

The Curwensville United Methodist Church was built in 1894 using native stone from the Roaring Run Quarry. This card was used as an attendance record for Sunday school in 1912. (Courtesy Zalno collection.)

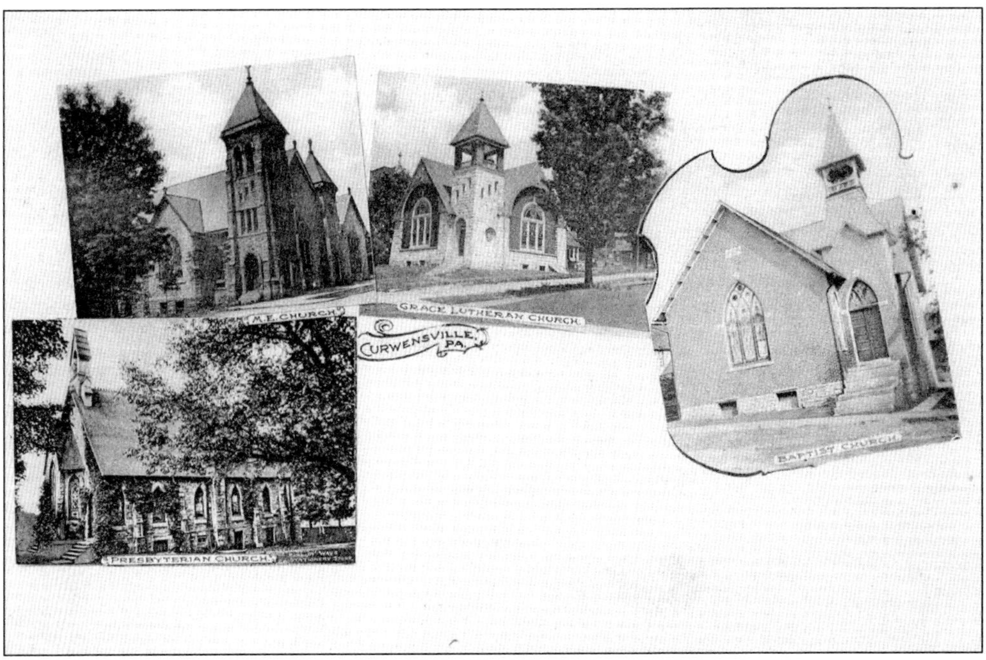

This collage features the Presbyterian, Methodist, Grace Lutheran, and Baptist churches in Curwensville. The Baptist church was built in 1905. (Courtesy Zalno collection.)

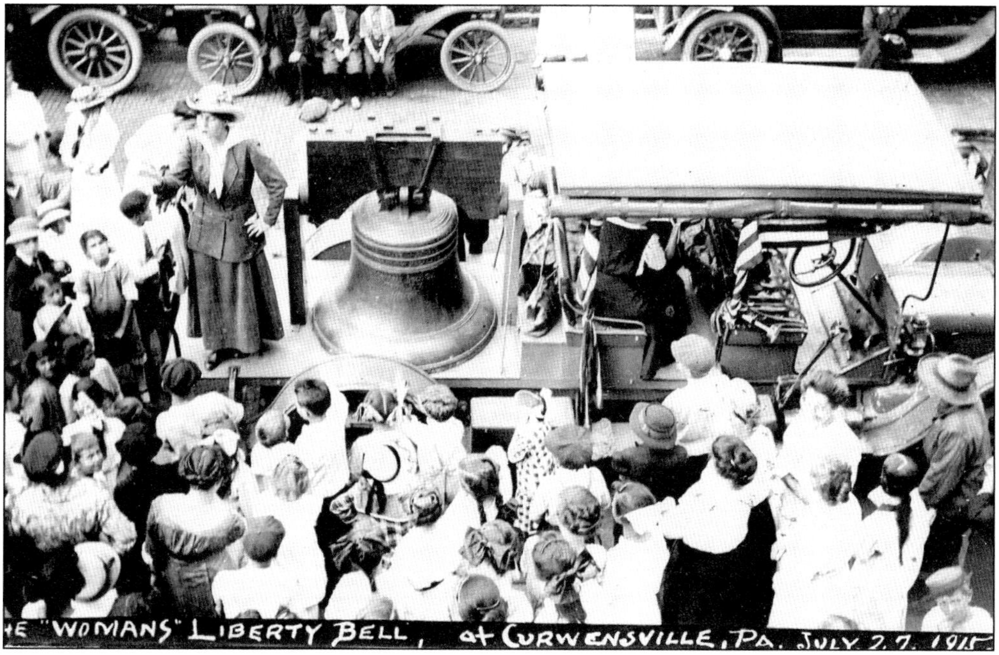

In July 1915, the "Woman's Liberty Bell" stopped by Curwensville to drum up support for voting rights for women. (Courtesy Test collection.)

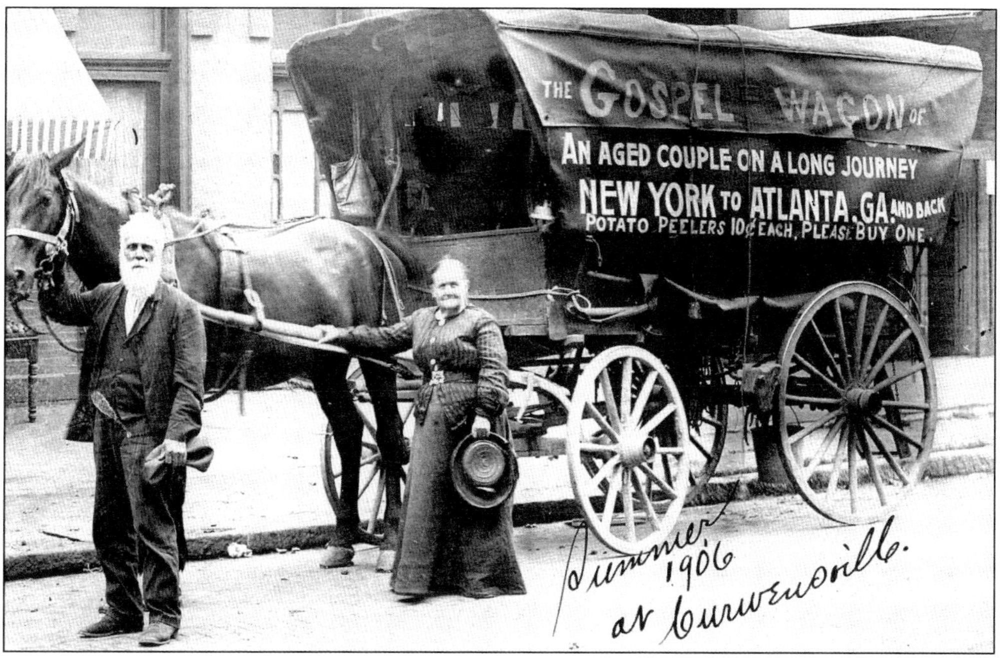

The "Gospel Wagon" traveled through Curwensville during the summer of 1906. According to the writing on the wagon, they also sold potato peelers along their way from New York to Atlanta. (Courtesy Test collection.)

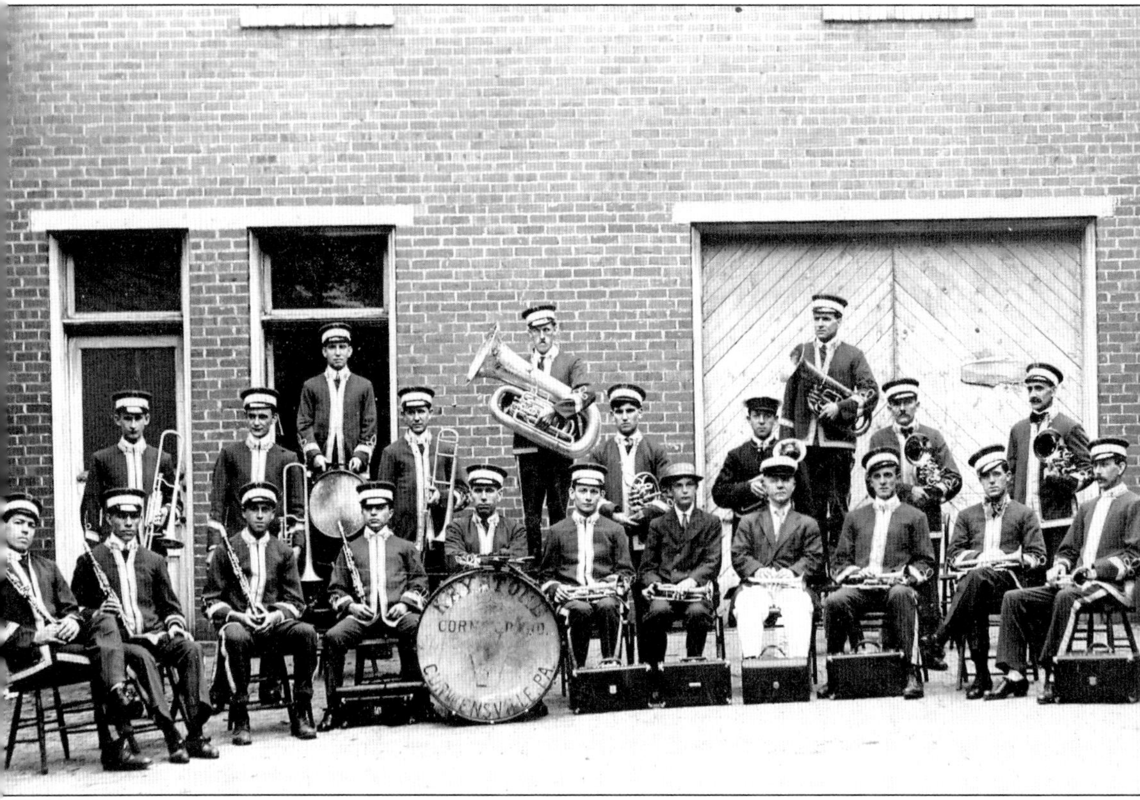

Shown here is the Curwensville Keystone Band. From left to right are the following: (front row) Obe Bloom, Joe Mallon, Jim Volpe, Vince DiPalma, Dock Smith, Russell Wright, Harper Dell, "Shorty" Mattis, Lew McKendrick, George Karndoff, and Tom Evans; (back row) Lew Vaughn, Lavoy Williams, John Way, Orie Hunter, Charles Spencer, John Deter, Mender Brunetti, Minner Bloom, Charles Strauss, and Charles Smith. (Courtesy Test collection.)

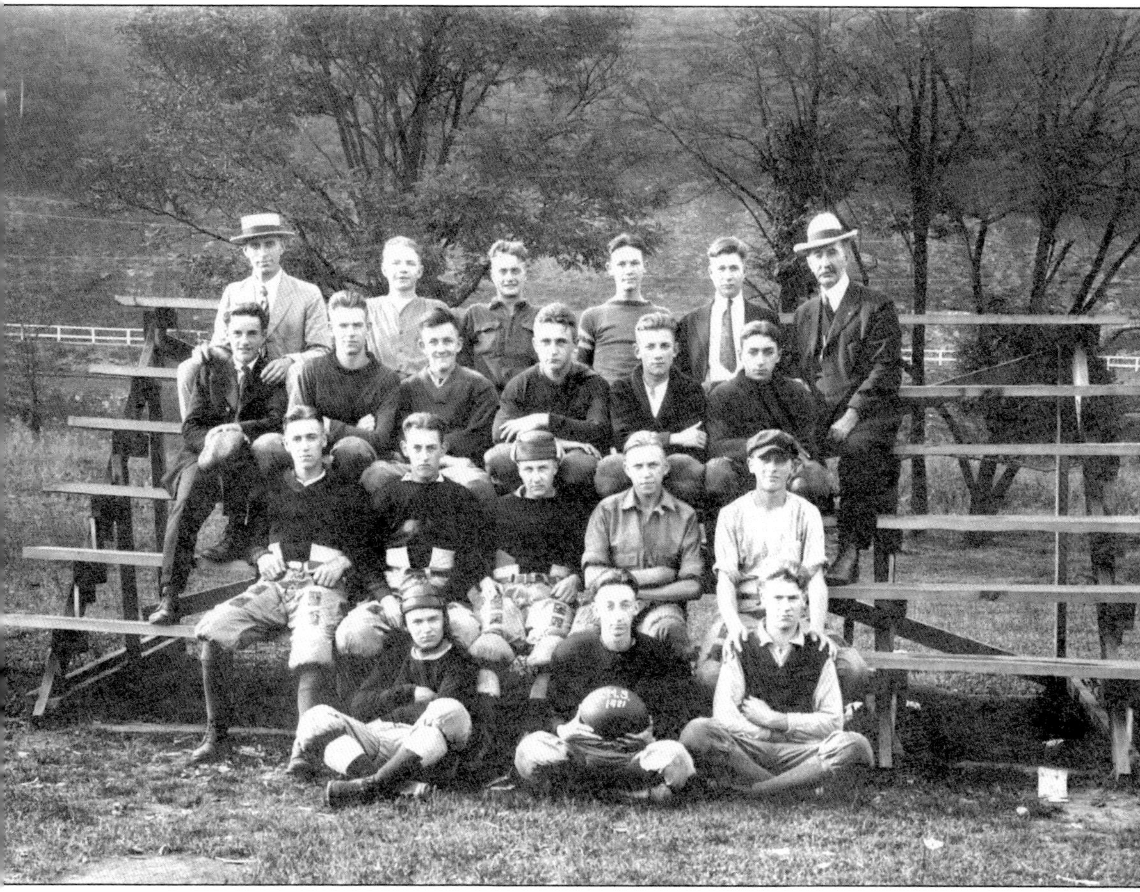

The Curwensville High School football team poses for a group photograph in 1921. Included with this team is collector J. Duane Test's father, Leon. (Courtesy Test collection.)

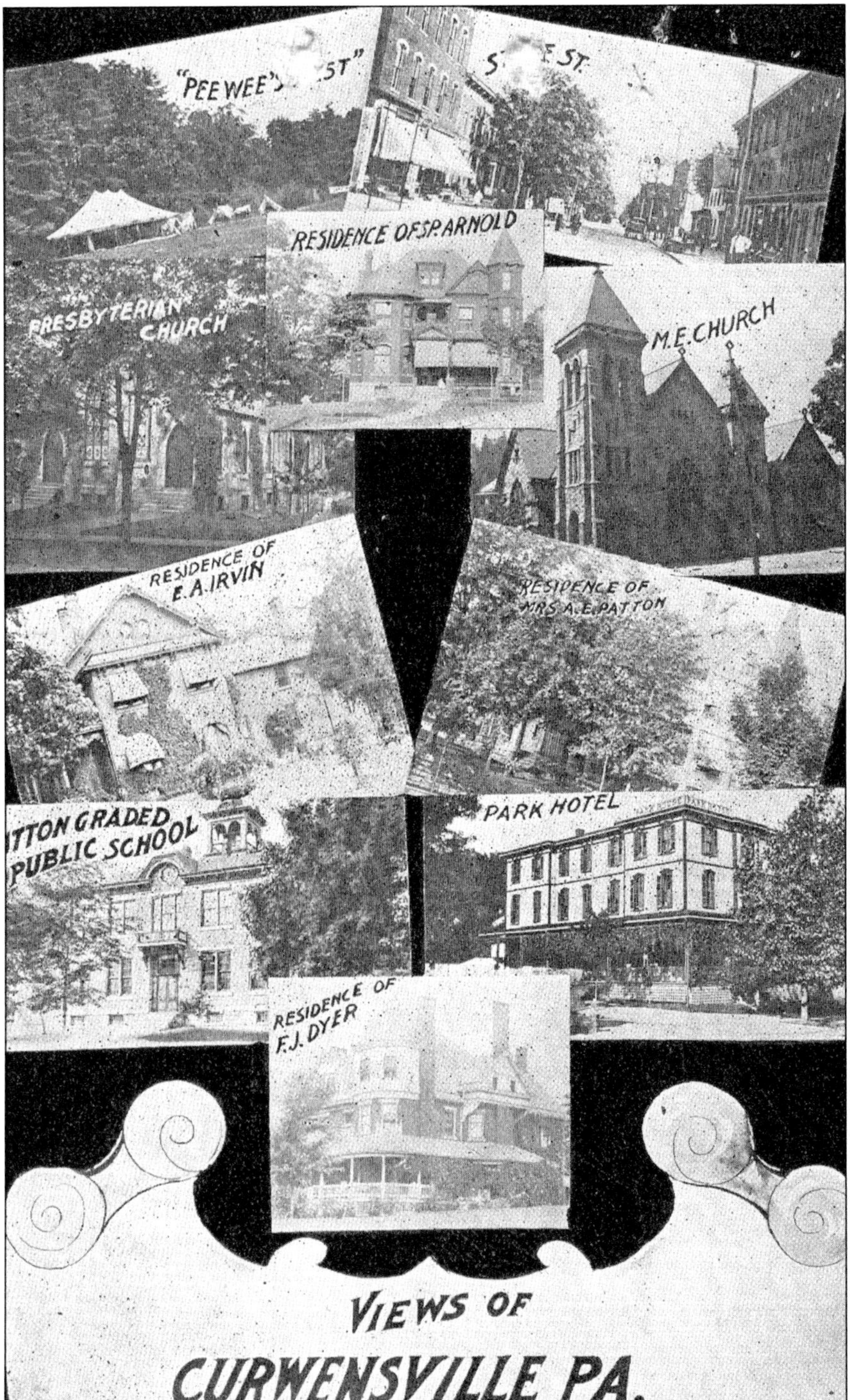

This card features scenes from many Curwensville sites, including Pee Wee's Nest, State Street, the Presbyterian church, the Methodist church, the Patton Graded Public School, the Park House, and the residences of S.P. Arnold, E.A. Irvin, A.E. Patton, and F.J. Dyer. (Courtesy Zalno collection.)

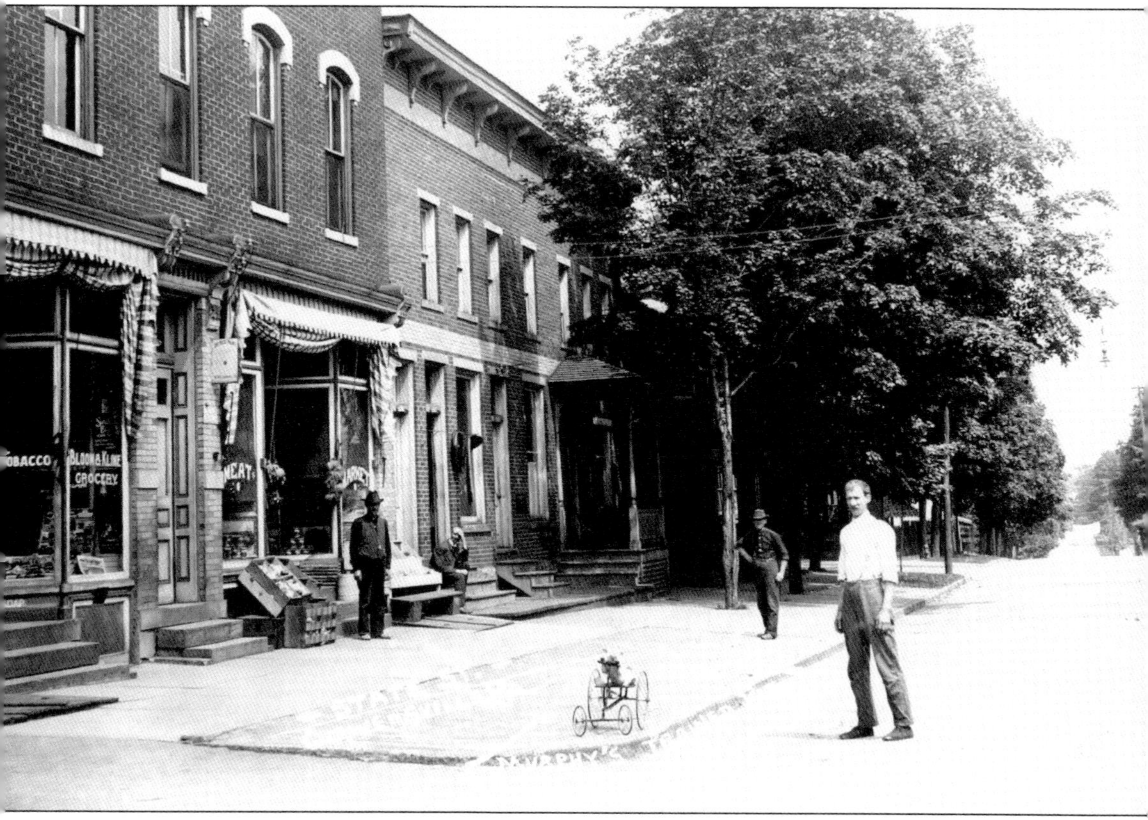

It is just another day on State Street as "Murphy's Trained Pig" takes a ride. (Courtesy Test collection.)

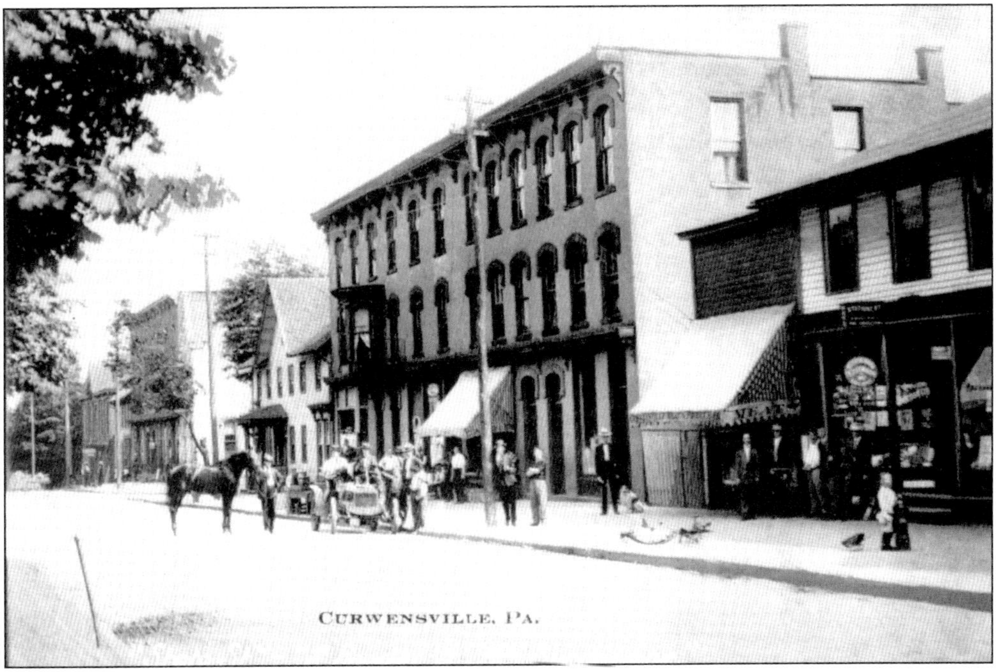

Several people on State Street admire what must have been one of the first cars in Curwensville as a horse stands by—or, as the bottom of the card states, "a roader and his successor"—in 1908. R.K. Way's Stationery Store, Murphy's Meat Market, and the John ("Tack") Way Store are on the right.

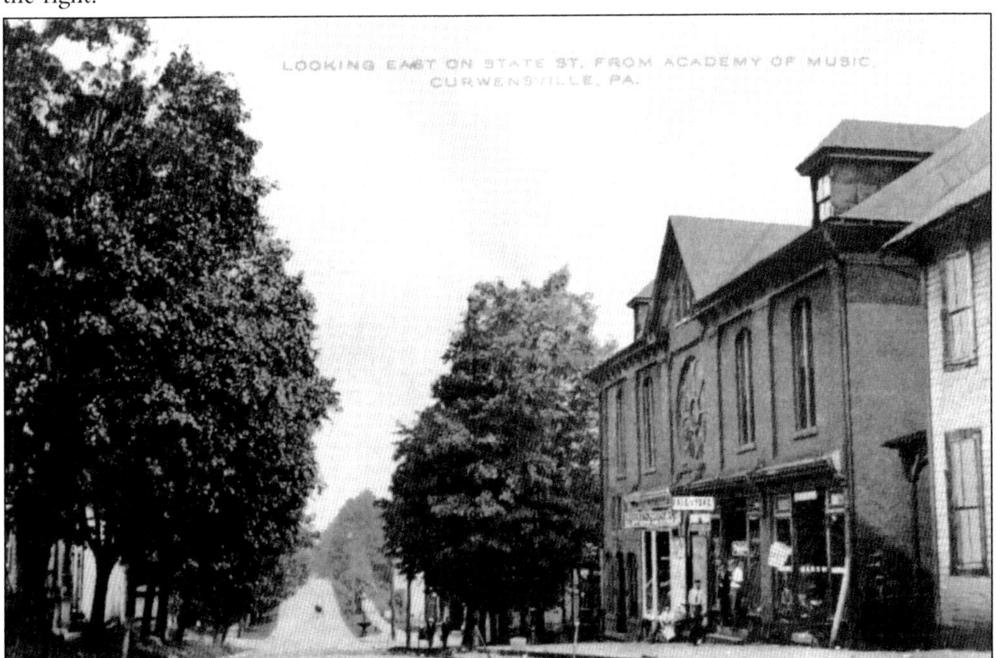

This view looks east on State Street from the W.F. Patton Academy of Music. The old opera house building (right) also included a watchmaker's store and Wrigley's Drug Store. The opera house was torn down in 1946. This location is now the CSB Bank.

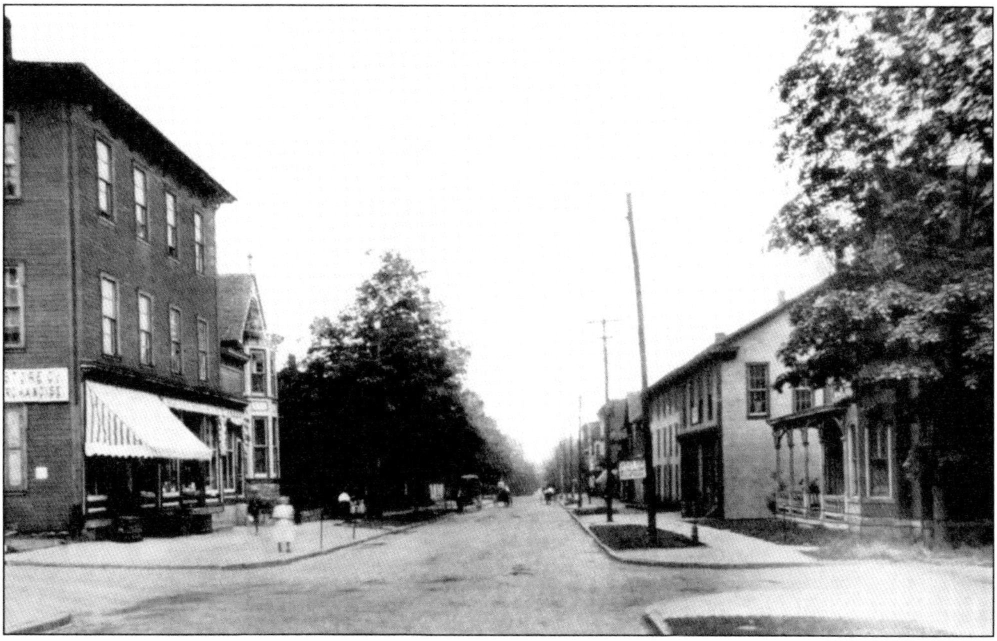

Shown here are State and Walnut Streets in Curwensville.

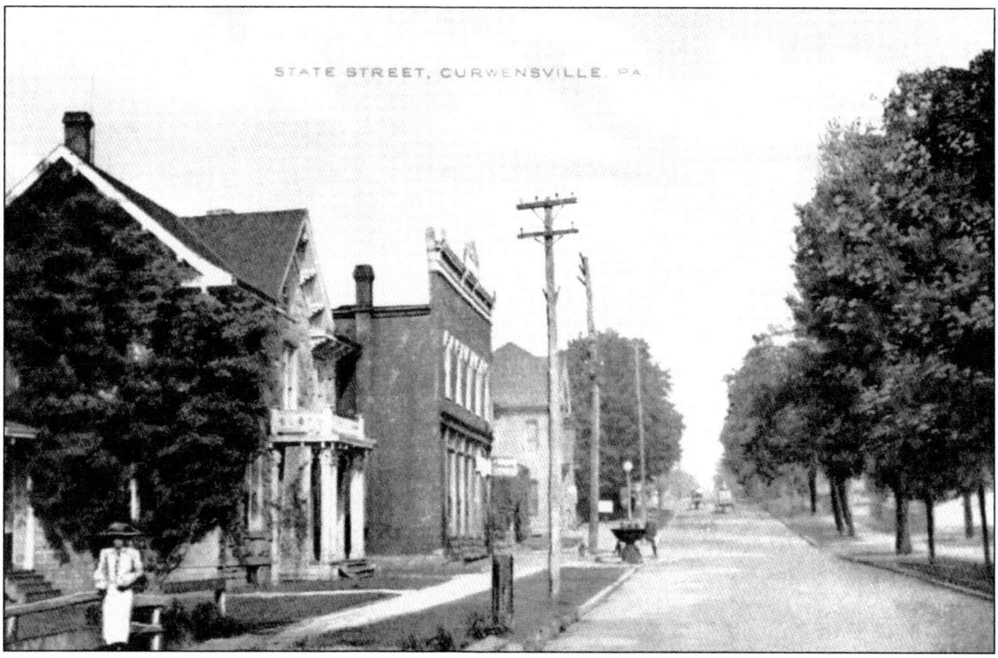

This view of State Street looks west toward Filbert Street.

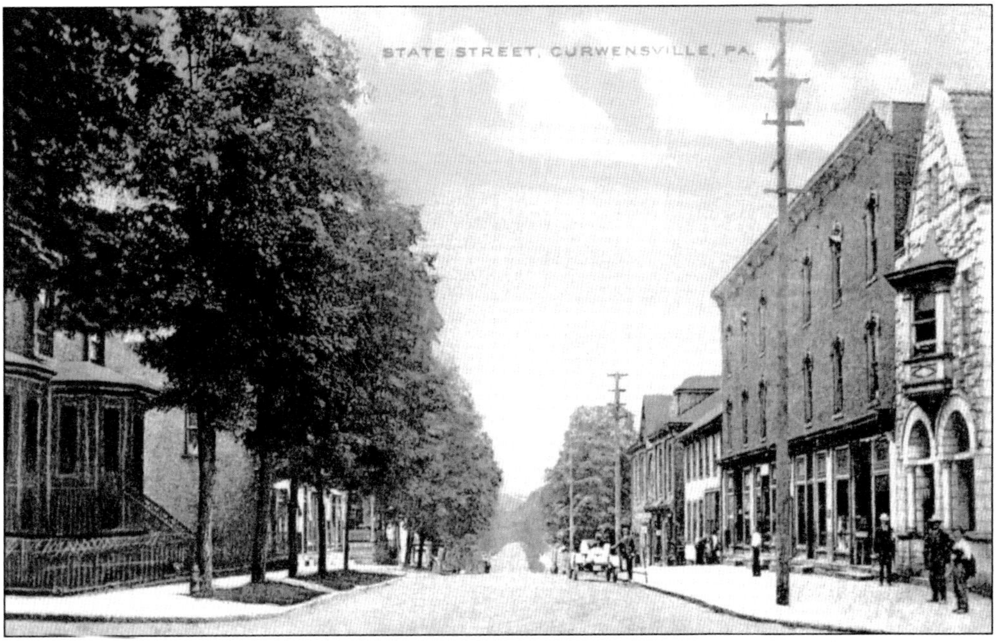

This view, looking east from Thompson Street, shows State Street. To the right is the Curwensville National Bank, the first bank in Pennsylvania to reopen during the Great Depression. Newspapers across the nation carried this news. The building is now the home of Bellmore Insurance.

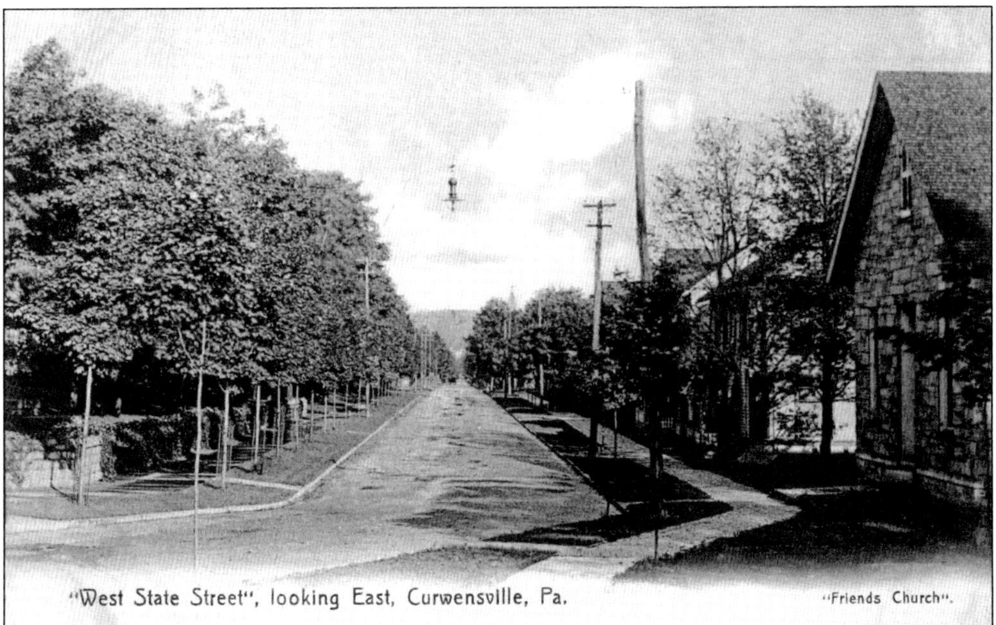

This view looks east on West State Street. On the right is the Friends Church, which was built in 1893 by the Quakers. Over the years, many other congregations used it while their churches were being completed. The church was also used to accommodate the overflow of students in the schools. The building is now Errigo's Antique Shop. Also on the right is the Korb House, home of the Curwensville-Pike Township Historical Society. (Courtesy Leitzinger collection.)

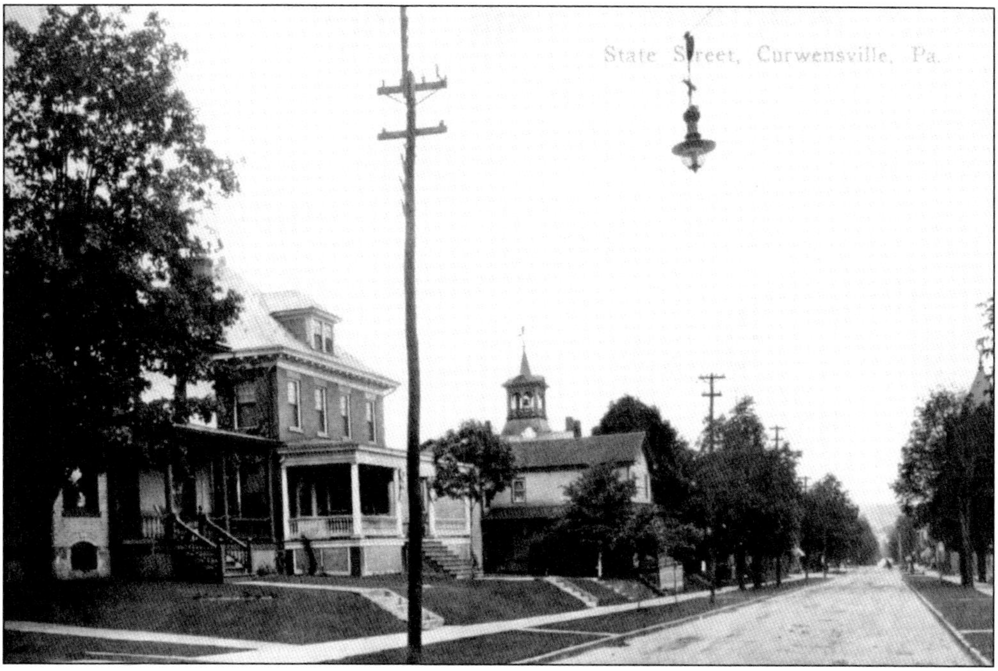

In this postcard of State and Pine Streets, the bell tower of the Patton School can be seen in the center.

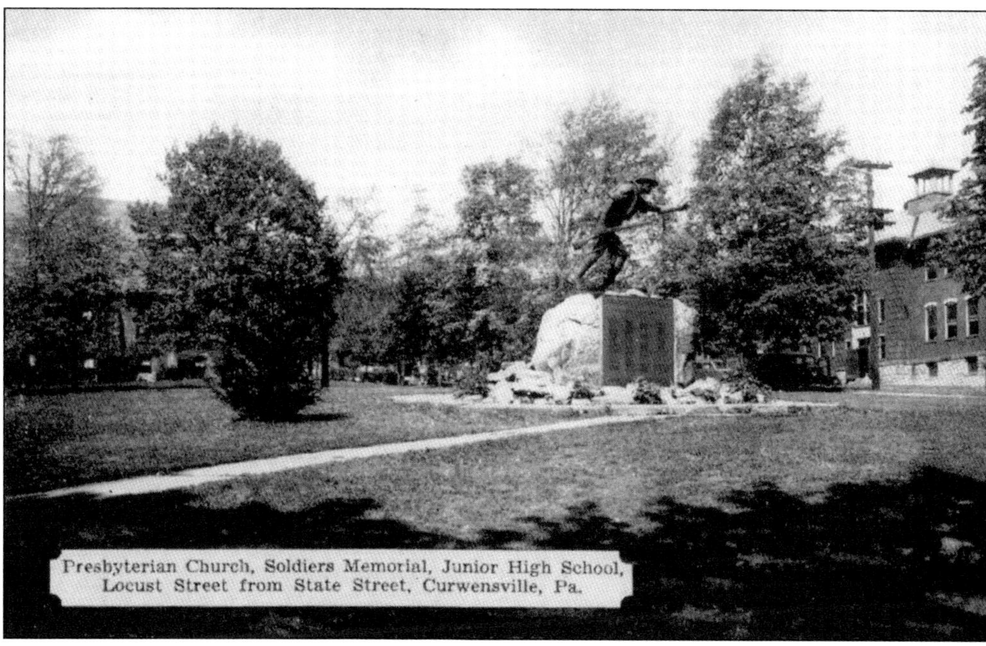

The "Doughboy" is one of the best-known features of Curwensville. Unveiled on Flag Day in 1925, it was dedicated to the veterans of all the wars. The plot, donated by Col. Edward A. Irvin, was originally intended as a memorial for his Pennsylvania Bucktails Company K, which served in the Civil War.

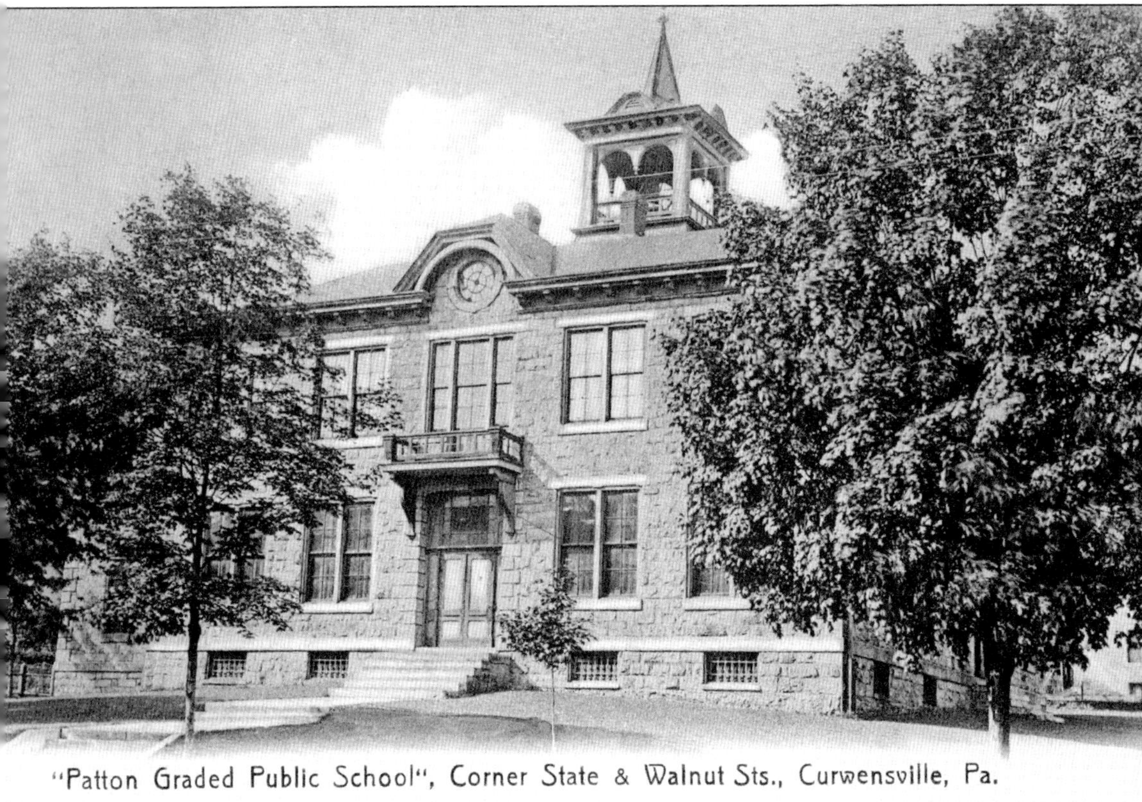

The Curwensville High School was originally known as the Patton Graded Public School when it was built in 1885. Later, it simply became known as the Patton Building. John Patton donated the money for the building, which was torn down in 1968. (Courtesy Test collection.)

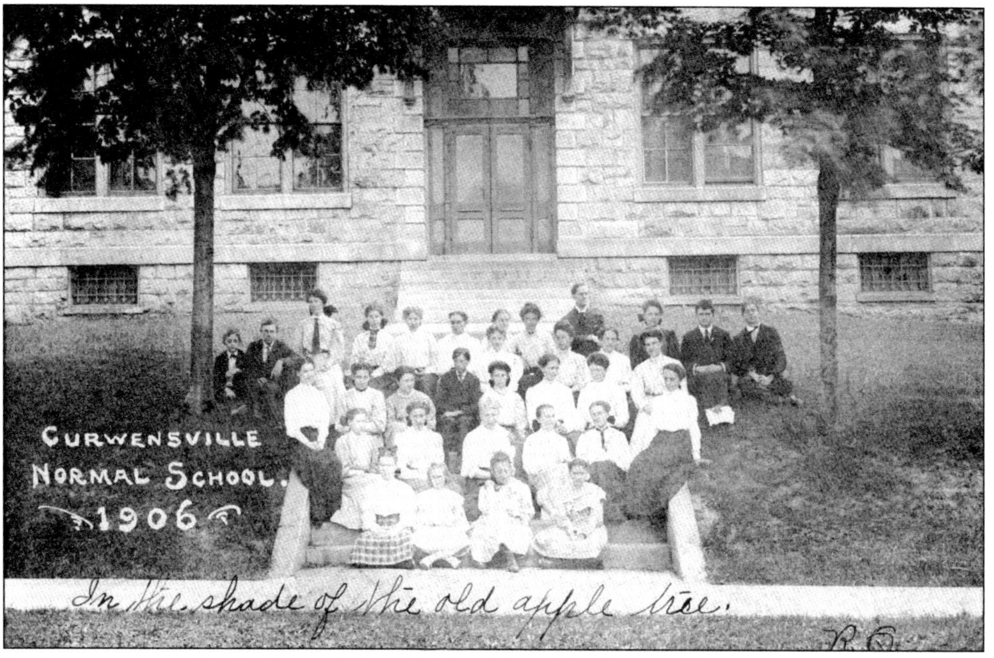

Students pose outside the Patton Normal School in 1906. "Normal" was a term used to refer to a school that trained teachers.

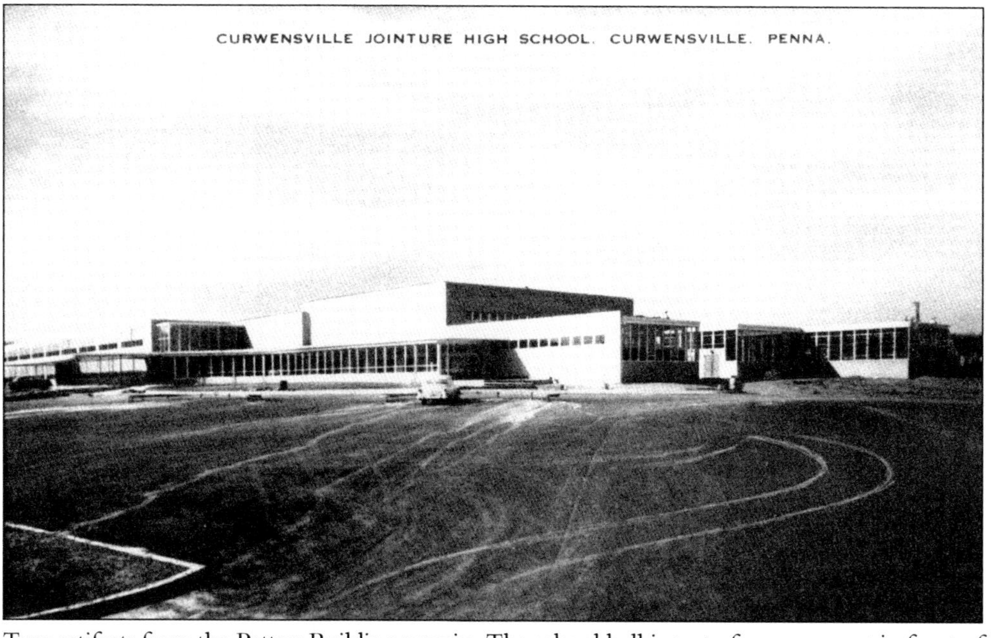

Two artifacts from the Patton Building remain. The school bell is part of a monument in front of the current Curwensville High School (above), and the Patton Eagle, which once perched above the school, is now sitting over the school's auditorium ticket office. This building was dedicated in May 1955. (Courtesy Zalno collection.)

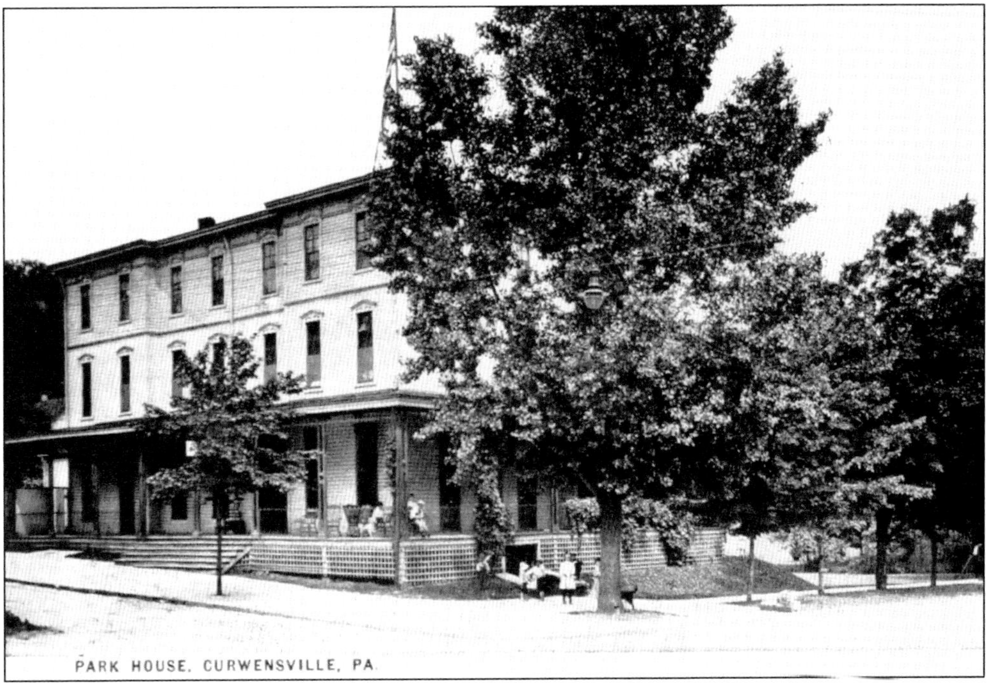

The Park House, located at State and Filbert Streets, was built in 1881 by a group headed by John Patton.

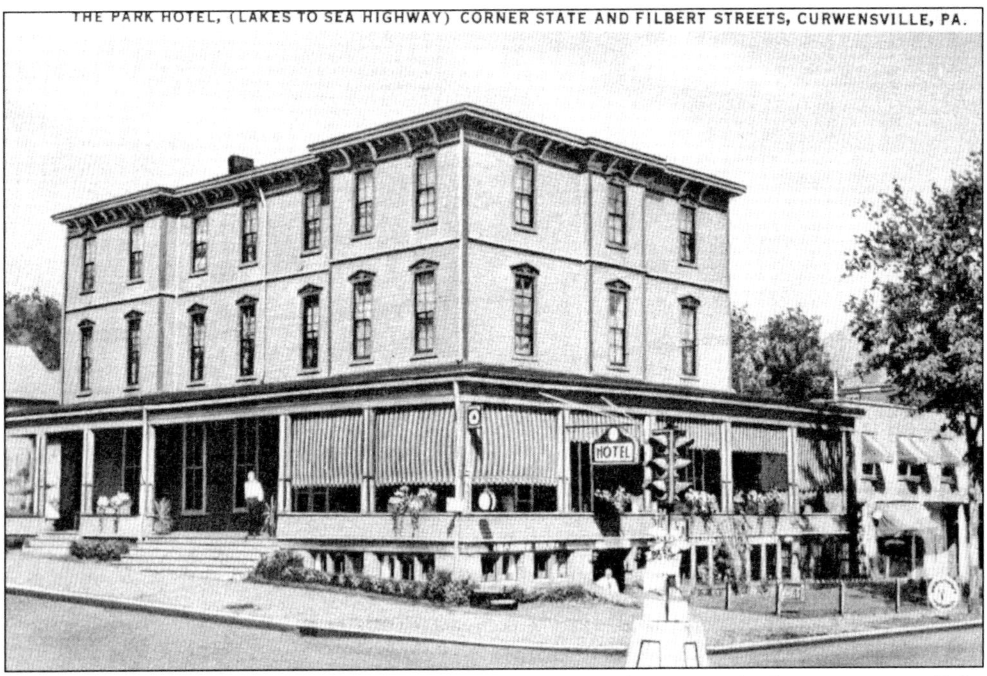

In this later photograph of the Park House—or the Park Hotel, as it was also known—a streetlight can be seen. The building was torn down in 1989. (Courtesy Test collection.)

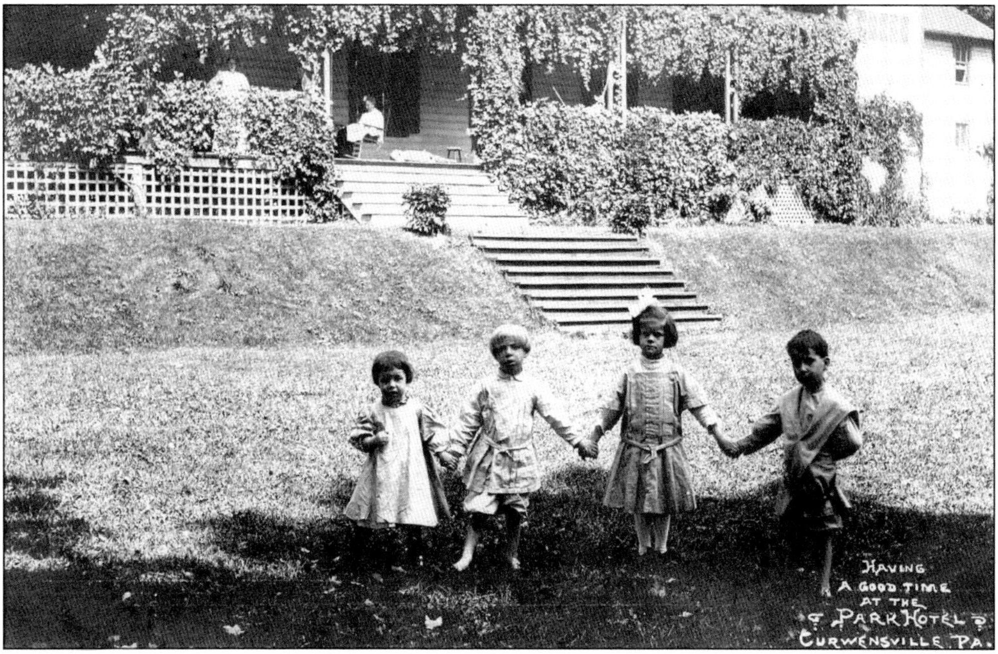

This 1907 postcard reads, "Having a good time at the Park Hotel in Curwensville PA." (Courtesy Test collection.)

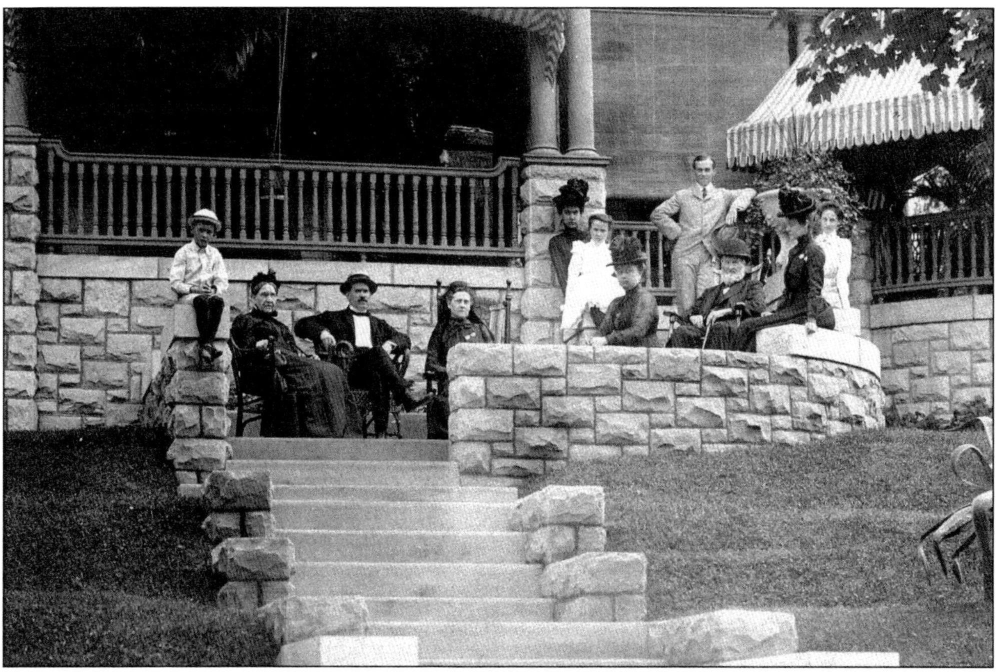

Shown here is a gathering at the Alexander E. Patton House *c.* 1917. Patton was a state senator and was on the board of directors for Dickinson College. In September 1890, he entertained Pres. Benjamin Harrison and his wife here. The house was destroyed by fire in 1942. (Courtesy Test collection.)

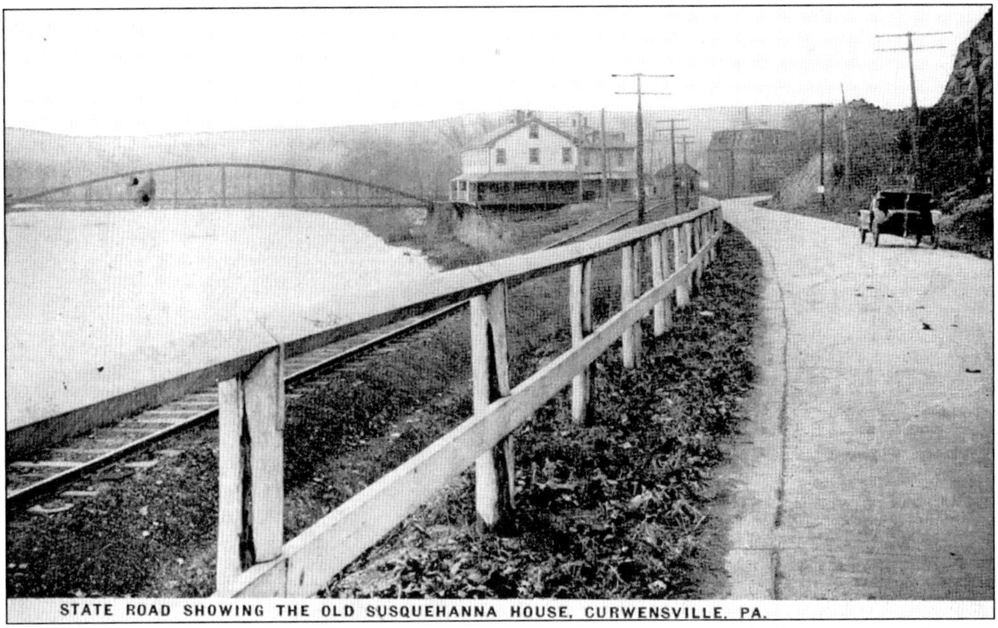

Another early Curwensville hotel was the Susquehanna House. Since it had an entrance located right on the river, this hotel was a favorite stop for the rafters. (Courtesy Test collection.)

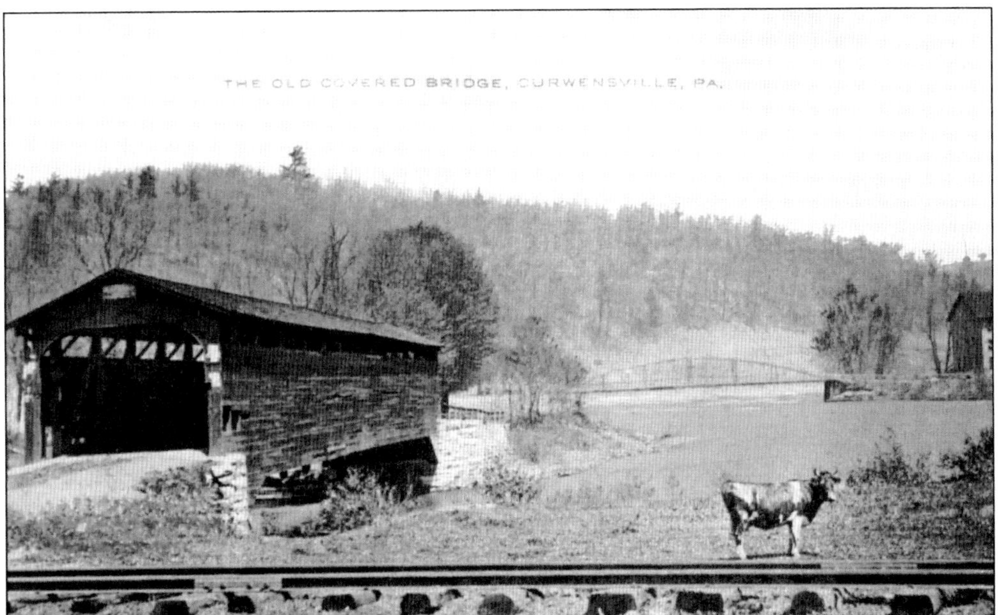

For 83 years, the Old Covered Bridge allowed travelers to cross Anderson Creek. The 120-foot-long structure was built in 1866. Original lumber from the bridge was used to create a replica that is on display at the nearby Veterans of Foreign Wars building.

Six

INDUSTRY

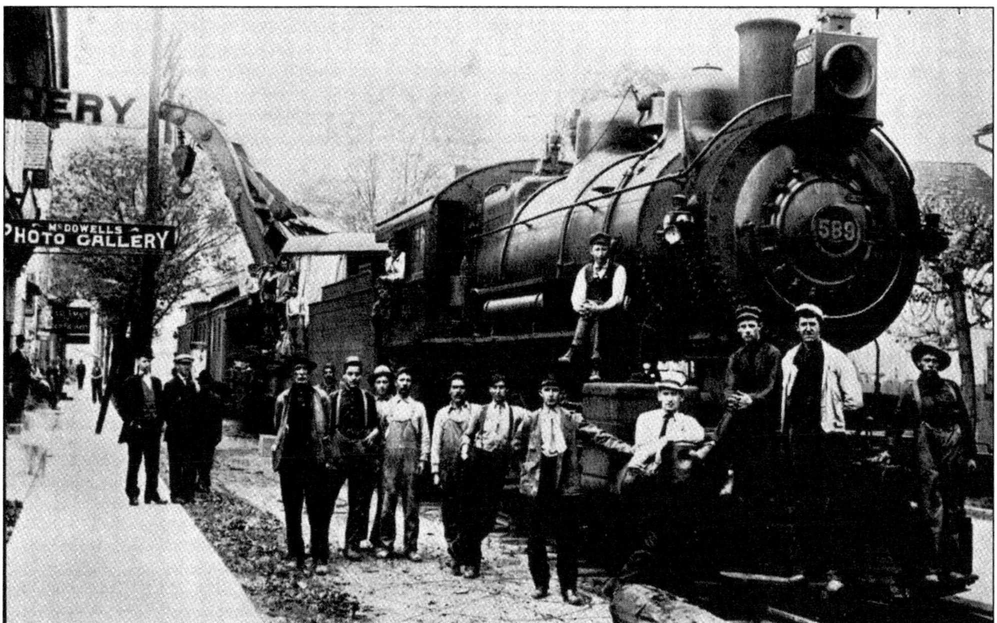

Many industries, including the railroad, called Clearfield home. The back of this card reads, "Pennsylvania Railroad, Clearfield PA. Work Extra 589 on pole setting during spring of 1917. Conductor Gartner is sitting on running board of engine and Engineer Harvey Huss is sitting in cab. Line Gang Foreman W.D. Black is leaning against pilot beam wearing Panama hat. Locomotive 589 was Class H6a."

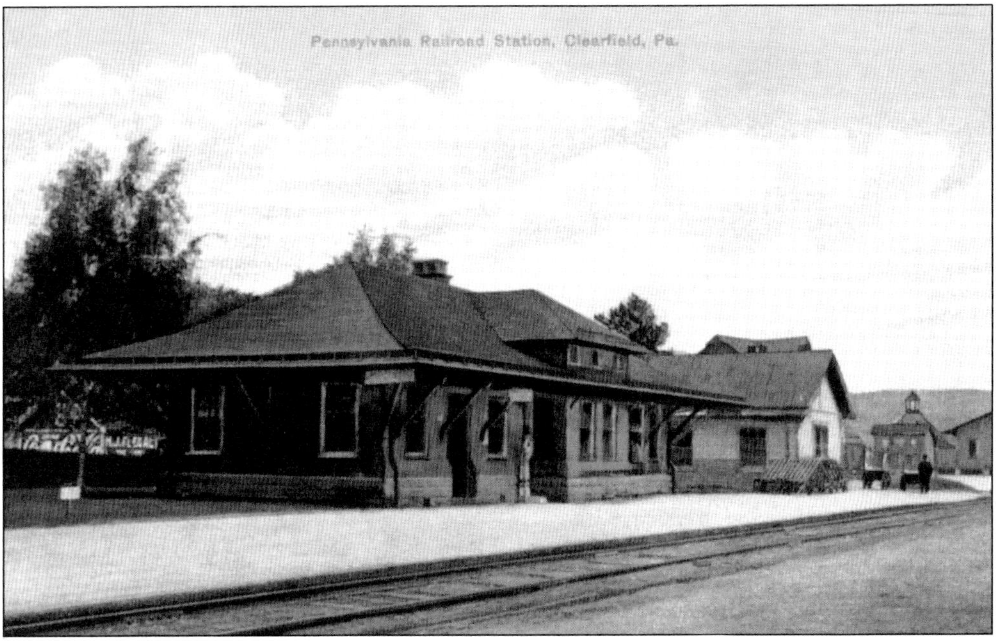

Shown here is the old Pennsylvania Railroad station on Third Street in Clearfield. Today, the building houses a laundromat.

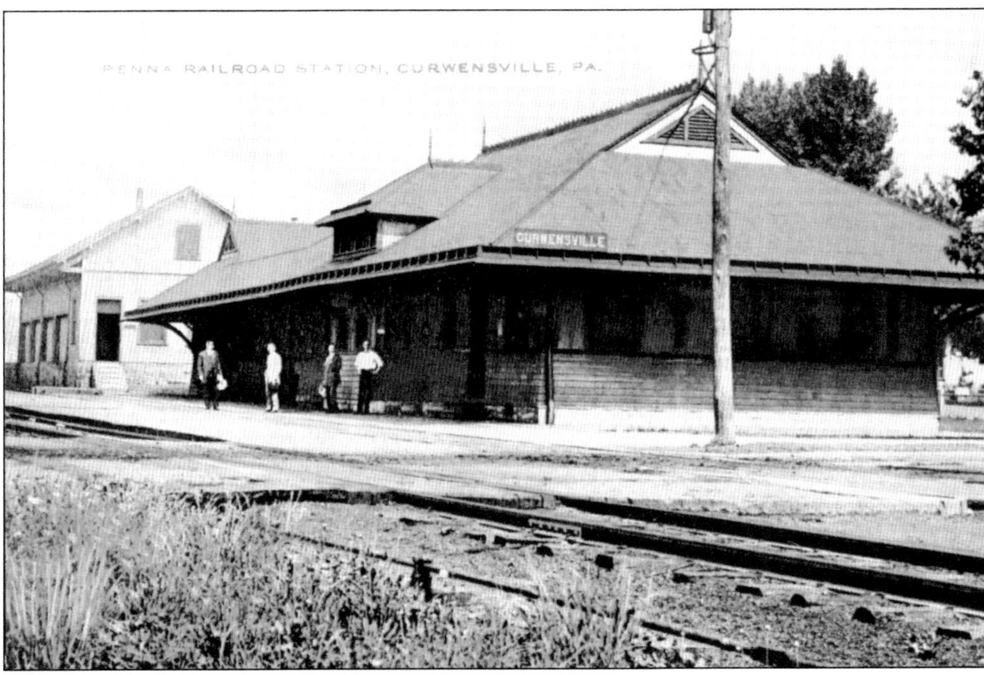

This Pennsylvania Railroad station in Curwensville was both a passenger and freight station. Today, it is home to the Curwensville Feed Store.

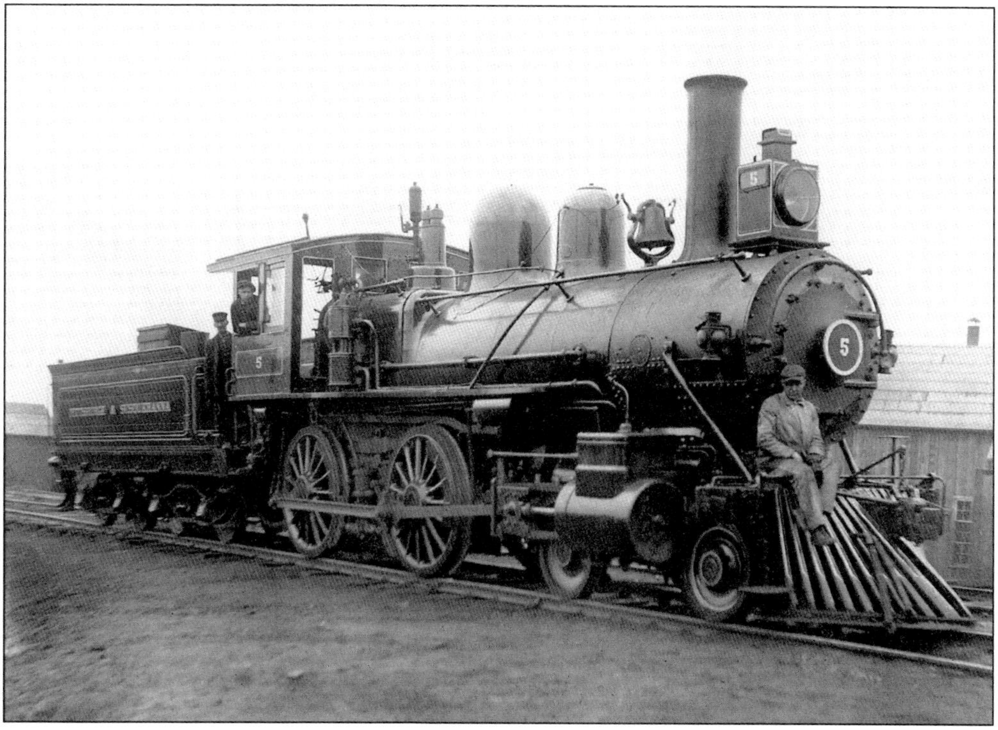

The Altoona and Philipsburg Connecting Railroad started in 1893 and became known as "the Alley Popper" due to its route from Al (Altoona) to PO (Philipsburg-Osceola). Later, it became the Pittsburgh and Susquehanna Railroad. It ran six trains daily and four on Sunday on a 15-mile track west of Philipsburg to Fernwood. The line was abandoned in 1936. The man in the cab is William Harley, and the man on the front is possibly John Edmundson. Below is a winter view of the train.

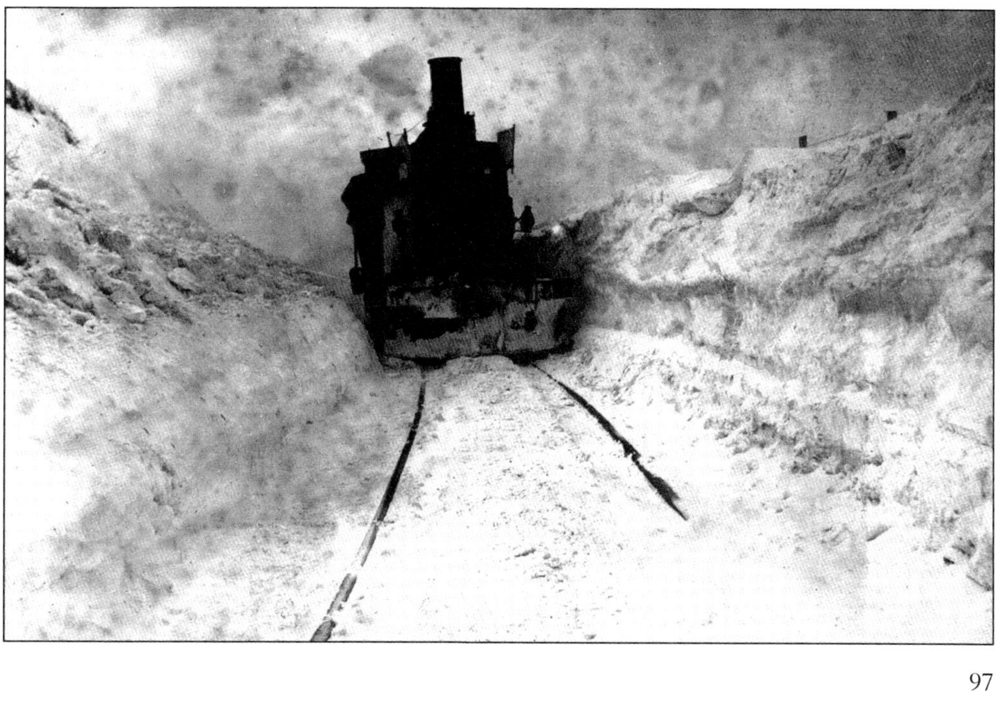

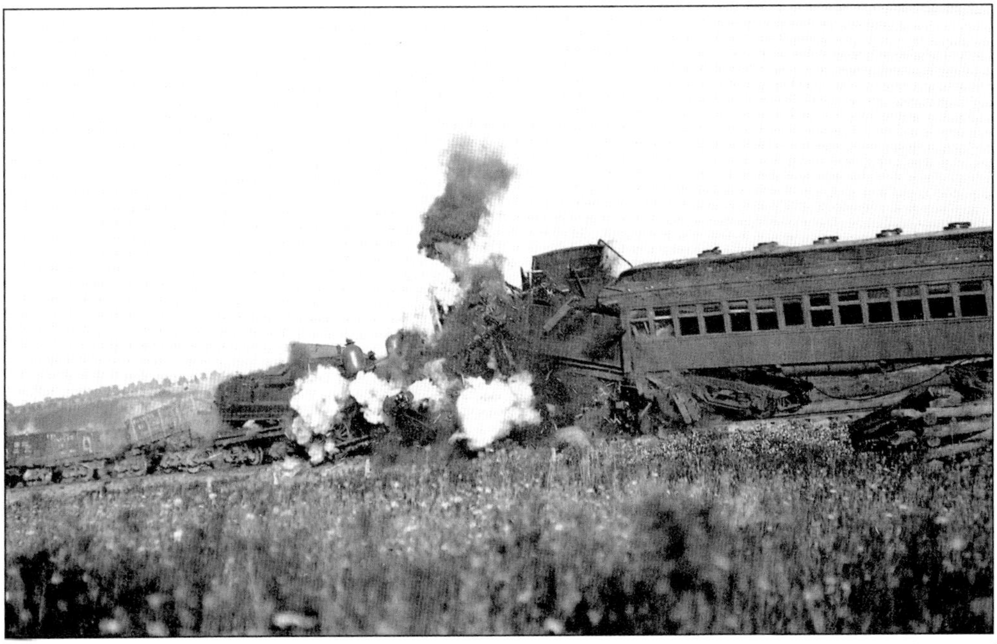

On September 8, 1914, some 10,000 people watched as the Alley Popper staged a collision of two locomotives for the Lubin Film Company of Philadelphia. The footage was used in the film *The Valley of Lost Hope* and several others.

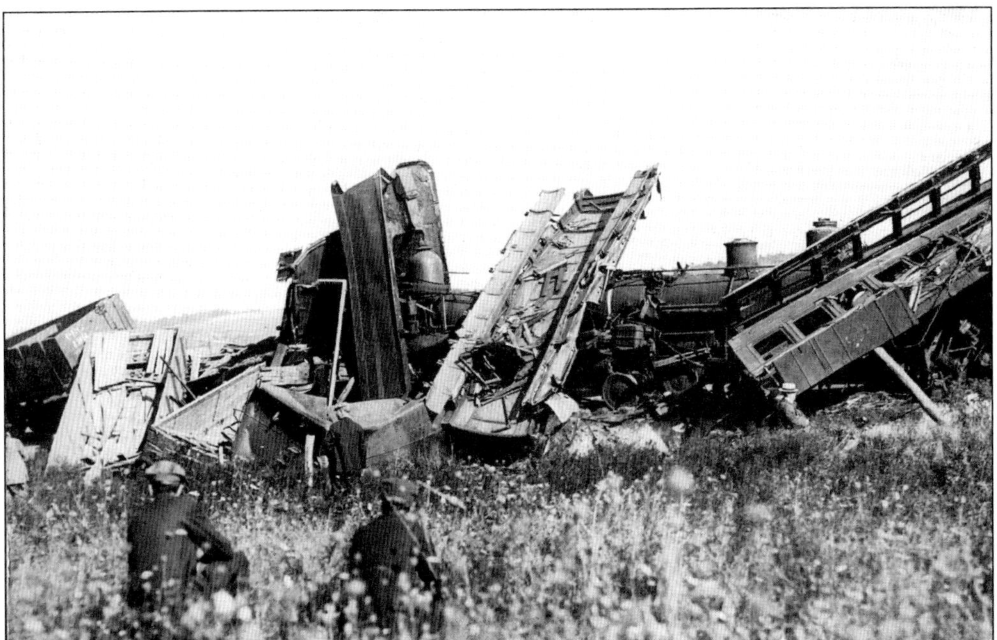

This view shows the aftermath of the staged wreck. These two cards were made by William F. Gable & Company of Altoona.

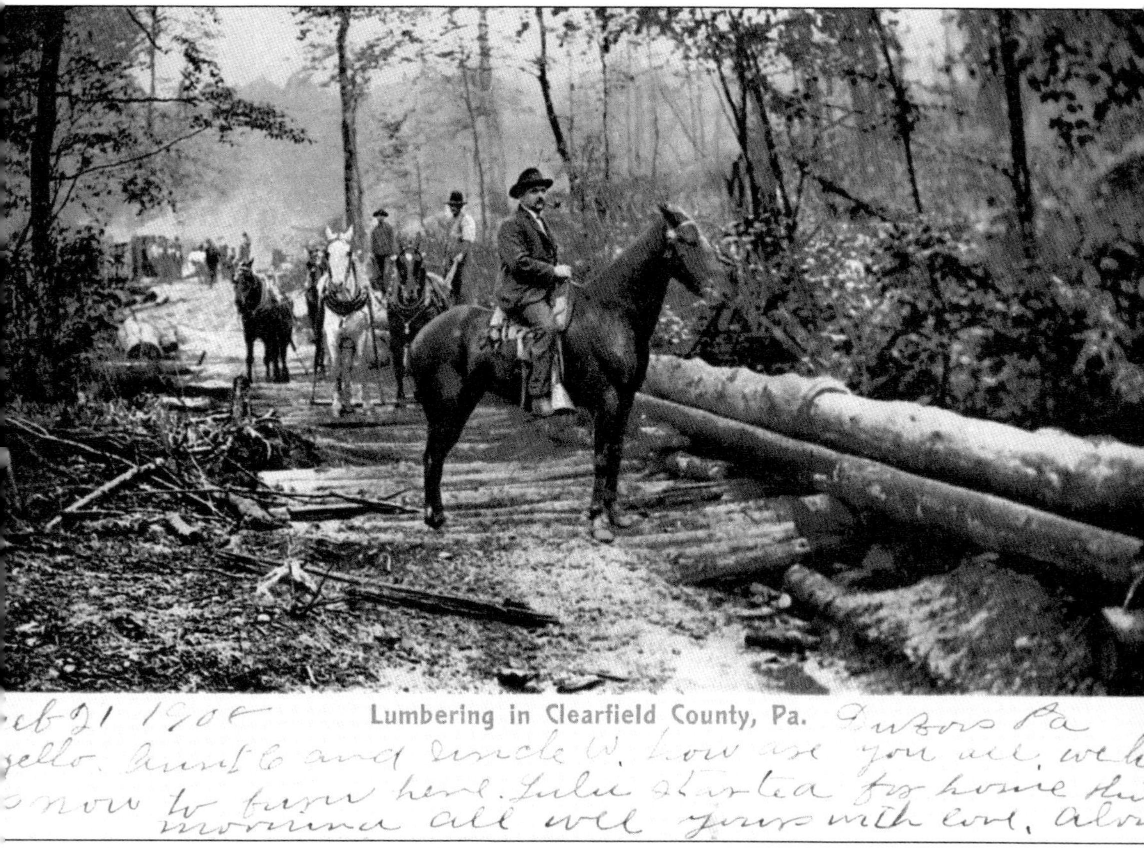

Lumbering was a very important industry in Clearfield County. This postcard was made when the post office did not allow any writing on the back of the card. The small space at the bottom was used for adding personal messages. (Courtesy Leitzinger collection.)

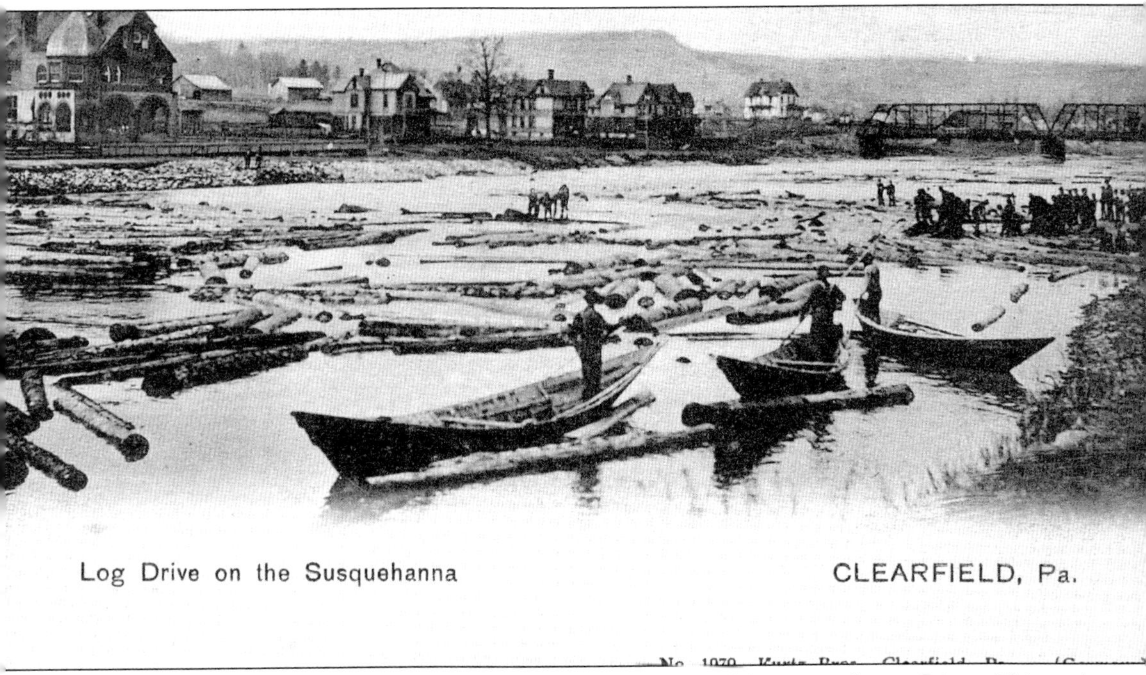

The easiest way to transport logs was down the west branch of the Susquehanna River. This card depicts a typical log drive. (Courtesy Test collection.)

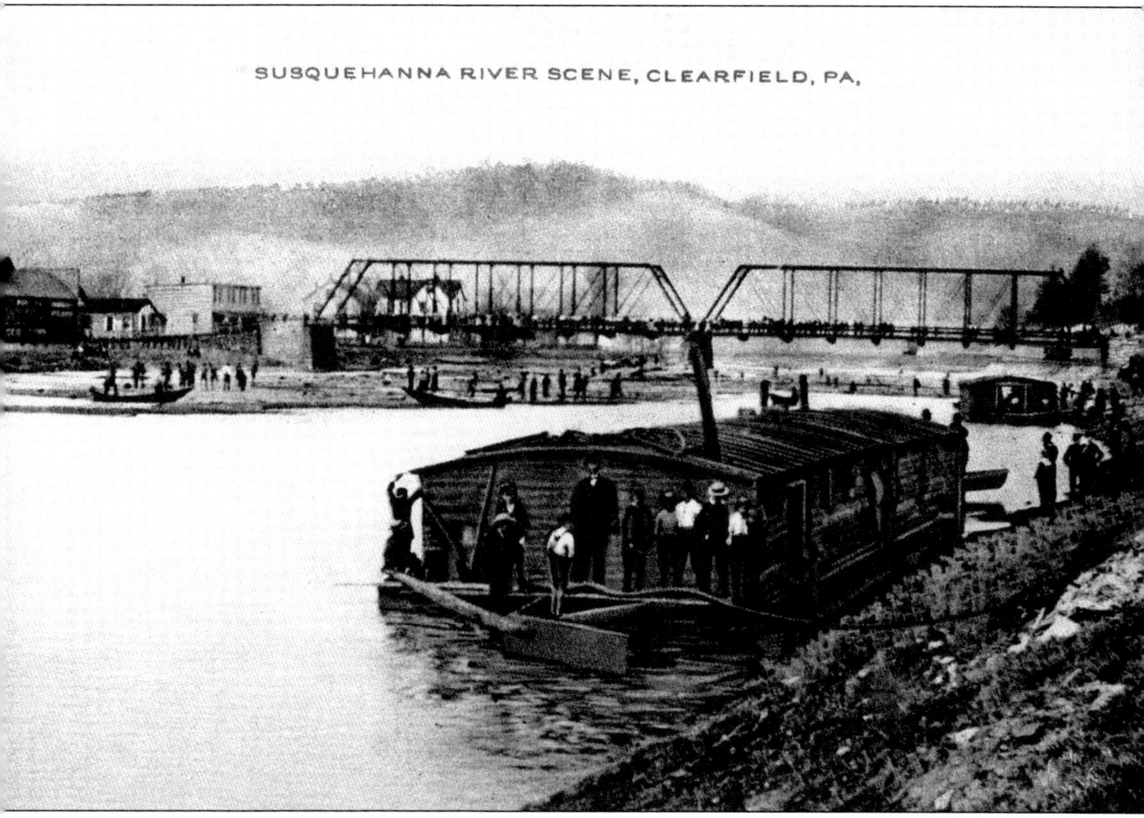

This *c.* 1910 postcard shows rafts as they are loaded with people and lumber. The Second Street (now Nichols Street) Bridge appears in the background.

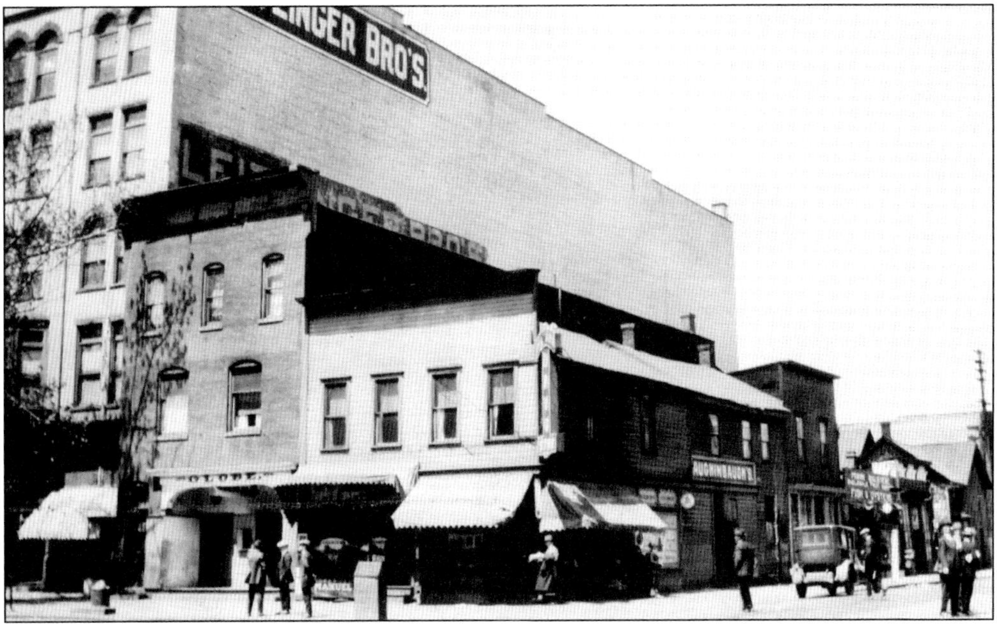

Kurtz Bros. has been a part of Clearfield since 1894. The original store location was on Third Street. In this shot of Market and Third Streets from 1923, we can see the building next to Aughinbaugh's Pharmacy. By then, it was Earl B. Guelich's barbershop. On Market Street from left to right are the Leitzinger Bros. Department Store, the Globe Theater, and the J.L. Shillenn cigar shop.

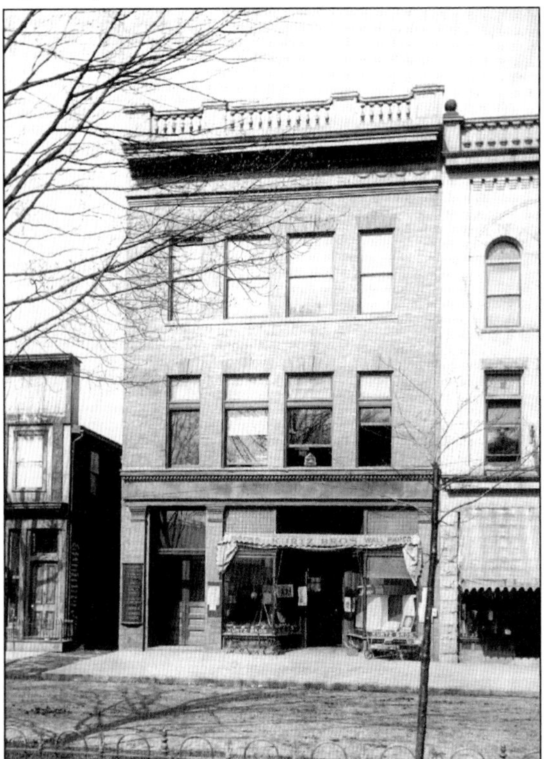

The business expanded, and founder Charles T. Kurtz built a new building on Second Street. Eventually, the growing business built at Fourth and Reed Streets and in Goldenrod. Today, the company is the biggest supplier of school products in the mid-Atlantic states and sells advertising specialties nationwide. (Courtesy Kurtz Bros.)

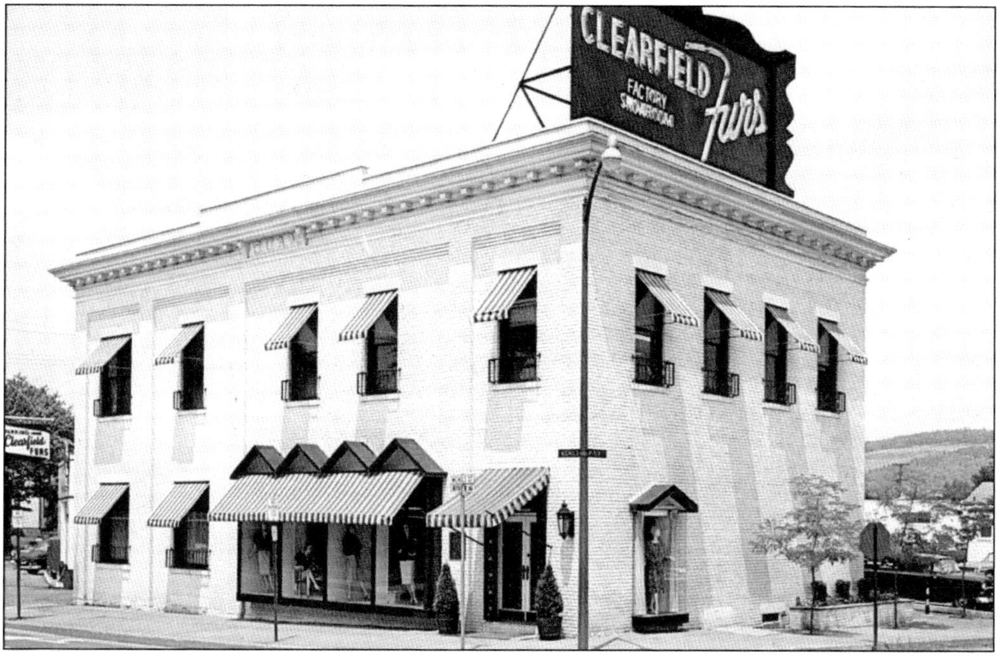

For more than 75 years, Clearfield Furs was one of the town's best-known businesses. It opened in 1915 and closed in 1992. (Courtesy Zalno collection.)

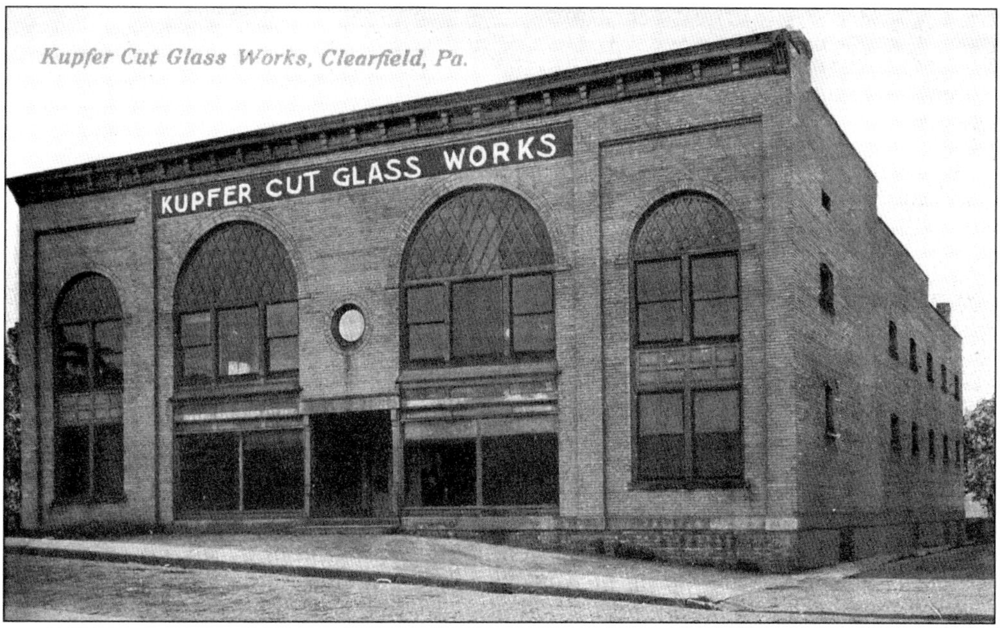

From 1912 to 1918, Kupfer Cut Glass Works was located on Market Street across from the old high school, which is the current location of Uni-Mart. (Courtesy Zalno collection.)

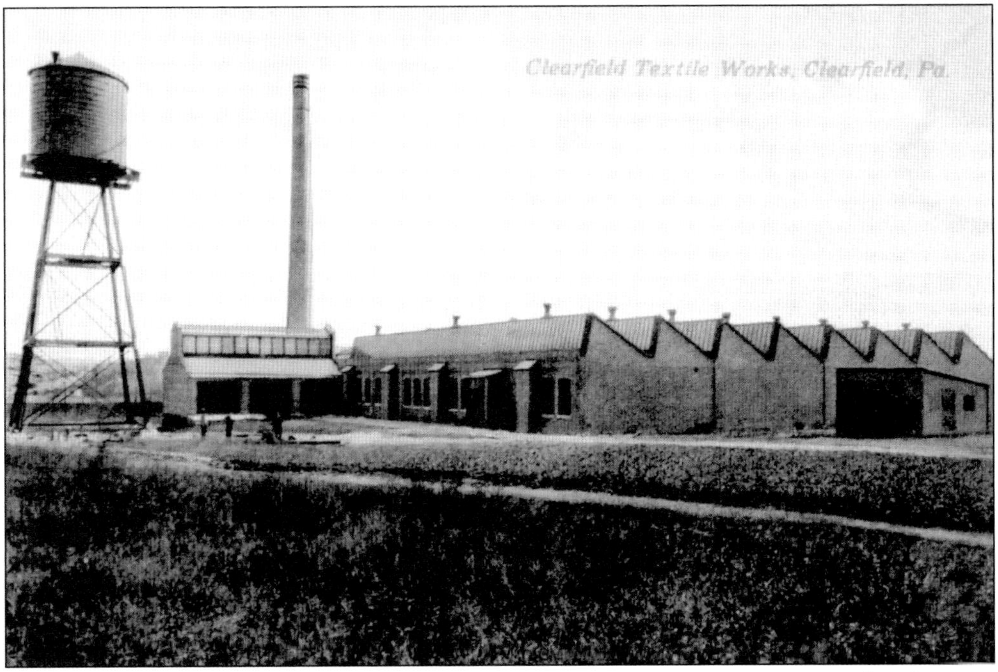

The Clearfield Textile Works was a silk mill located on the West Side. Later, it was the Shortway plant. The site is now used as the Expo II building in the Driving Park.

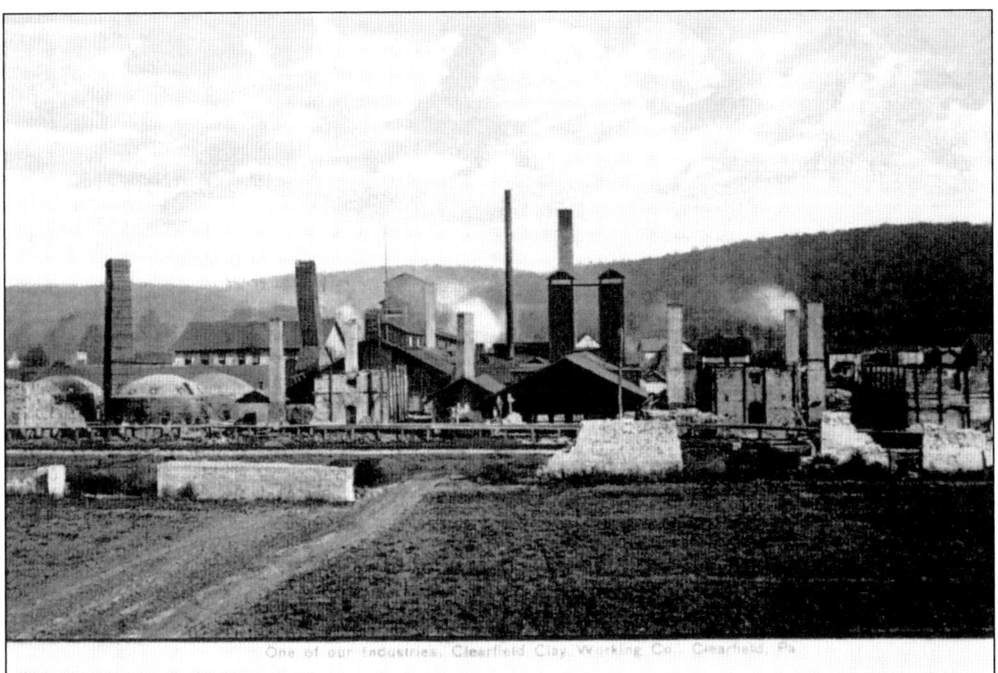

The Clearfield Clay Working Company was located at Spruce and Latimer Streets. The company manufactured paving bricks.

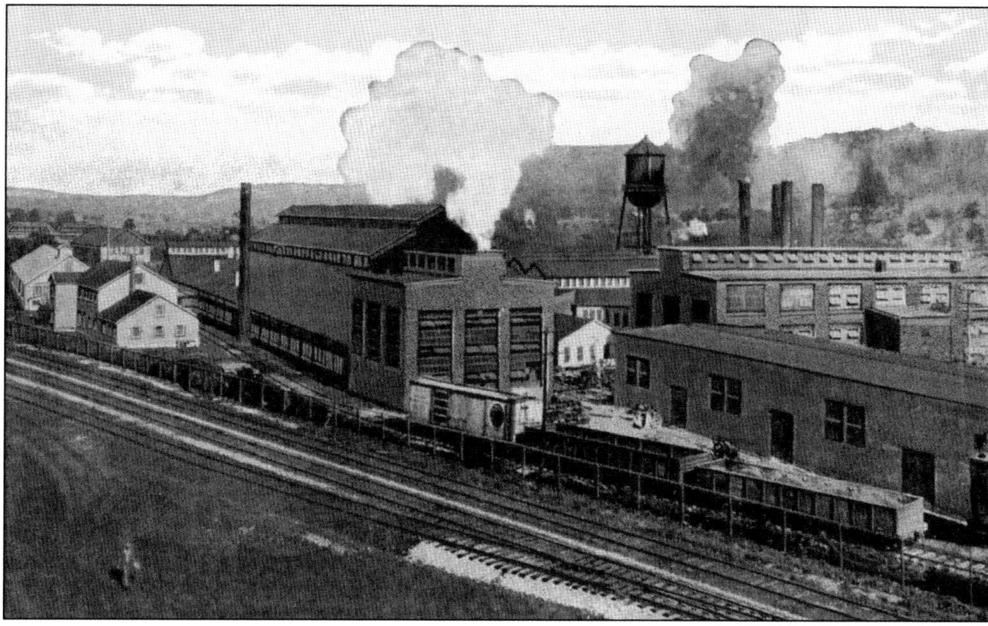

The American Nickel Corporation was actually located outside Clearfield in Hyde in 1909. It manufactured many items, from rivets to bread pans. The building was later Tafco and is now TMP Acquisitions.

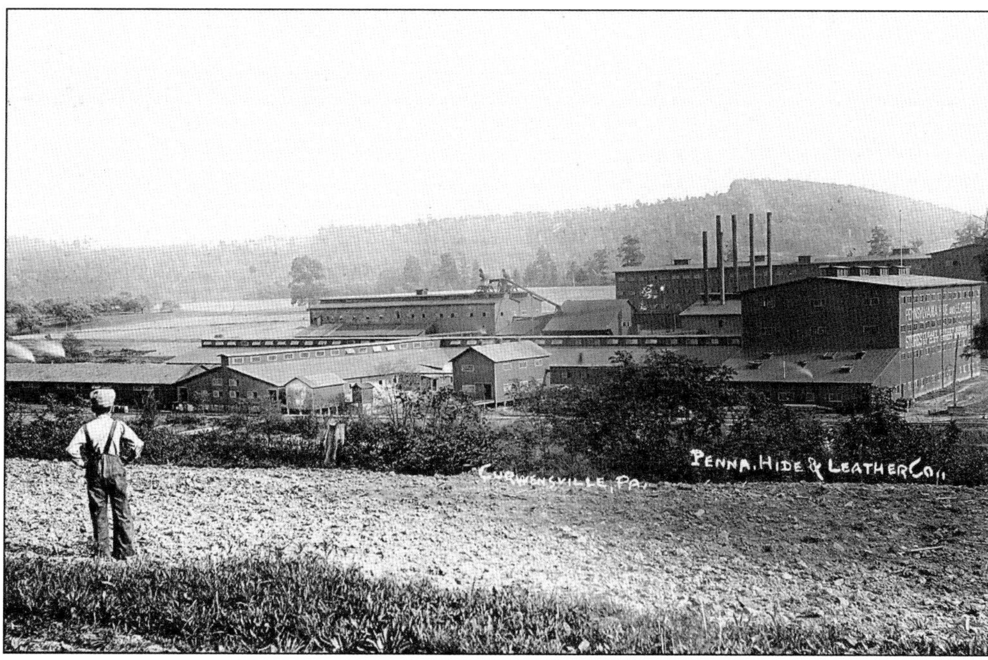

A young man admires the Pennsylvania Hide and Leather Company in Curwensville in 1912. Tanneries are the oldest continuous industry in Curwensville, starting in 1819. Today, the company is known as Howe's Leather. (Courtesy Test collection.)

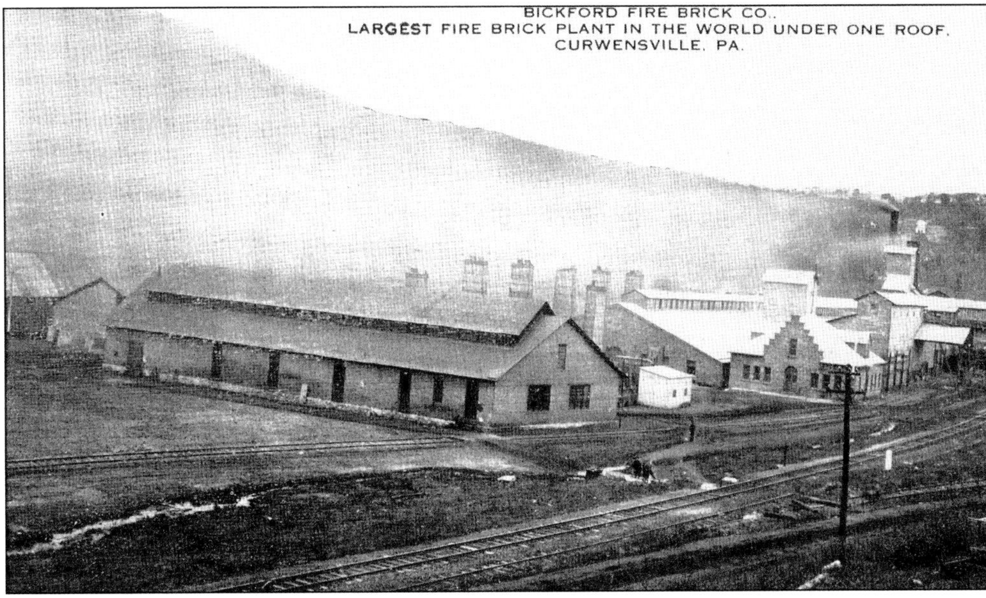

The Bickford Fire Brick Company of Curwensville is described as "the largest fire brick plant in the world under one roof." Begun in 1900, it was originally called the Curwensville Fire Brick Company. (Courtesy Test collection.)

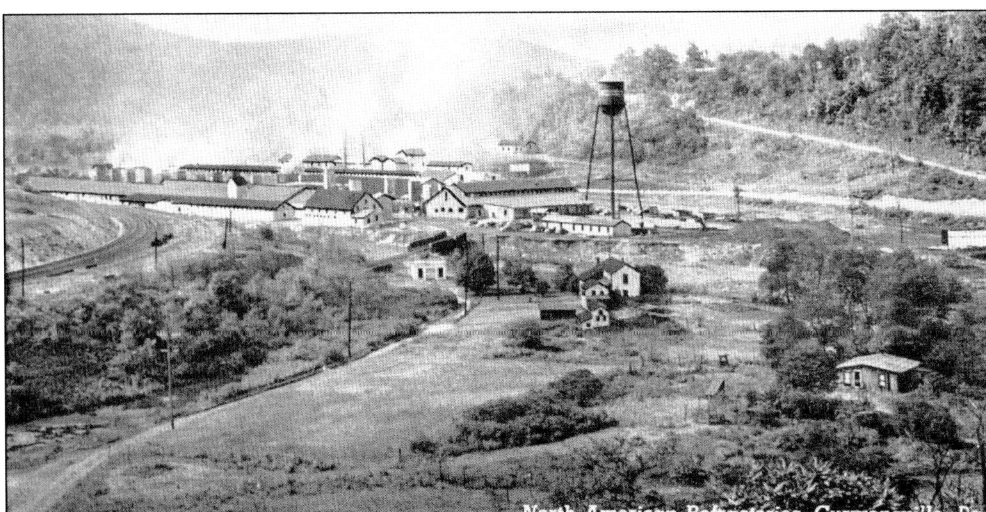

In the 1940s, the Bickford Fire Brick Company became North American Refractories and eventually NARCO. (Courtesy Test collection.)

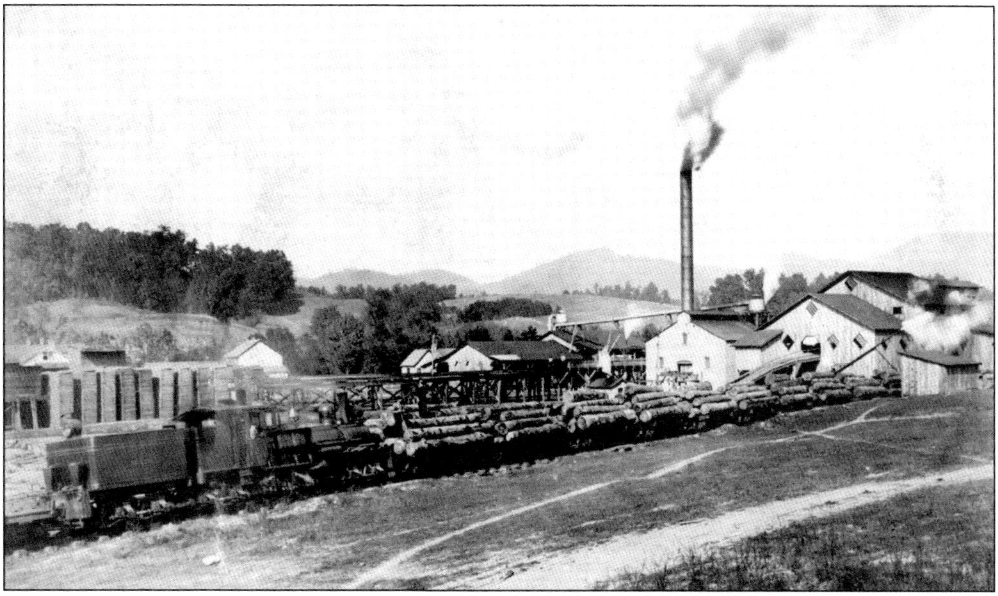

The "Big Mill" was the largest lumbermill in the area from 1889 to 1895. It was once owned by Hoover, Hughes, and Company of Centre County.

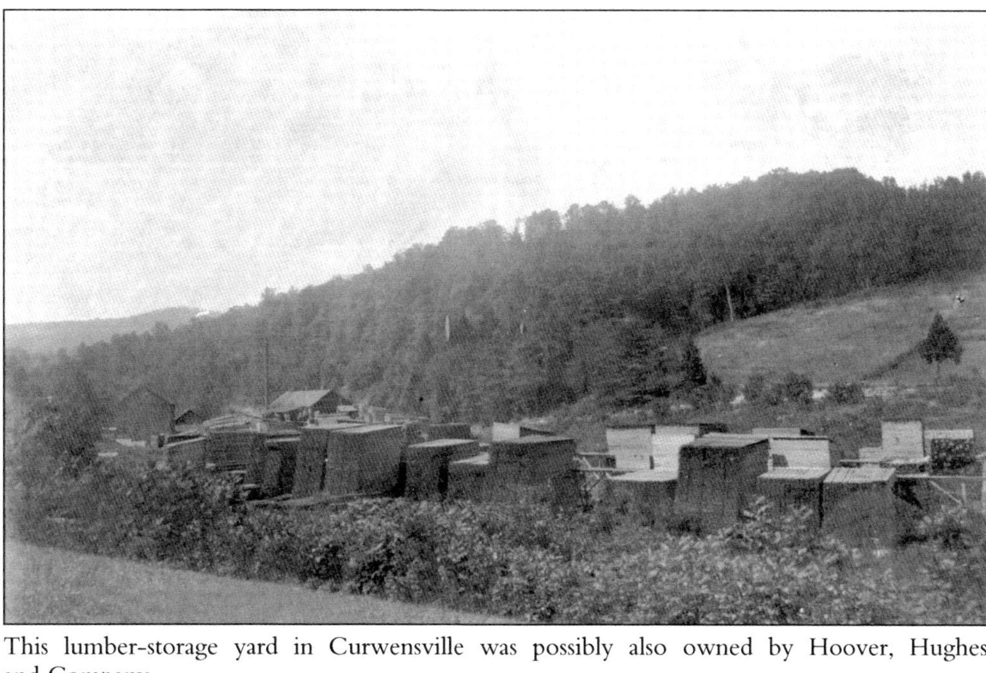

This lumber-storage yard in Curwensville was possibly also owned by Hoover, Hughes, and Company.

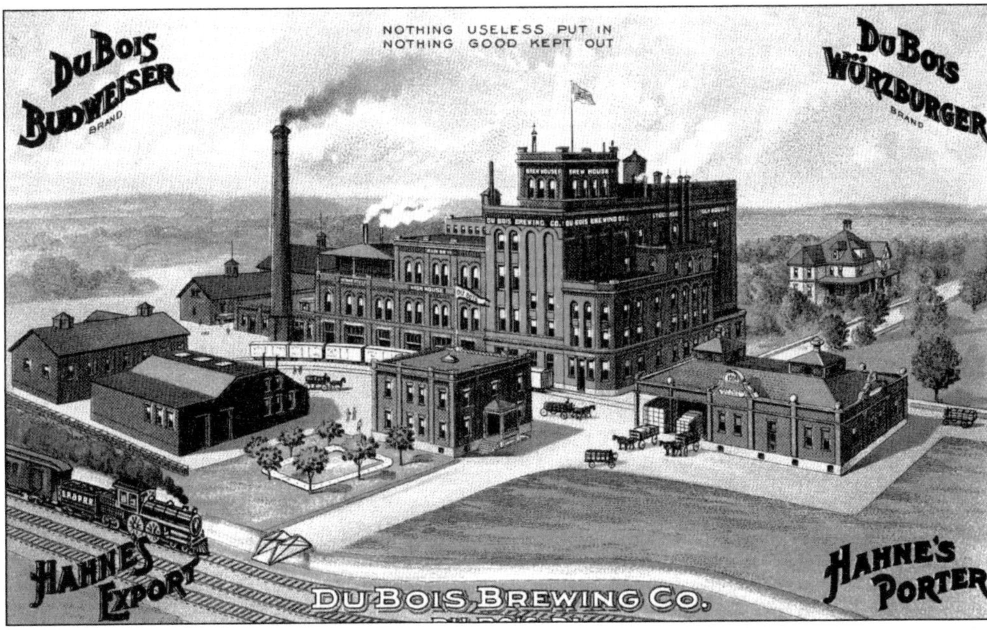

The DuBois Brewing Company was a distributor of the Budweiser brand of beer but eventually lost out to the Anheuser Busch Company. Note the company's slogan at the top of the card: "Nothing useless put in. Nothing good kept out." The company closed in 1972. (Courtesy Leitzinger collection.)

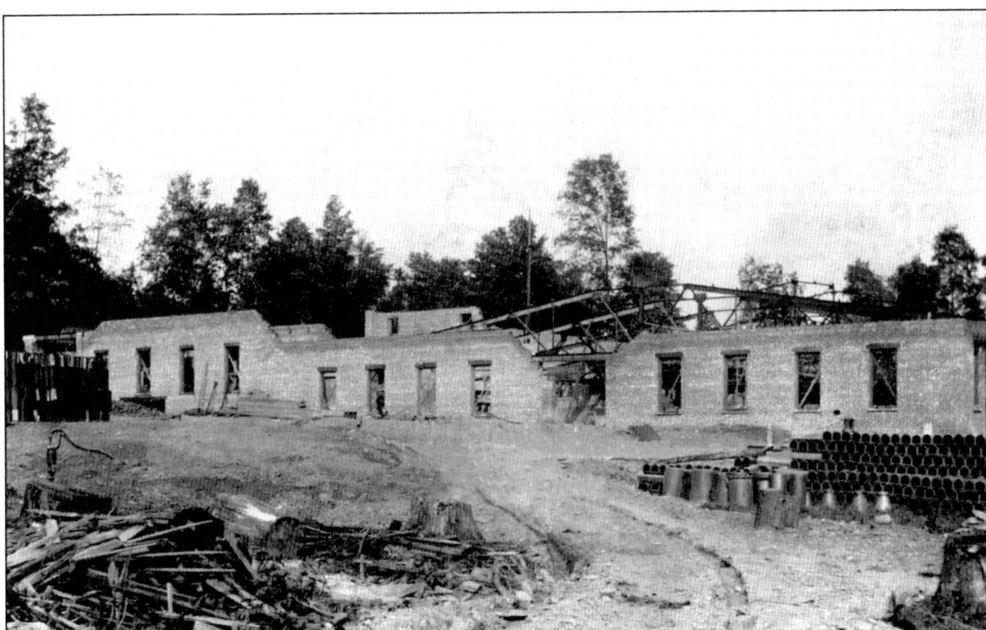

Shown here is the Good Brick Works Company in Lumber City.

Seven

The View from Above

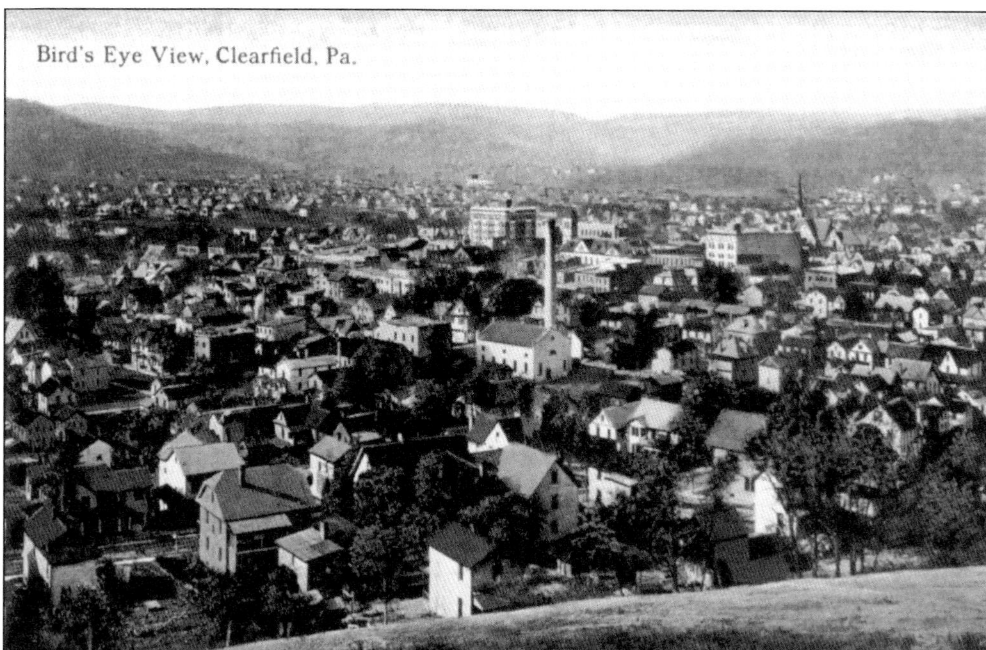

Another way of looking at the town is from the many hills around Clearfield. This bird's-eye view of Clearfield was one of many cards using the idea. In the photograph, one can see the Dimeling, the courthouse, and the Leitzinger Bros. building in the upper center.

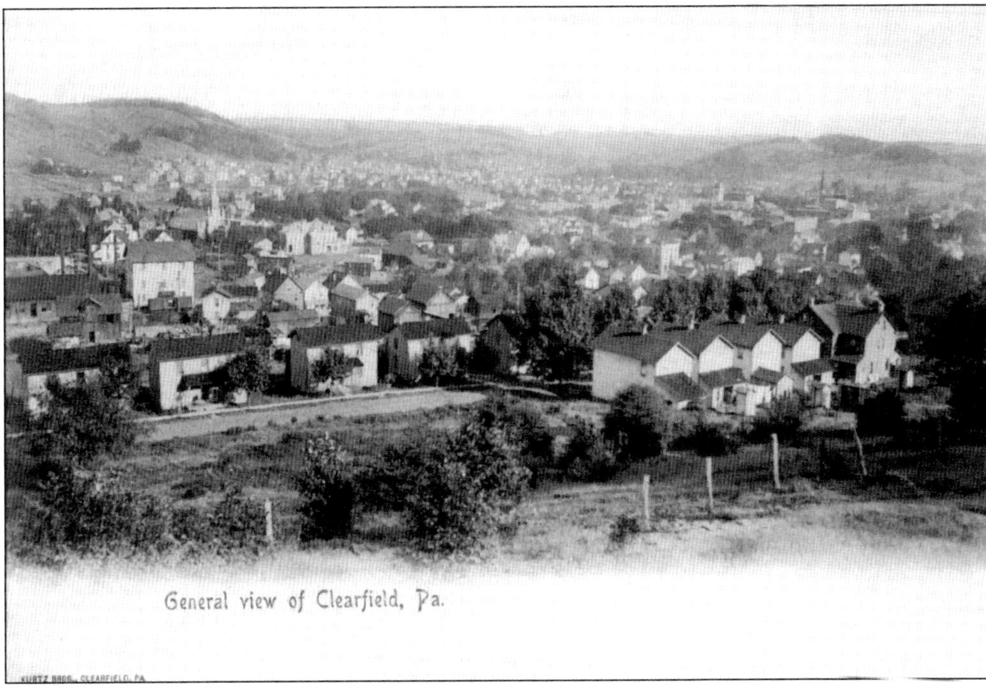

In this general view of Clearfield from 1903, the St. Francis Church appears in the upper left, and in the upper right, the tower of the courthouse can be seen. Farther to the right is the steeple of the Presbyterian church. At the time, the Dimeling Hotel and the Leitzinger Bros. five-story building had not yet been built.

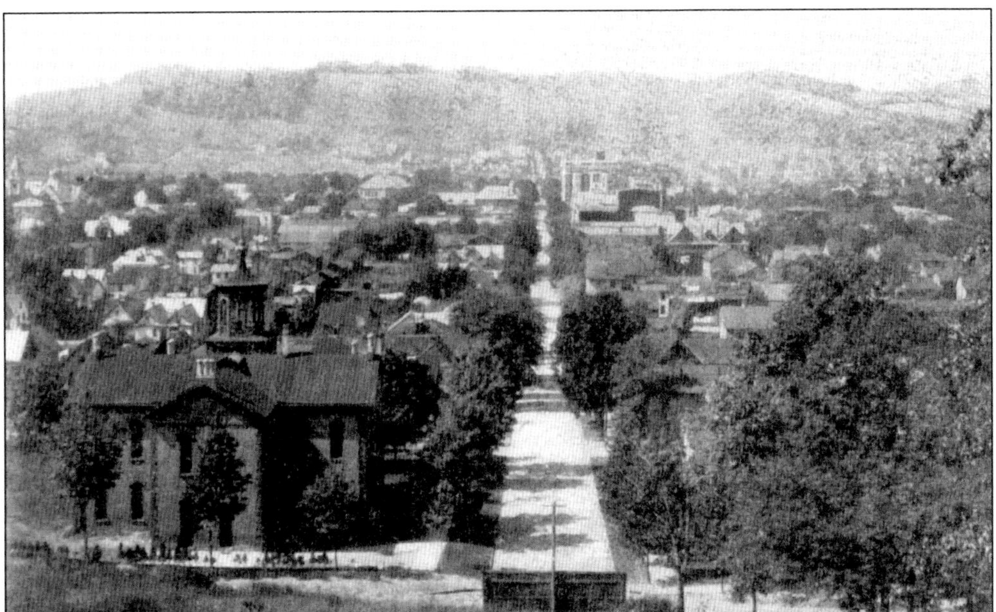

This view looks down at the town from the top of Market Street. On the left is the old Leonard Graded School.

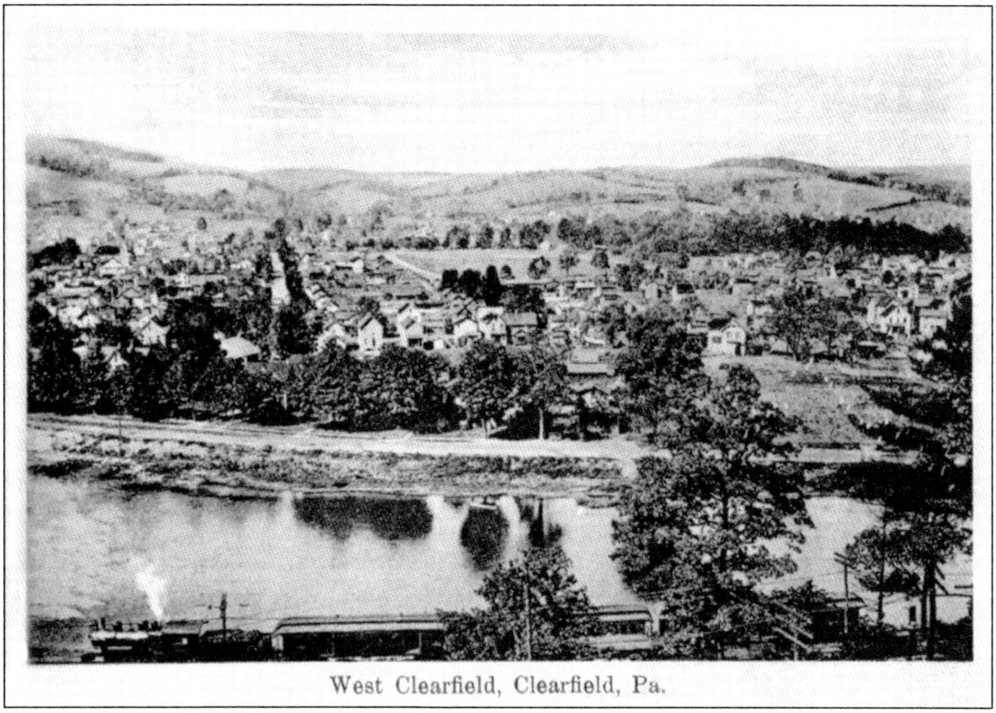

West Clearfield borough was established in 1883. Only a few years later in 1900, it was combined with Clearfield borough. In the upper center is the Driving Park, or Fairgrounds, and the train running along the bottom is from the New York Central Railroad.

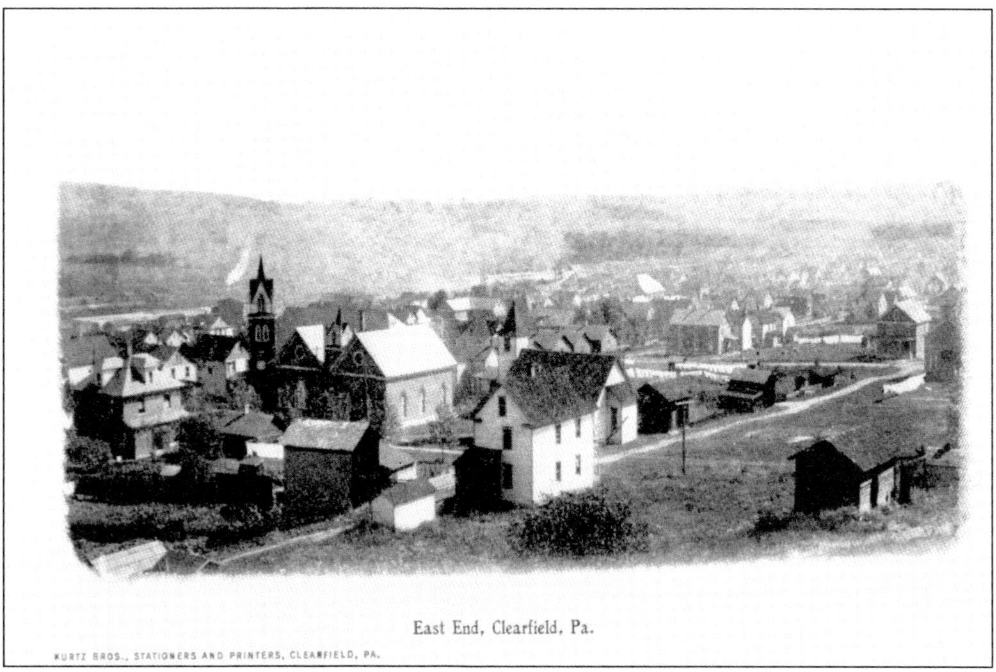

This card features the East End of Clearfield.

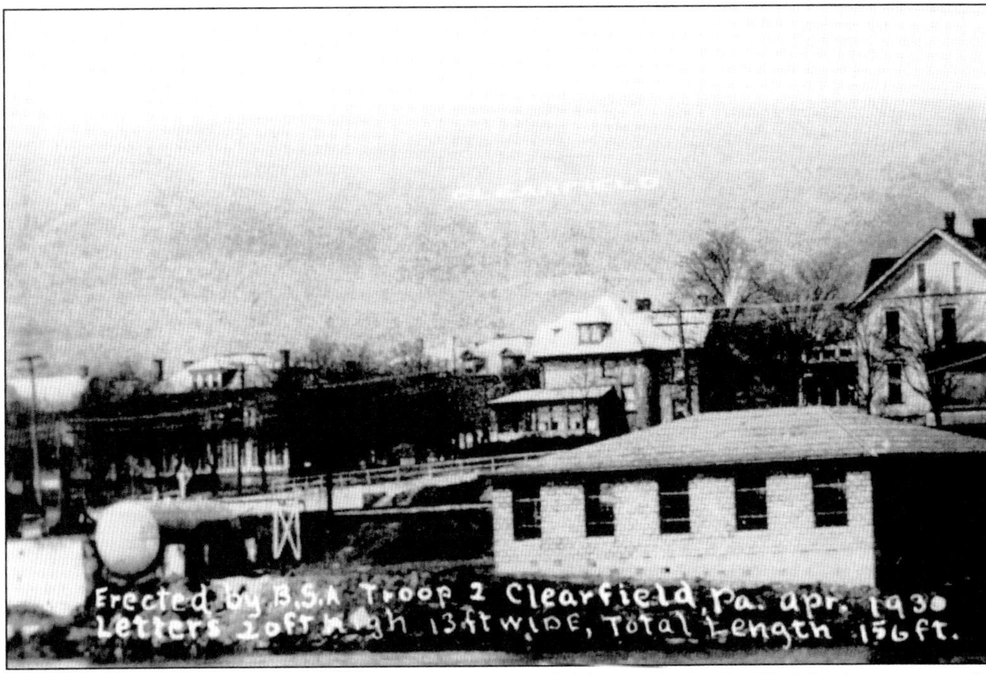

In April 1930, Boy Scout Troup 2 erected this Clearfield sign on Coal Hill. The letters were 20 feet high and 13 feet wide. The total length of the sign was 156 feet. During World War II, the sign was destroyed as a security precaution. This sign is also visible in the upper left corner of the below view of downtown Clearfield.

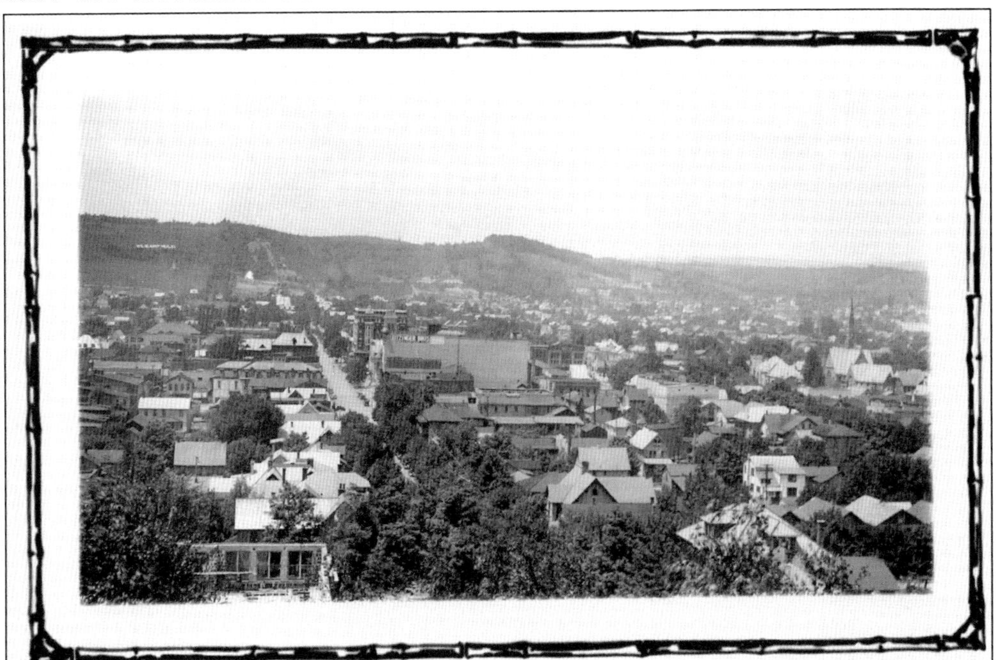

Eight

Neighbors

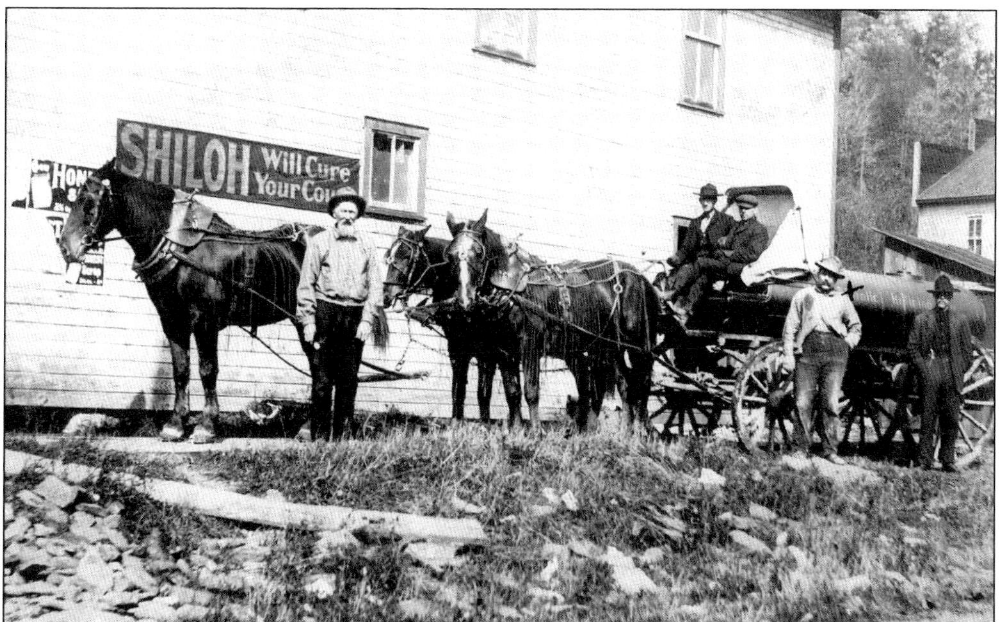

Many of the other communities in Clearfield County were also featured in postcards. Here, men pose outside a country store in Olanta. This building is now a private home.

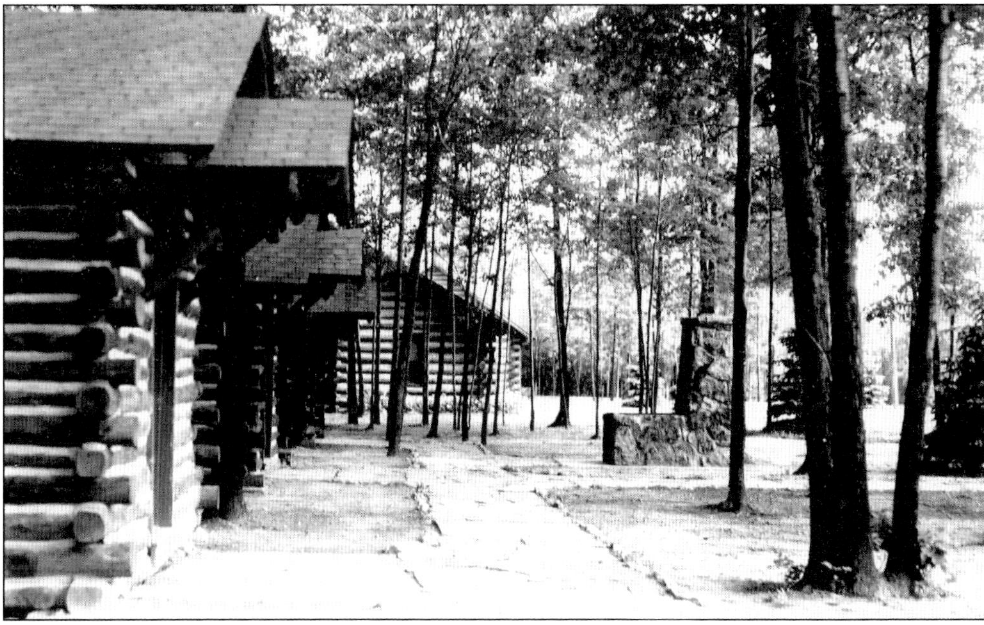

Shown here are cabins at Camp Elliott. S.B. Elliott State Park was named for conservationist Simon B. Elliott, who helped establish the Clearfield State Forest Nursery. The Civilian Conservation Corps (CCC) set up the cabins, pavilions, roads, and trails on the 318-acre park. (Courtesy Zalno collection.)

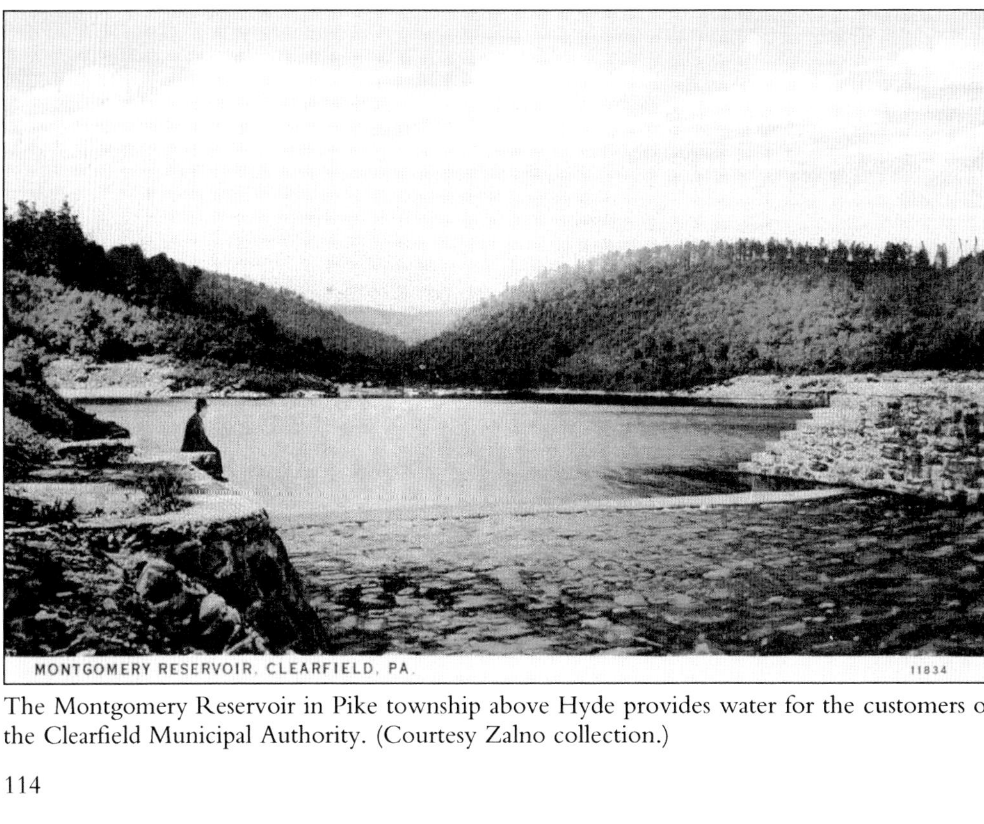

The Montgomery Reservoir in Pike township above Hyde provides water for the customers of the Clearfield Municipal Authority. (Courtesy Zalno collection.)

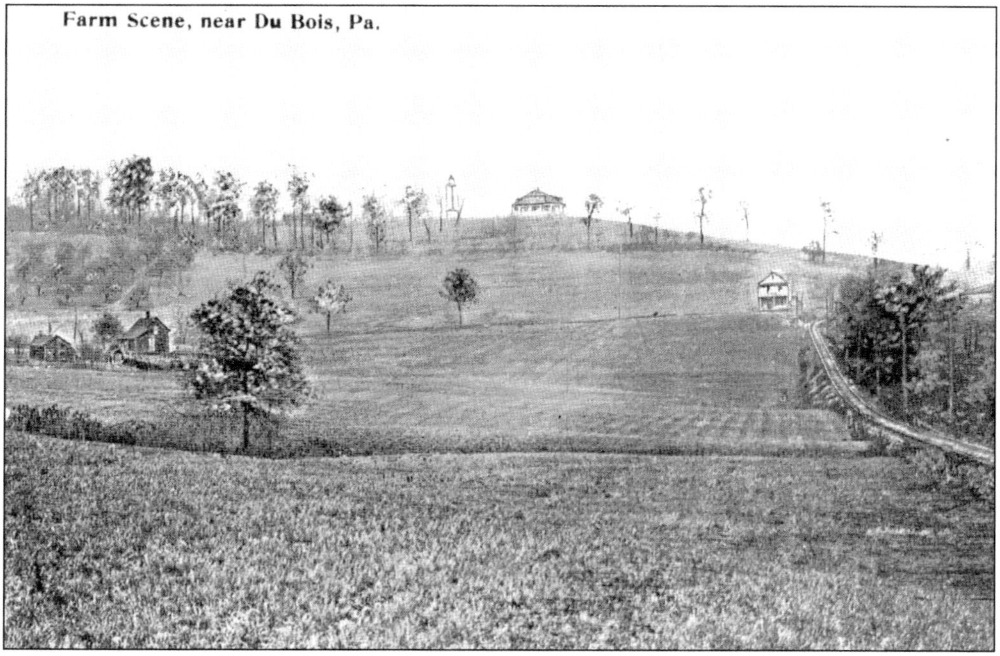

This farm was located near DuBois. (Courtesy Test collection.)

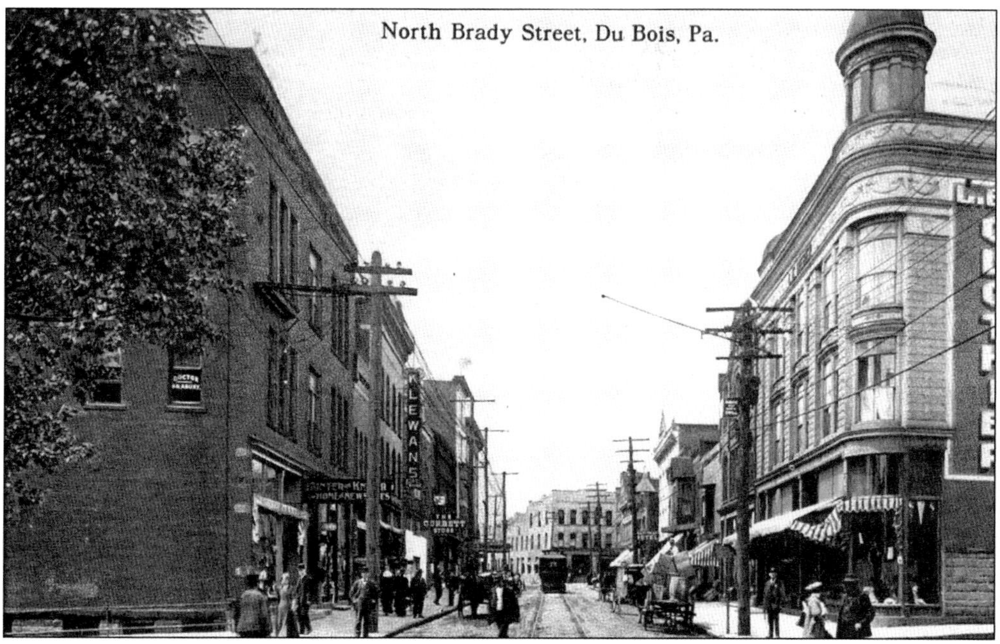

Shown here is North Brady Street in DuBois. (Courtesy Test collection.)

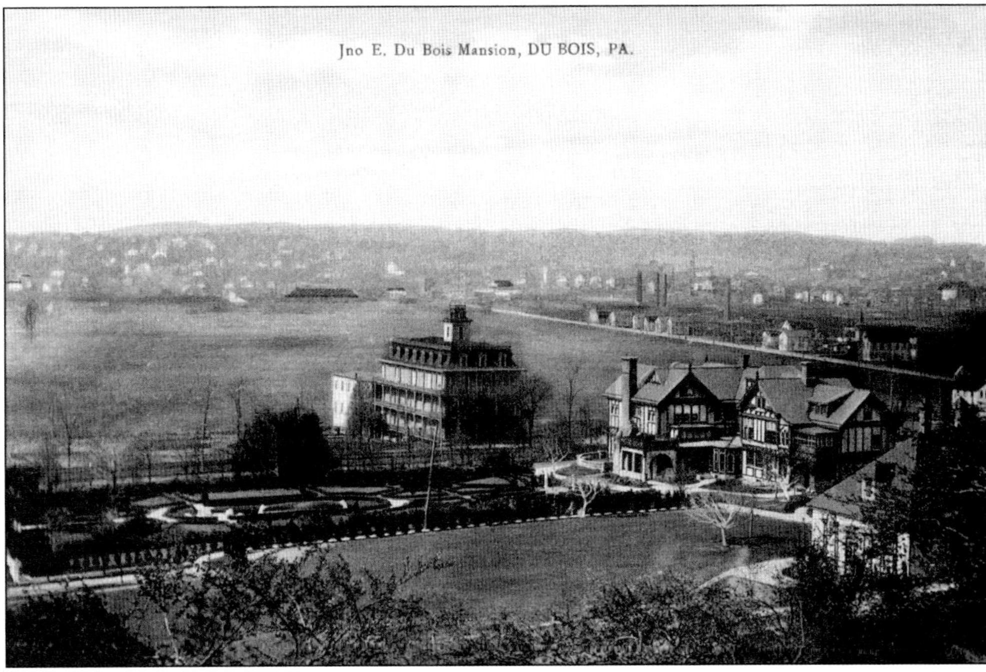

John E. DuBois was the nephew of John DuBois, the lumber merchant who came to this area in 1871. His mansion was donated to and became the home of the DuBois Penn State campus. (Courtesy Leitzinger collection.)

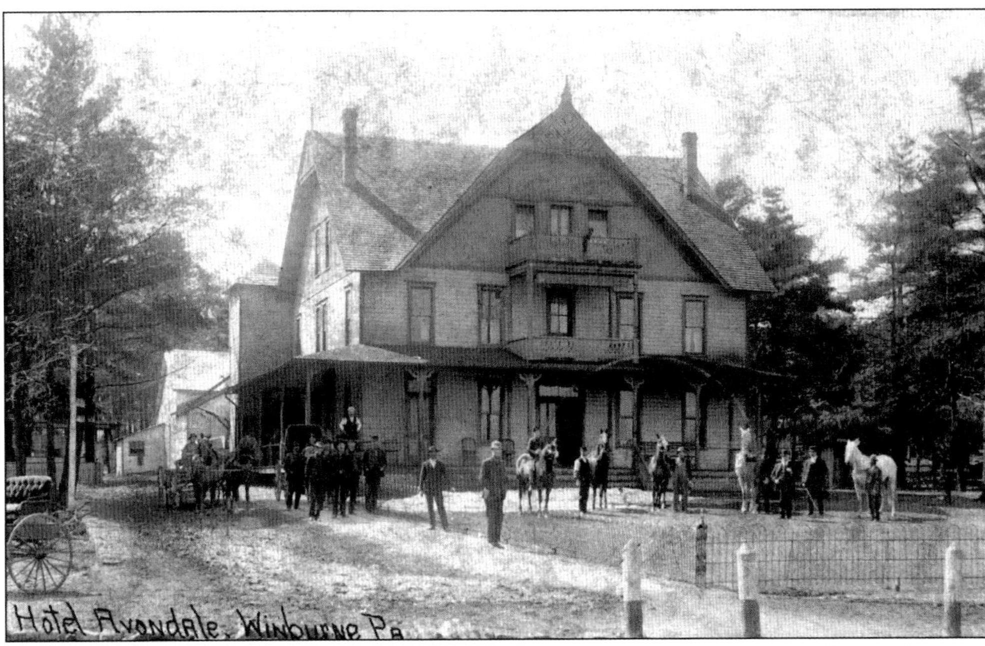

This postcard shows the Hotel Avondale in Winburne. (Courtesy Leitzinger collection.)

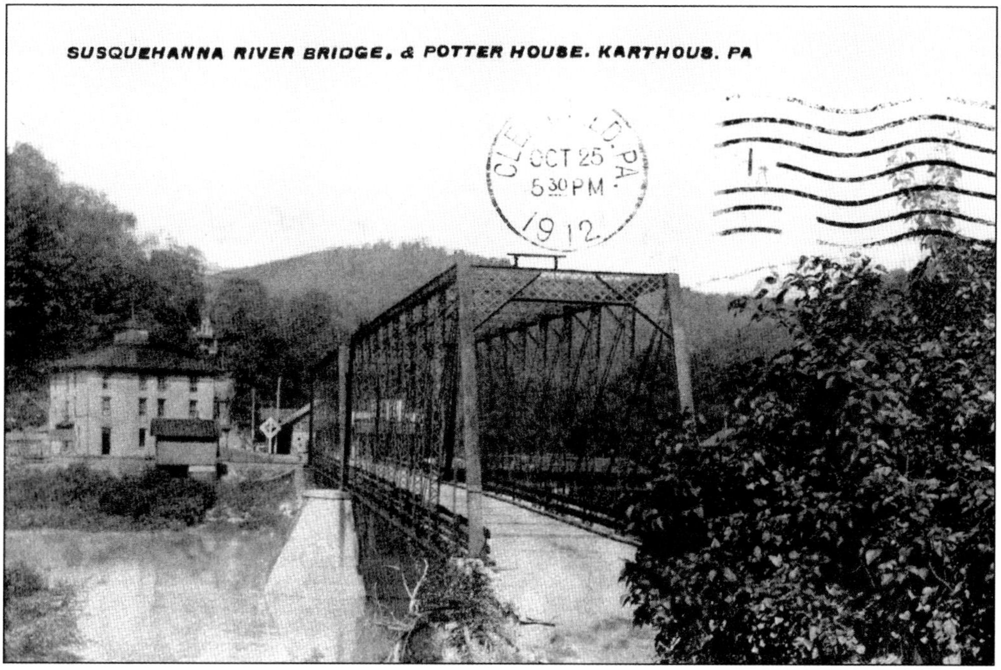

The Potter House, located by the Susquehanna River Bridge in Karthaus, was built in 1883 by Dr. J.W. Potter. Raftsmen were the biggest customers, stopping on their way down the river. The hotel later became known as "the Ring Rock" because of the large iron ring used to tie the rafts. It burned down in 1979. (Leitzinger collection)

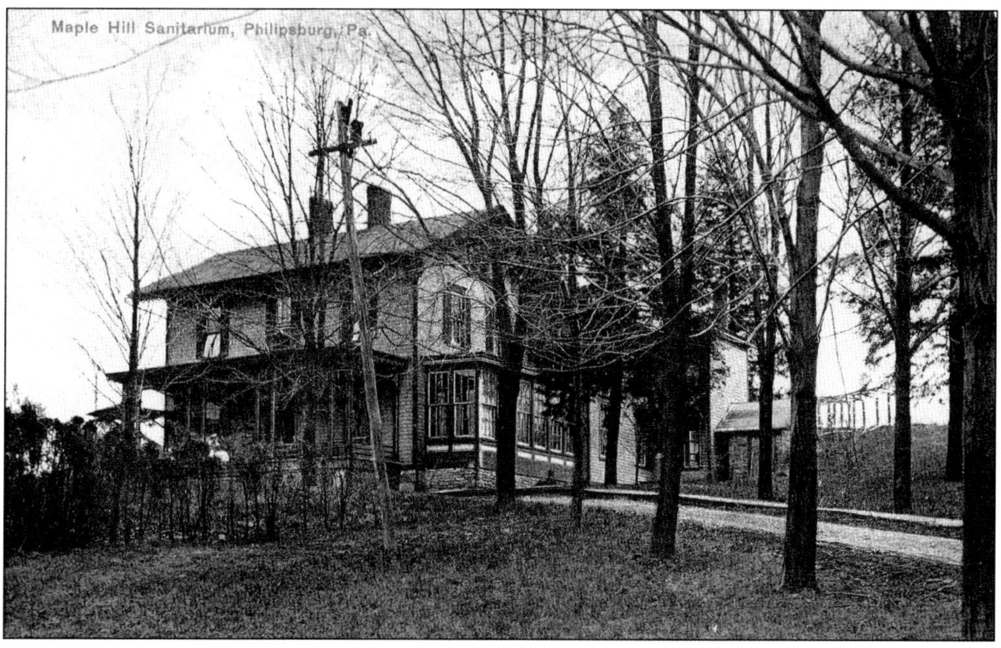

The Maple Hill Sanitarium in Philipsburg operated as a hospital from the late 1800s until the early 1900s. It later became a nursing home and is now a private home. This card was sold by B.F. Hoffer in Philipsburg. (Courtesy Zalno collection.)

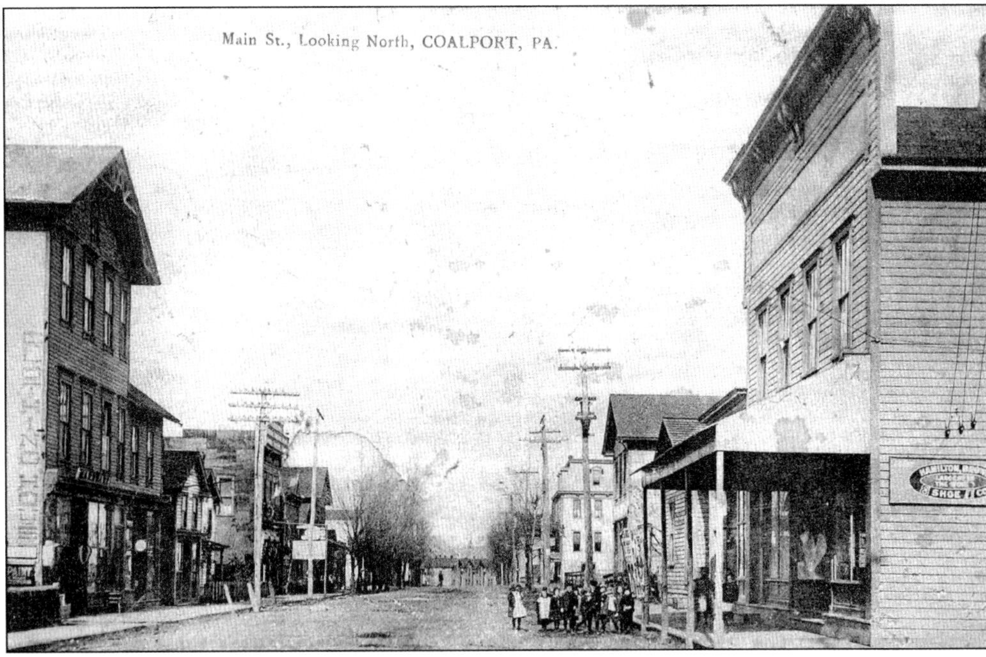

This 1910 view looks north upon Coalport's Main Street. (Courtesy Test collection.)

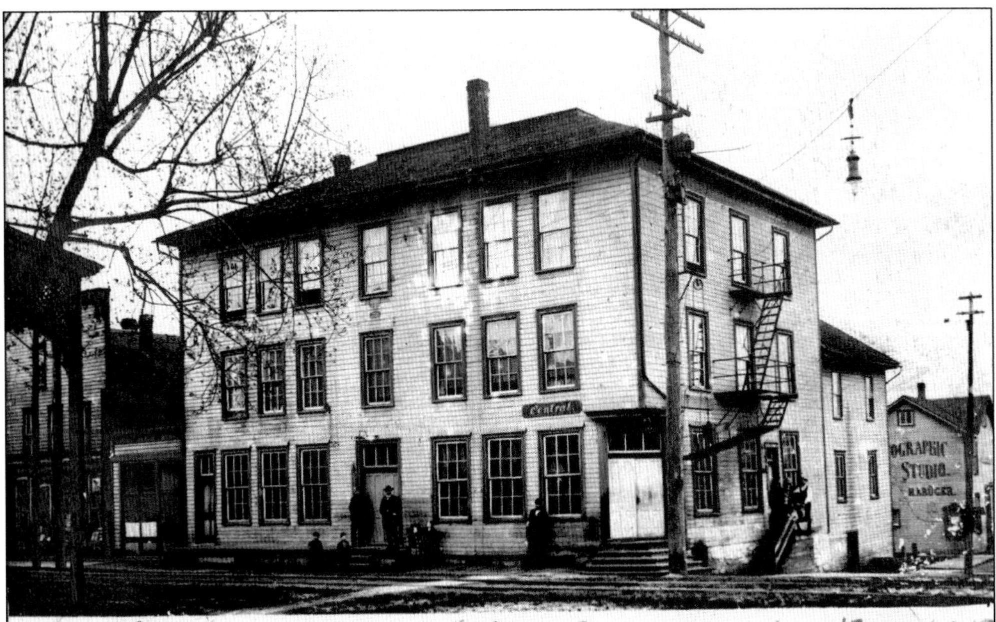

Shown here is the Central Hotel in Houtzdale in 1907. (Courtesy Leitzinger collection.)

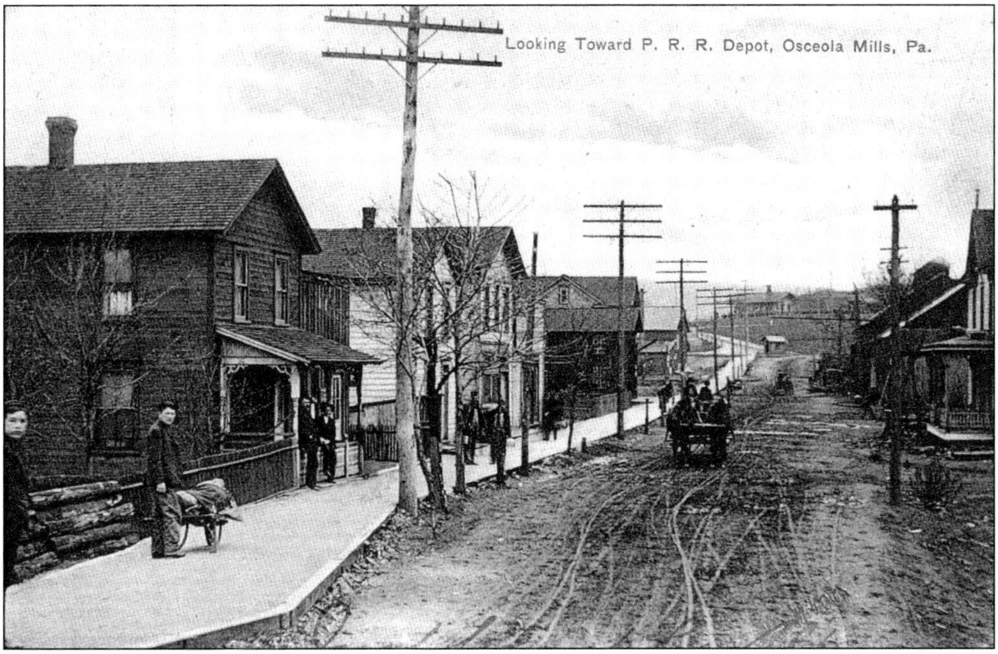

This 1906 view looks toward the Pennsylvania Railroad depot in Osceola Mills. (Courtesy Test collection.)

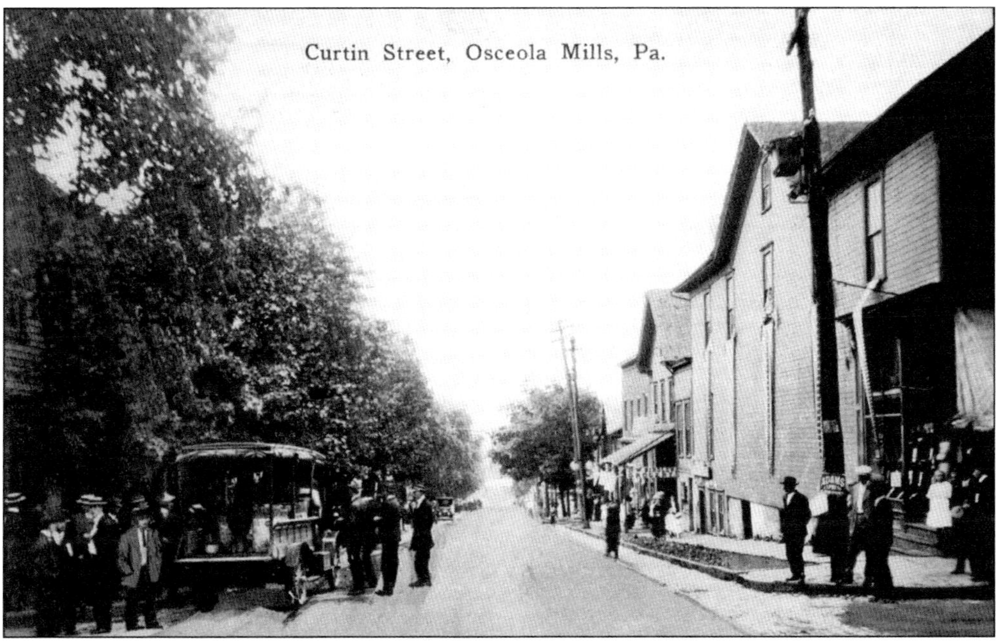

Pictured here is Curtin Street in Osceola Mills in 1913. (Courtesy Leitzinger collection.)

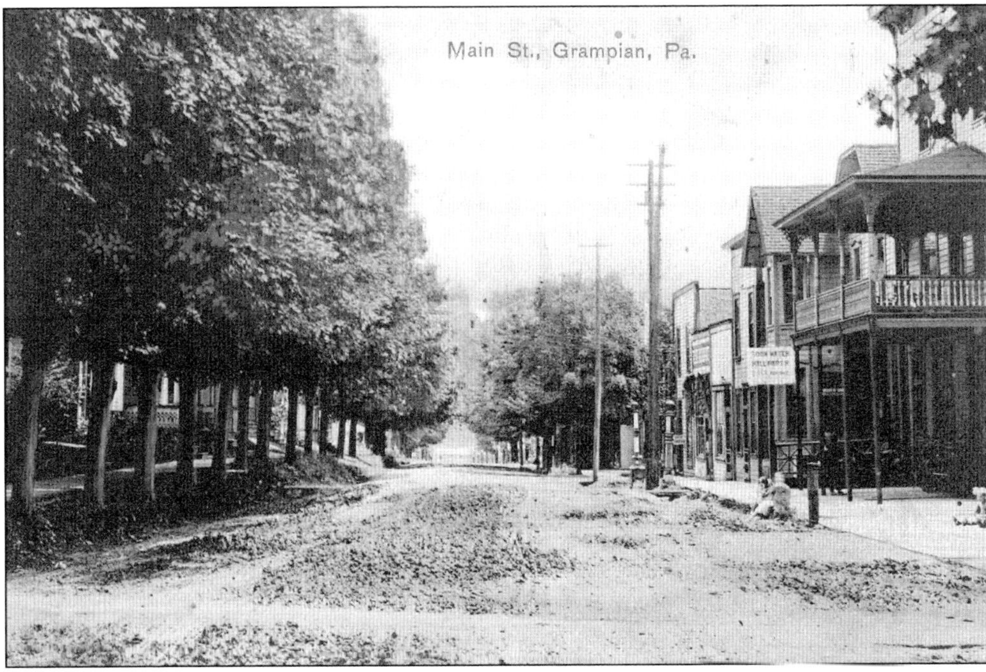

This postcard, dated 1913, depicts Main Street in Grampian. (Courtesy Test collection.)

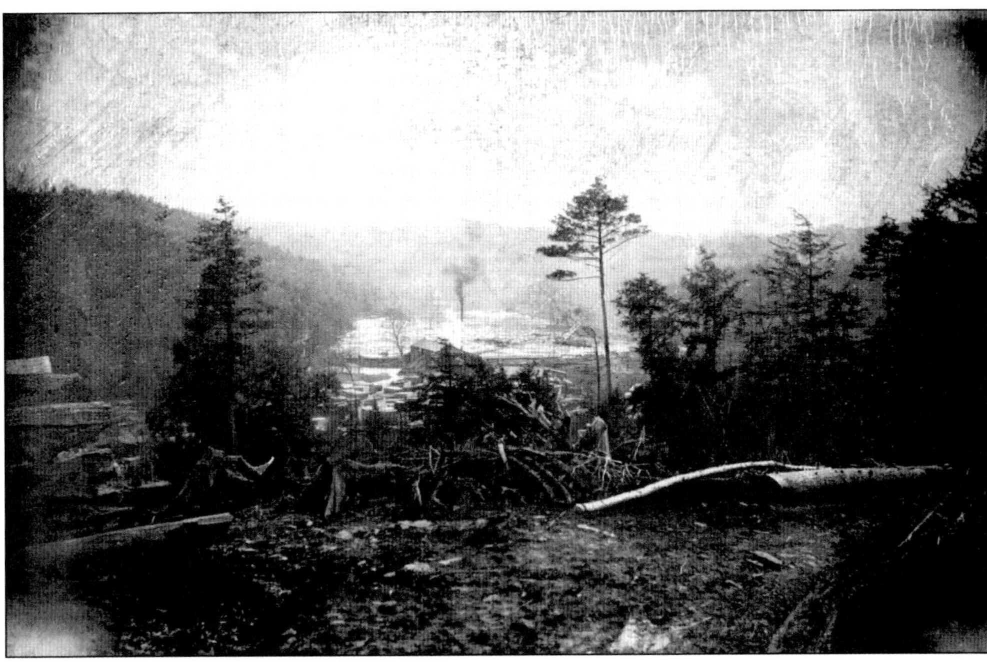
This logging camp was located near Kermoor.

The Presbyterian church in Cherry Tree was dedicated in 1856. It later became the United Presbyterian Church.

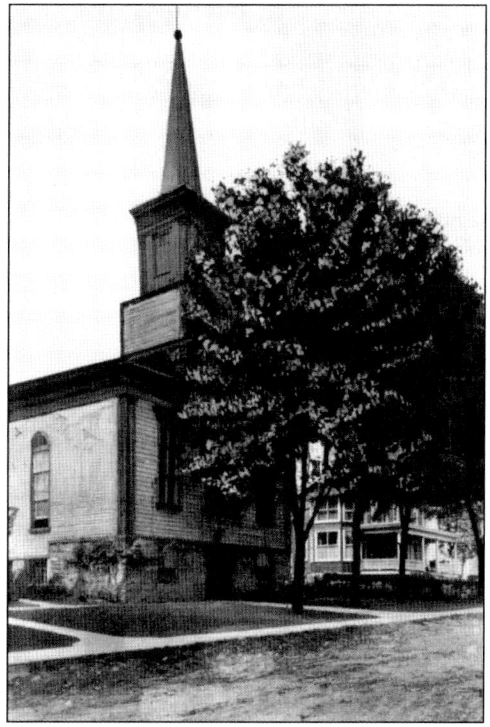

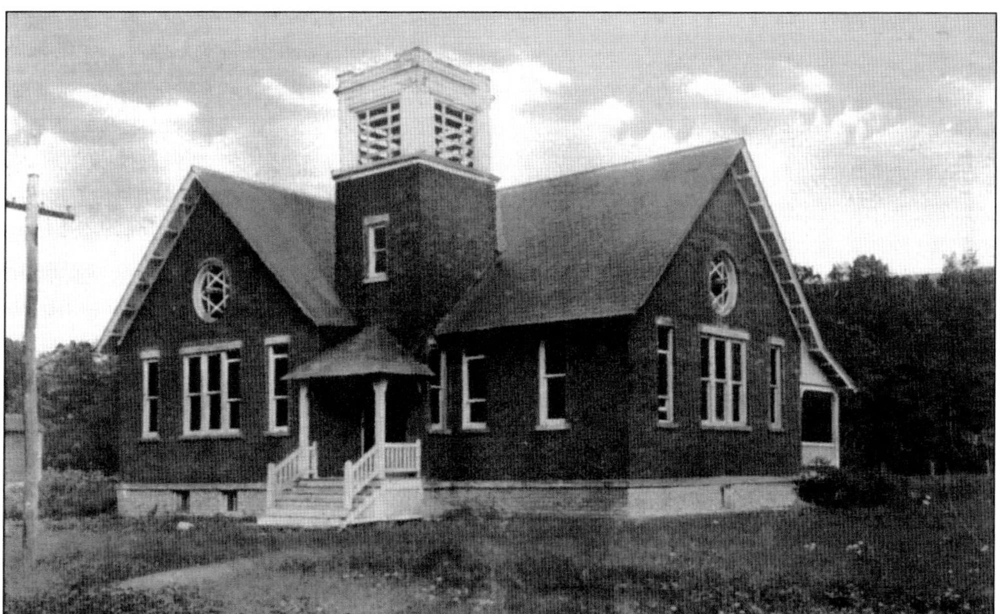

J.M. Byers and Cyrus Knupp built the Methodist church in Cherry Tree in 1911.

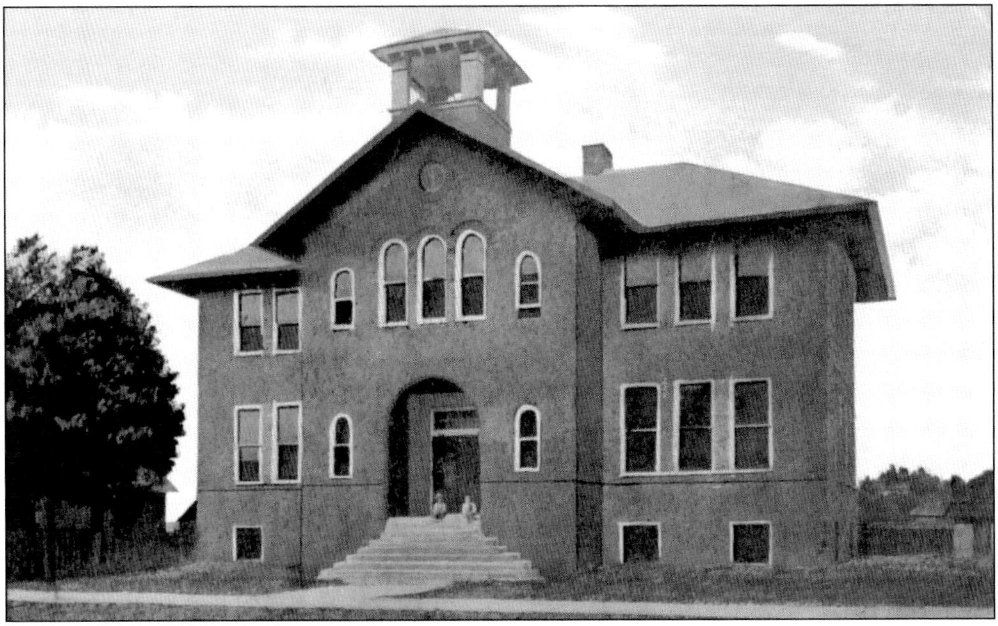

Cherry Tree's public school was constructed in the early 1900s and was in use until the 1950s.

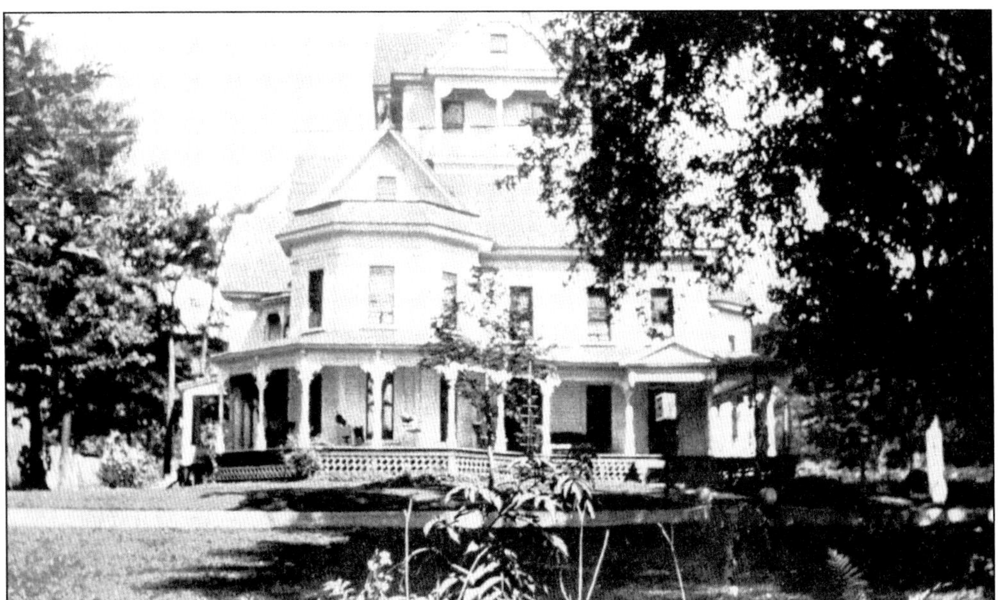

Snyder's Place, McGee's Mills, Pa.

Snyder's Place in McGee's Mills became the Snyder Hotel. It included 19 sleeping rooms, a cocktail lounge, a bar, a dining room, and an enclosed sun porch for private parties.

Nine

MISCELLANEOUS GREETINGS

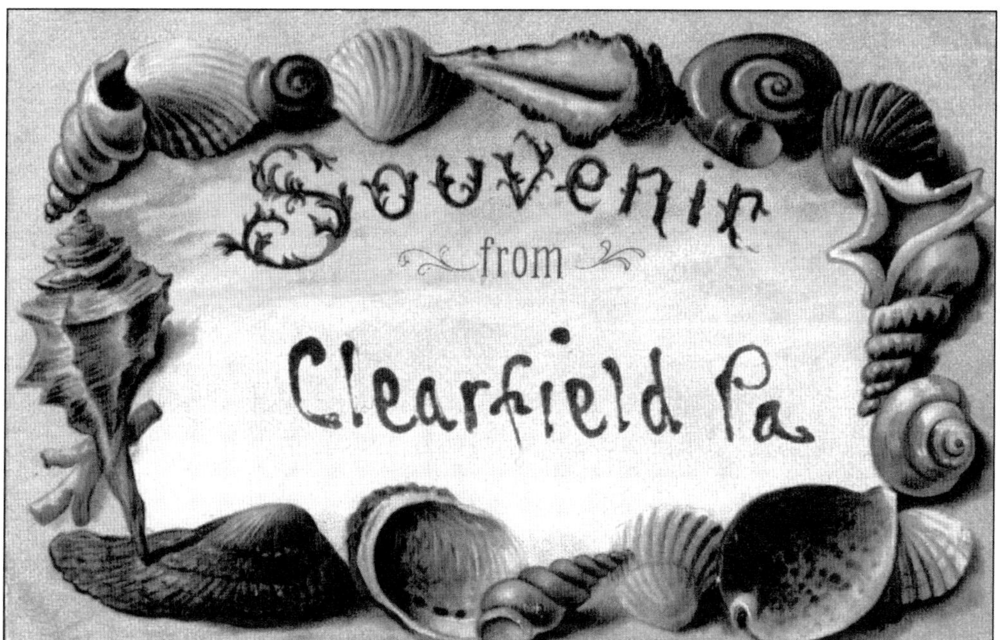

In addition to scenic and historic photographs, postcards feature many different and various greetings, some of which were mass-produced with no real local connection. For example, this "souvenir of Clearfield Pa" leads one to ask this question: Where in Clearfield can you find seashells?

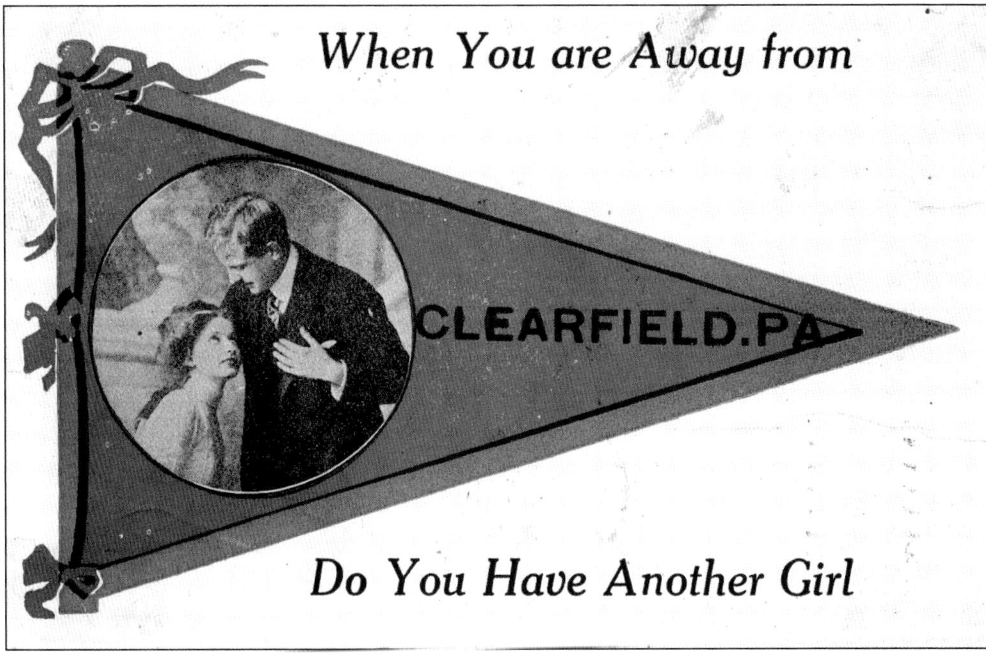

This card from 1913 represents the fear of every girl who has a traveling salesman for a beau. (Courtesy Zalno collection.)

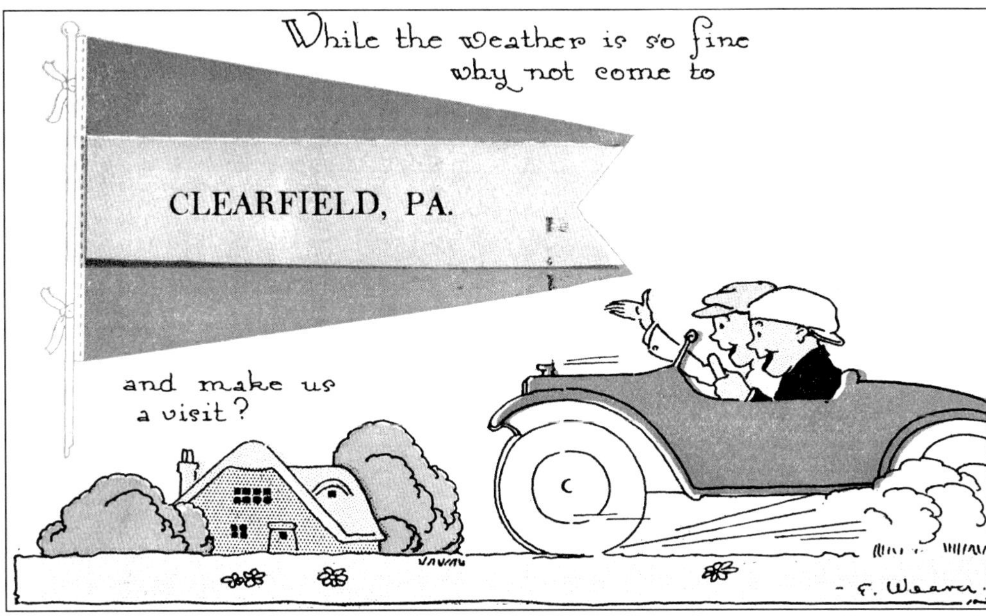

Shown here is either an early effort at creating more tourism or a relative's way of fostering guilt. (Courtesy Zalno collection.)

The Clearfield Trust Company used this postcard as a promotional device in 1907. Today, the Clearfield Trust Company is known as the Clearfield Bank & Trust Company. (Courtesy Zalno collection.)

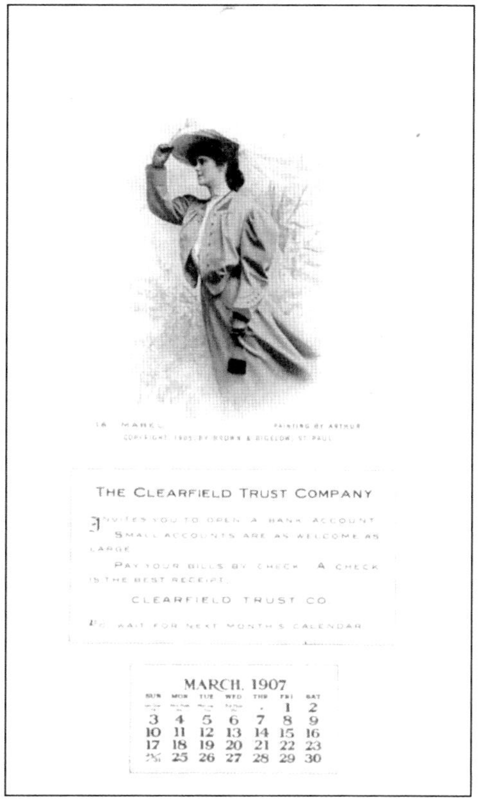

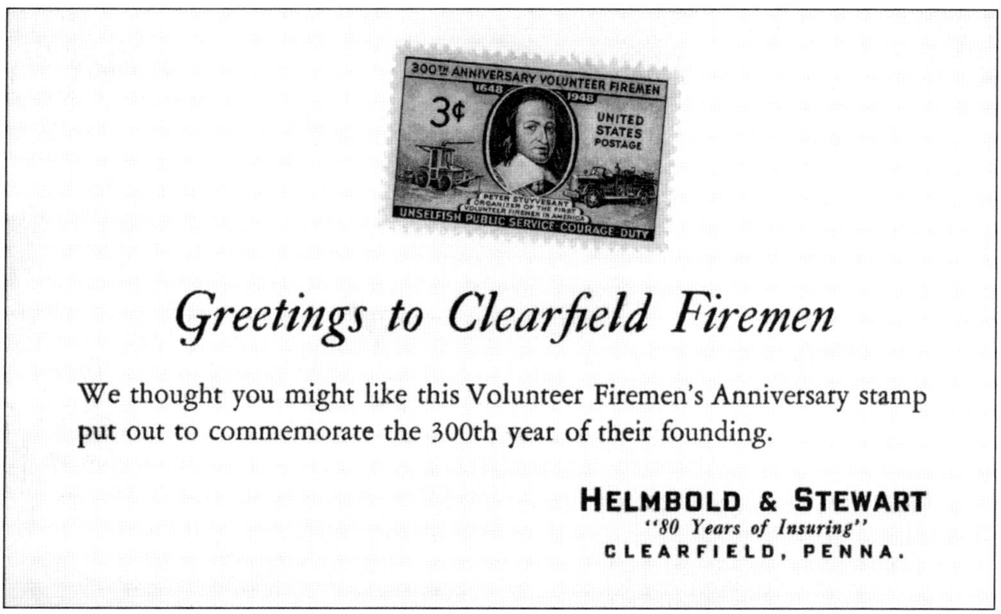

This promotional postcard features a stamp honoring the 300th anniversary of volunteer firemen; it was sent out to local businesses in December 1948. Hembold & Stewart still does business in Clearfield today. (Courtesy Leitzinger collection.)

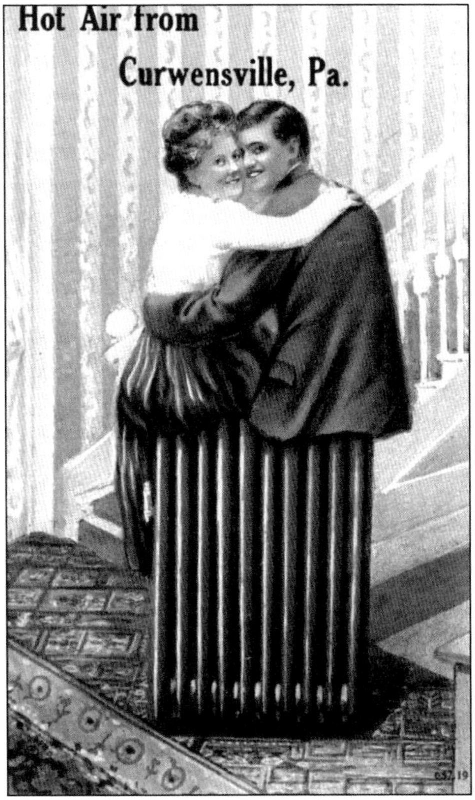

This hot air was mailed from Curwensville in 1913. (Courtesy Test collection.)

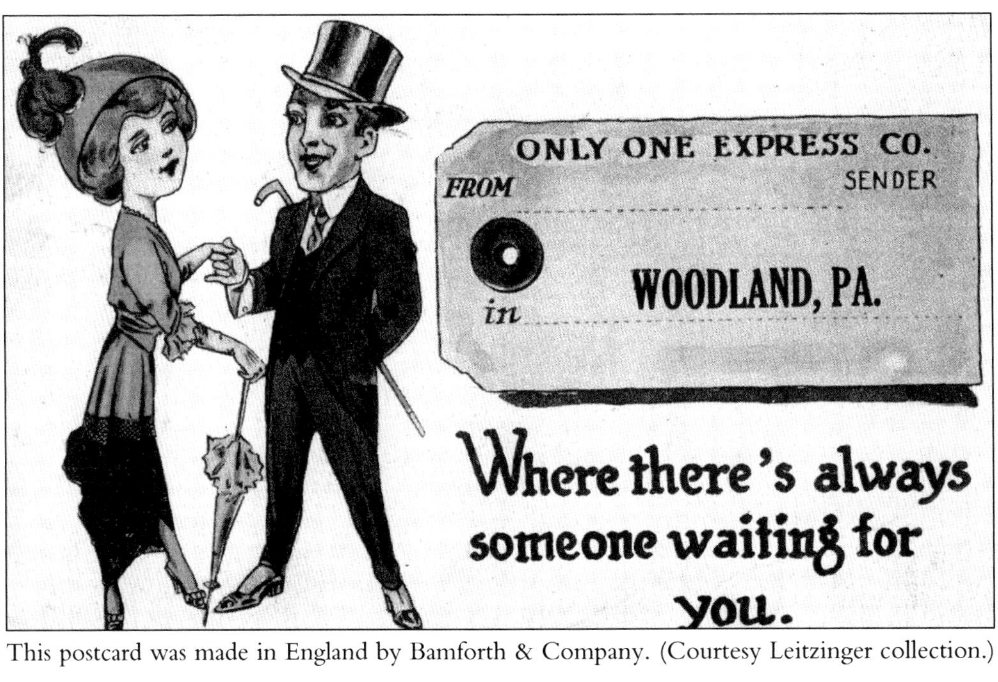

This postcard was made in England by Bamforth & Company. (Courtesy Leitzinger collection.)

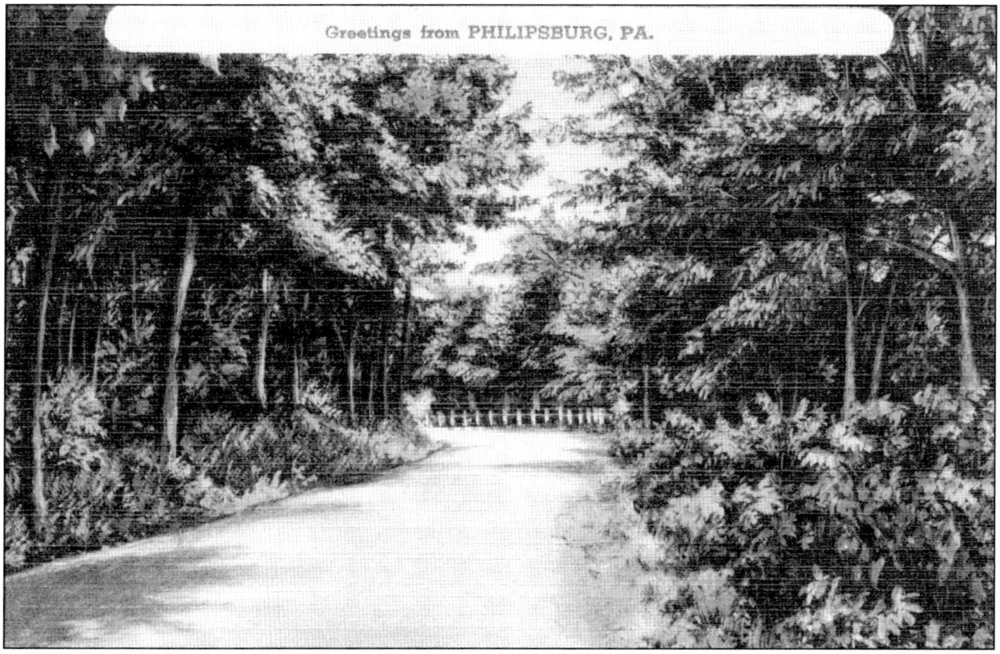

This greeting from Philipsburg was made by Landscape Panal Locals 20 Designs. (Courtesy Test collection.)

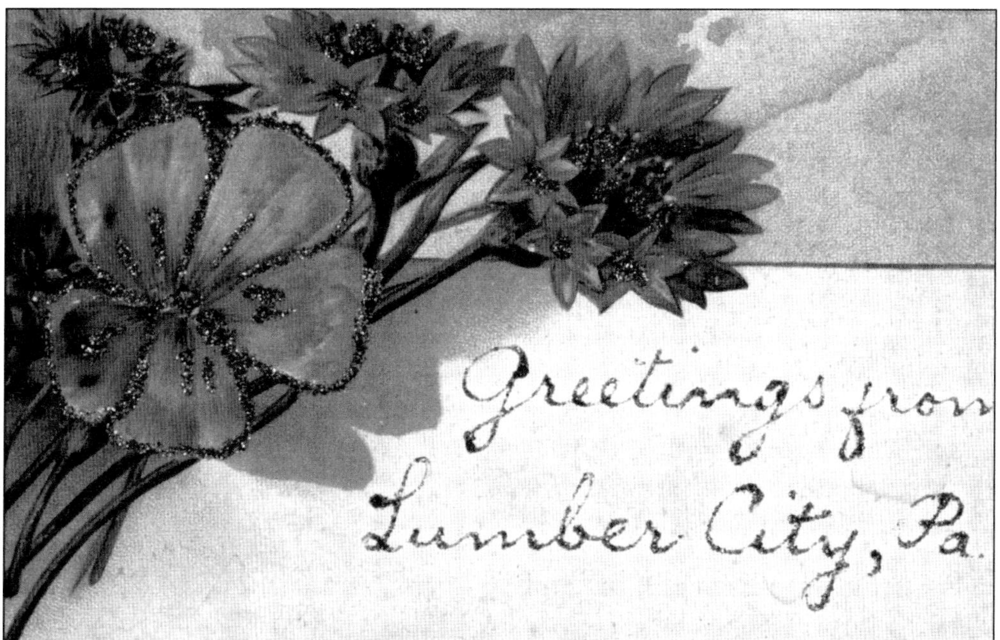

Shown here is a simple yet pretty greeting from Lumber City.

Historical Society and Author Information

The proceeds from this book go to support the Clearfield County Historical Society, at 104 East Pine Street, Clearfield, PA 16830. Telephone: (814) 765-6125.

The museum and its library are open free to the public every Sunday and Thursday from 1:30 to 4:30 p.m., beginning the first Sunday of May and ending the last Sunday in October.

For more information on the Clearfield County Historical Society, go to http://www.rootsweb.com/~pacchsm.

For more information on author Julie Rae Rickard, go to http://thedestinyofmiro.tripod.com. Send e-mail to thedestinyofmiro@yahoo.com. Write to Julie Rae Rickard, P.O. Box 565, Clearfield, PA 16830.